Ariel Manzur
George Marques

Sams **Teach Yourself**

Godot Engine Game Development

in **24** Hours

CONTRIBUTORS:
Poommetee Ketson
Thomas Herzog
Emmanuel Leblond
Tiamo Pastoor (Pandaqi)
Anna Daubenspeck
Jakob Schwab

Pearson

800 E. 96th St., Indianapolis, IN 46240 USA

Sams Teach Yourself Godot Engine Game Development in 24 Hours

ISBN-13: 978-0-13-483509-9

ISBN-10: 0-13-483509-3

Library of Congress Control Number: 2017963657

1   18

Trademarks

All terms mentioned in this book that are known to be trademarks or service marks have been appropriately capitalized. Sams Publishing cannot attest to the accuracy of this information. Use of a term in this book should not be regarded as affecting the validity of any trademark or service mark.

Warning and Disclaimer

Every effort has been made to make this book as complete and as accurate as possible, but no warranty or fitness is implied. The information provided is on an "as is" basis.

Special Sales

For information about buying this title in bulk quantities, or for special sales opportunities (which may include electronic versions, custom cover designs, and content particular to your business, training goals, marketing focus, or branding interests), please contact our corporate sales department at corpsales@pearsoned.com or (800) 382-3419.

For government sales inquiries, please contact governmentsales@pearsoned.com.

For questions about sales outside of the U.S., please contact intlcs@pearson.com.

Publisher
Mark Taub

Acquisitions Editor
Laura Lewin

Managing Editor
Sandra Schroeder

Project Editor
Prathiba.R/
Pearson CSC

Copy Editor
Pearson CSC

Indexer
Pearson CSC

Proofreader
Pearson CSC

Technical Editor
Ariel Manzur

Editorial Assistant
Courtney Martin

Cover Designer
Chuti Prasertsith

Compositor
Pearson CSC

Contents at a Glance

Table of Contents

Foreword

Ariel Manzur, co-creator of the Godot Engine

Godot Engine[1] was conceived around the end of 2007, at a time when we (Juan Linietsky and Ariel Manzur) noticed two big changes in the hardware available for game development. The first was simply an improvement in hardware, which made it more available on lower-end and portable devices, like the PlayStation Portable (PSP) and the first iPhone. Of course, portable gaming existed before 2007 (the Nintendo DS was out at the time), but those devices were so low end that games had to be made specifically for them, and it was not viable to use a general purpose game engine there. In the case of the iPhone and PSP, for the first time they were "normal computers," but portable.

The second change was the way central processing units (CPU) were built. Before, we were used to a "computer" being a single CPU with some memory, storage, and a graphics processing units (GPU), and as time went by, the CPU became faster and the GPU more capable. But suddenly, we started seeing the CPU being split into multiple cores. It was new and also a bit unpredictable, as the industry started experimenting (for example the cell architecture on PlayStation 3). This meant that the classic "game engine main loop," which consisted of "collect user input > update game logic > update graphics > go back to start", was no longer the most effective way to run a game, so parallel processing was necessary.

These two factors led to a decision: We had to drop the current low-level engine architecture we were using, and start over with a design that was better suited for multi-core systems and systems with a high variety of capabilities, from the low-end portable devices to the big exotic consoles. We adopted an architecture where each core system is handled by a "server" in an asynchronous way. The servers operate at a higher level of abstraction than usual (for example the VisualServer does its own spatial indexing, as opposed to the old rendering abstraction, which simply draws objects), but they can be better implemented in ways that take advantage of the underlying hardware.

At the time, our engine was around its fourth generation and was used to make a few games, including the MMORPG *Regnum Online* and the PC Minecraft-like title *Atmosphir*. But not everything was thrown away and a number of features were kept, with the most important being the Scene Tree.

While Godot's architecture is based on a server system, on the surface, the content is organized in a way that is very friendly to humans. This was very important for us because we knew that

---

[1]Godot Engine is published as an open source project under the MIT License.

during the development of a game, most of the time (and money) will be spent integrating content into the game. This means every member of the project needs to be able to use the tools to integrate this content, and they all need to be responsible for their own content, from its creation to its implementation in the running game. The Scene Tree system works great for this, because it's the way humans are used to seeing the world already.

Imagine you wake up in the morning, grab your backpack, put your computer in it, along with the charger, an umbrella, and a water bottle. You put your phone in your pocket, which has 20 apps on it, and put the phone charger in the backpack as well. When you go out, you don't think, "I need to take my phone with the 20 apps, and my backpack, my computer, my umbrella, the water bottle, and the chargers." You think, "I need to take the backpack and the phone."

You take the bus with 20 other people, the bus driver knows how to drive around the city, and he's not thinking, "I'm driving 20 people with 5 backpacks, 7 purses, 6 briefcases, 12 computers, 5 books, 7 lipsticks, etc." He's thinking, "I'm driving a bus."

We organize things in different levels of abstraction, we worry about each level separately, and we specialize in each level. When you pack the backpack, you worry about what goes in it and later you just carry around a backpack. The bus driver knows how to drive a bus, he doesn't have to worry about what's in it, and all the passengers on the bus are in charge of carrying their things.

The Scene Tree in Godot is a great way to organize the content of your game, and to let all of the members of the team contribute to it, specialize in different levels of the tree, and not be distracted by other levels that are someone else's responsibility. A programmer calls the "explosion" animation and forgets about it, the artist is in charge of the contents of the animation, without depending on help from the programmer. This is crucial during the development of a game, not only because it saves money by using the programmer's time more efficiently, but by giving the artist more control over their assets, they are able to deliver higher-quality content for the game.

This book is aimed at all of the members of a game development team, and each one will take away a different piece of knowledge relevant to their discipline. But there's an area where we hope we can help everyone learn together, which is how to take advantage of the tools provided by the engine to design the most efficient workflow, so that everyone on the team can work to the best of their ability and produce a great game. We'll cover all of the main areas of the engine: 2D, 3D, Physics, and the UI, plus a few example games to put all of the knowledge into practice. Programmers will have code examples, but everyone else will also learn about the features and processes of the engine to integrate their content in the best possible way.

We'll use the upcoming version 3.0 of Godot, which includes huge improvements to 3D rendering, the GDNative module, a C# module, and a lot of work done by our wonderful community of contributors over the past two years.

Preface

The Godot Engine is a powerful open source tool tailored to help you make video games. The Godot 3.0 version brings a revolution to its structure, using modern techniques and increasing the user-friendliness of the editor. Due to its variety of features and ability to accommodate a plethora of different game genres, Godot can be quite complex for a beginner.

This book will guide you to use the Godot editor interface while explaining topics pertaining to the game development field. Each chapter covers a different subject, featuring important information about the process of creating 2D and 3D games. Details about the general context and how to apply them inside Godot are explained. Three of the chapters (Hour 5, Hour 17, and Hour 23) are dedicated to sample games so you can see the content being used in practice.

All the code for the sample projects in this book can be found at https://github.com/vnen/ Godot-24-Hours.

Who Should Read This Book

If you want to learn how to use the Godot Engine to develop complete games, this book is for you. Whether you are an experienced game developer wanting to dive into a new engine, or a beginner who's just scratching the surface of this field, you'll feel comfortable in these pages. This book is meant for people of all ages, cultures, and degrees of knowledge.

How This Book Is Organized

Following the Sam's Teach Yourself approach, this book is divided in 24 chapters that should take about an hour each to work through. There's also a bonus 25th chapter for advanced users, covering how to use native code to complement the scripting language by replacing the slow bits. Here is what's covered in the chapters:

 ▶ **Hour 1, "Introducing the Godot Engine":** This hour gets you started, explaining how to download and run the editor, and guides you along the interface components.

▶ **Hour 2, "Scene System":** This hour talks about a specific Godot idea, which is how the projects are organized into scenes that are composed of other scenes and based on fundamental blocks, called "Nodes."

▶ **Hour 3, "2D Graphics":** In this hour, you get started with general 2D graphics knowledge, including a bit of vector math. You learn how to use Godot nodes made specifically for 2D games.

▶ **Hour 4, "Scripting":** This hour teaches you about GDScript, the Godot custom scripting language. You learn how to add scripts to nodes and how things interact with each other.

▶ **Hour 5, "Game 1: Space Shooter":** In this hour, you make your first full game. It guides you in the creation of a simple 2D space shooter, including how to organize your scenes and make the scripts.

▶ **Hour 6, "More Scripting":** This hour complements what you learned in Hour 4, teaching you how to create global game objects and tools that run inside the editor itself.

▶ **Hour 7, "Handling Input":** The player input is very important for the interaction. In this hour, you learn how to get it from a keyboard, mouse, and joystick.

▶ **Hour 8, "Physics System":** In this hour, you learn how to use the Godot physics engine to create realistic movements and not-so realistic ones that are often used in games of all kinds.

▶ **Hour 9, "User Interface":** This hour shows you the Godot graphical controls, like buttons and text boxes, are used to create user interface in your games.

▶ **Hour 10, "Animation":** In this hour, you learn about the animation system offered by the Godot Engine. You learn how to create your own simple animations and how to make properties change over time.

▶ **Hour 11, "Game Flow":** This hour is responsible for teaching you how to make transitions in your game. You learn how to go from one scene to another, how to pause the game, and how to handle the exit request gracefully.

▶ **Hour 12, "File System":** In this hour, you see how you can create and save configuration files and save games. You also learn how to load resources from the disk and how to encrypt your files.

▶ **Hour 13, "3D Graphics":** This hour shows you basic concepts involved in a 3D game. It teaches you which nodes are part of a 3D environment, such as the Camera, which gives vision to the player. You also learn how to load your own models into the game.

▶ **Hour 14, "Project Management":** This chapter gives you tips about how to structure your game project files. It shows you how to import files into the project and how to use a version control system to keep the project safe from irreversible changes.

▶ **Hour 15, "Shaders and Materials":** In this hour, you learn how to create and use materials for objects inside Godot, both in 2D and 3D environments. You also learn the basic concepts about shaders and how to create them inside the editor.

▶ **Hour 16, "Lights and Shadows":** This hour shows you how to add light in the scenes, which is vital in 3D and an interesting effect in 2D, too. You also see how to enable and configure shadows.

▶ **Hour 17, "Bloxorz Clone":** This hour gives the second game project. You learn how to make a simple 3D puzzle game with a rolling block.

▶ **Hour 18, "Environments and Reflections":** In this hour, you learn how to customize the environment of a 3D world, using panoramic skies or simple colors. You also learn how to use global illumination and how to improve reflections with a probe node.

▶ **Hour 19, "Sound":** In this hour, you see how to add sound to your game. You learn about positional audio in 2D and 3D, how to use the buses and effects, and how to take advantage of the calculated Doppler effect.

▶ **Hour 20, "Particle System":** This hour teaches particles effects in Godot, both in 2D and 3D environments. These are useful in creating visual effects, such as smoke, fire, and sparks.

▶ **Hour 21, "Viewports and Canvas":** In this hour, you see the uses of the Viewport node, such as how to make a split-screen game and take screenshots. You also learn how the canvas layers can organize your 2D scene.

▶ **Hour 22, "Networking":** This chapter guides you through the networking functionality inside Godot. You see how to connect with other peers and synchronize the game status across the network.

▶ **Hour 23, "Game 3: Networked Bomberman Clone":** This hour shows you the recreation of the classic game with the added feature of networked multiplayer.

▶ **Hour 24, "Exporting the Project":** In this hour, you learn how to pack everything and make a final binary set that can be distributed as your game for every platform Godot supports.

▶ **Hour 25, "Native Code":** This bonus chapter gives you instructions about the use of native code with Godot to optimize the performance-critical bits of your game. It teaches you how to use the provided API and how to compile C code.

All the code for the sample projects in this book can be found at https://github.com/vnen/Godot-24-Hours.

About the Authors

Ariel Manzur is co-creator of Godot and is currently maintaining the open source project.

George Marques is a full-stack developer at Open Journal Solutions. He is an active contributor to the Godot game engine. His projects include the plugin to import Tiled Map Editor levels. He is the author of two blog posts on Godot published by Packt Pub titled, "How to create a breakout game with Godot engine," and "How to make 2D navigation with Godot engine." He is a former student of Information Systems at the University of São Paulo and his interests include general programming and writing. He can be found on Github at: https://github.com/vnen.

Contributors

Poommetee Ketson is a Godot committer.

Thomas Herzog is a Godot committer.

Emmanuel Leblond is a software engineer living in France. He co-founded Scille SAS (http://scille.eu), a company that's specialized in open source software. Besides his daily job, he is deeply involved in the Python ecosystem and chases his childhood's dream of one day becoming a true game developer with Godot.

Tiamo Pastoor (Pandaqi) doesn't really know what his profession is. He's finishing his bachelor degree in applied mathematics, but is most likely to pursue a career in writing, music, or game development. He currently lives in the Netherlands, and is desperately trying to get a novel published.

Anna Daubenspeck and Jakob Schwab are an illustrator/product designer and a software engineer team living in Germany. Besides their day jobs, the married couple operates a tiny gamedev studio called SnailSpaceGames where they can wield the power of Godot to make fun games.

Dedication

George: To Thaís: the love of my life who's always by my side.

Emmanuel Leblond: To my wife Jie; while still hoping she will grow her hair a bit longer . . .

Anna & Jakob: To our friends and family, because one must still have chaos around oneself to be able to give birth to a dancing star.

Tiamo: To battling illness; writing's the only thing left that I can do at the moment, so that's what I'll do.

Acknowledgments

George Marques: Big thanks to all the Godot Engine contributors, without whom this amazing engine wouldn't get to this level. And special thanks to Juan Linietsky, Ariel Manzur, and Rémi Verschelde, who maintain the project with great ability. Another thanks for the great, vibrant community that keeps the Godot Engine alive by using it and sharing knowledge. Thanks to Thaís, my significant other, who provided me with care and food while I dedicated my time to this book, and who comforted me in the difficult hours.

Emmanuel Leblond: Nothing of this incredible project, Godot, would have been possible without Juan Linietsky and Ariel Manzur and their hard work throughout numerous years and their willing to release their game engine on open source. But a great codebase is only half of what makes an open source project successful. On this topic, Rémi Verschelde should be greatly praised for his dedication to build a strong and living community.

Anna Daubenspeck and Jakob Schwab: We would like to thank all of the Godot Engine founders, contributors, and the community as a whole for developing such great piece of software. We also would like to thank George Marques, Christina Rudloff, and Troy Mott for giving us the opportunity to be part of this book and to contribute to the Godot Engine project this way. Last but not least, we want to thank all our friends and family and especially our cats Walter and Wilma for their great support and patience.

Tiamo Pastoor (Pandaqi): An enormous thanks to the Godot Engine creators/contributors and the community that helped shape it into the ambitious piece of software that it is today. Also thanks to Jan, a friend of mine, who forced me to pick the Godot Engine for a new game project we were starting together (even though I didn't want to try something new at first). Thanks to my parents, who provide me with food and shelter during these trying times, asking for nothing in return. And lastly, thanks to my bunnies, who are always there to cuddle.

We Want to Hear from You!

As the reader of this book, you are our most important critic and commentator. We value your opinion and want to know what we're doing right, what we could do better, what areas you'd like to see us publish in, and any other words of wisdom you're willing to pass our way.

We welcome your comments. You can email or write to let us know what you did or didn't like about this book—as what we can do to make our books better.

Please note that we cannot help you with technical problems related to the topic of this book.

When you write, please be sure to include this book's title and author, as well as your name and email address. We will carefully review your comments and share them with the author and editors who worked on the book.

Email: feedback@samspublishing.com

Mail: Sams Publishing
ATTN: Reader Feedback
         800 E. 96th St.
         Indianapolis, IN 46240 USA

Reader Services

Register your copy of *Sams Teach Yourself Godot Engine Game Development in 24 Hours* at informit.com for convenient access to downloads, updates, and corrections as they become available. To start the registration process, go to informit.com/register and log in or create an account*. Enter the product ISBN, 9780134835099, and click Submit. Once the process is complete, you will find any available bonus content under Registered Products.

---

* Be sure to check the box that you would like to hear from us in order to receive exclusive discounts on future editions of this product.

HOUR 1
Introducing the Godot Engine

What You'll Learn in This Hour:

▶ Installing and running the Godot Engine
▶ Creating a blank project
▶ Using the visual editor
▶ Running a simple scene
▶ Setting the main scene of the project

The Godot Engine is software designed to make games. It contains many tools to make all kinds of 2D and 3D games, with varying levels of complexity. This all comes in a very small download compared to other engines, without strings attached. Since Godot is available under the MIT license, you can use it for free and redistribute your games in any way that you want to.

This first hour (this chapter) gets you started with the Godot Engine. It shows you how to download, install, and run the editor for the first time. You'll look at the project manager at first and learn how to create and open a new project. Then you'll see the editor, put together a simple scene, and run it for testing. Finally, you'll set up a main scene for the game and change a few other common settings for projects.

Installing Godot

Unlike most computer software, Godot doesn't require an installation wizard. After downloading it from the website (see Figure 1.1), all you need to do is to put the executable in a folder anywhere and it can be launched from there all the time. There's also an installer available for Windows users if you prefer the usual method. Another option is to install it via the Steam store, which has the advantage of easier updates.

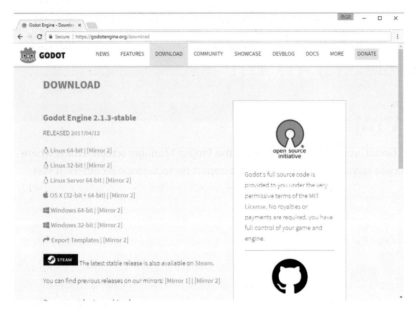

FIGURE 1.1
Godot Engine download page

Downloading and Installing the Godot Engine

Godot is very lightweight. The editor has only about 30MBs of size and that includes all of the features. It can run on pretty much any computer, as long it has a relatively recent operating system and a graphics card that supports OpenGL 3.3 (supported by most current integrated graphics processors).

1. Go to the Godot Engine website (https://godotengine.org).

2. Click on the "Download" link on the top bar.

3. Select the option for your current platform.

4. Wait for the download to finish.

5. Extract the zip contents to a local folder in your hard drive.

TIP

Self-Contained Mode

Godot usually stores the user settings in a global folder for the user profile (`%APPDATA%` on Windows, `~/.local/share` on Linux and `~/Library/Application Support` on macOS). If you are running multiple versions or want a portable mode this behavior might not be desired. To fix this, you can run the editor in a self-contained mode. This is easily accomplished by adding an empty file called ._sc_ (or just _sc_ if you're on Windows) in the same folder as the executable. Godot will then create an `editor_data` folder in the same place where all the settings will be stored. Note that temporary files are also stored there, so the folder can become quite heavy if there are many projects or big ones.

Creating a Project

The first time you open Godot, you will be greeted with the Project Manager screen. This is where you can see the projects you have, create new ones, and import projects made by others. If you click the "Templates" tab, you'll get access to Godot's Asset Library where you can download templates and demo projects.

Project Manager Interface

The main portion of the Project Manager (see Figure 1.2) shows the list of your projects. You can see the name, icon, and path of every game you are working on. It's also possible to favorite projects, which will make them appear before the others. To find a specific one, you can use the search box to the right of the Name dropdown list to filter the list. At the right of the window you can see the main buttons. The names are quite descriptive: you can edit or run the selected item(s), scan a folder to import all projects there, create a new game project, import an existing one, and remove the selected item(s) from the list (which does not exclude the project's files from the hard drive).

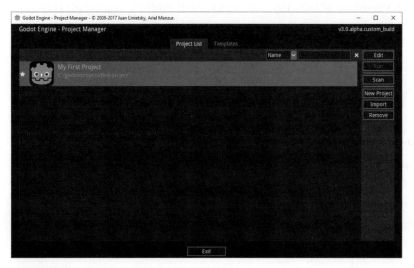

FIGURE 1.2
The Godot Project Manager with a single project.

▼ TRY IT YOURSELF

Create a New Project

You can create a project anywhere in your system. They are contained in a single folder and are as large as your assets, so only big games will occupy much of your hard drive space. Godot can recognize a project by the presence of a file called project.godot, where your project settings are stored. Here is how you do it once you first open Godot:

1. In the Project Manager, click on the **New Project** button.

2. Type or browse to the place where your project will be. The dialog can create folders if they are needed. The folder should be empty and it's a good practice to keep projects together.

3. Type the name of your project. Godot will autofill with the folder name, but you can change it as you wish. Note that the name can be changed later.

4. Click on the **Create** button.

5. The new project will be created and the editor will launch automatically.

NOTE

Console Window

If you are running Godot on Windows, you may notice the console window that opens alongside the engine. This window shows errors, warnings, and messages related to the engine itself and your game. If you're having problems, be sure to check if anything important appears there. On Linux and Mac, you can see those messages if you open Godot from a terminal window.

Don't worry about this window on your published game, because it does not appear on release builds, which are used in the final export of the project.

Using the Visual Editor

Once you create a project and open the editor, you'll be greeted with the main Godot Engine Interface. There are a few menus and buttons at the top, a few docks around the interface, some buttons at the bottom, and the main viewport is in the middle where the scene is created. Everything is quite empty at first, but soon we will add content to our first project. We'll cover the Godot Editor Interface, shown in Figure 1.3, in the following sections.

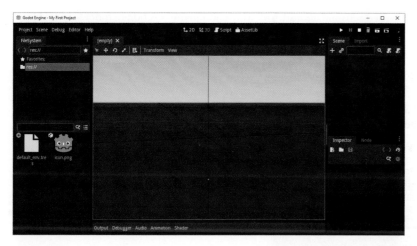

FIGURE 1.3
The main Godot Editor window.

The Main Viewport

In the central area of the screen you see the game viewport. It shows the current level you're editing, which is quite close to the final game, except for some additional visual cues and gizmos to help you edit the scene.

This viewport changes depending on the context. At the top, you can see a bar with the current viewport editor context. You can change between **2D**, **3D**, **Script**, and **AssetLib**, though most of the time the editor will change automatically based on what kind of file you open.

Above the actual viewport and below the scene tabs you can find some buttons and menus related to the current context. These are useful tools that help you edit the scenes and scripts with ease. The tools are covered throughout the book in the specific sections.

TIP

Asset Library

Though not directly related to game editing, the Asset Library is also shown on the main editor viewport. This is the place where you find community-created content to help you prototype and develop your games. These can be directly downloaded to your current project's folder and used right away. There is a variety of content available, such as code snippets, editor plugins, and game assets for prototyping. You can also check the content with your internet browser by going to https://godotengine.org/asset-library.

Editor Docks

Around the main editor viewport, there's a few docks with options to manage and edit your game. They are the most used interface portions when making scenes. We will now cover briefly each one of them so you can get used to the editor.

While the layout comes with a sensible default, you may change the position of a dock by clicking on the icon with three dots at the top-right corner of it. You can also save, delete, and change the layout by going to the **Editor** > **Editor Layout** submenu.

FileSystem

By default, at the left side of the FileSystem doc (Figure 1.4) you can see the files in your project. You can also see previews of the scenes and assets, and navigate within the project folder. A few actions are possible with this dock, such as renaming, moving, and deleting files.

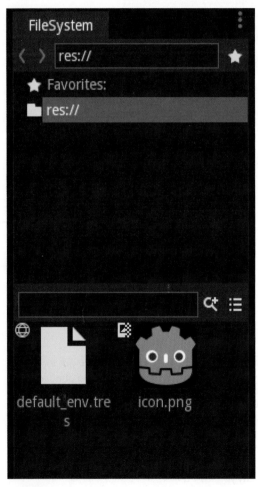

FIGURE 1.4
The FileSystem dock.

Scene Tree

The Scene Tree dock (shown in Figure 1.5) is where the hierarchy of the current scene is done. Most of Godot is based on Scenes and Nodes, as will be made clear in the next Hour. The Scene Tree dock is used most of the time, where you can add nodes to your scene, add scripts, and reorganize the hierarchy. This dock also helps you to select a specific node without having to scavenge for it in the main viewport.

FIGURE 1.5
The Scene Tree dock.

NOTE

Scenes and Nodes

Hour 2, "Scene System," covers the Scene System of Godot, explaining how nodes are put together to make game scenes. For now, you just need to understand the scene works as a tree of nodes where the root node is the base of the scene. Also, the bottom ones are drawn on top for 2D scenes (in 3D they respect the world position).

Node Dock

Right below the scene dock, along with the Inspector, you find the Node dock (see Figure 1.6). This is a helper dock that is used both for signals and groups (which will be properly covered later in the book). Here you can connect the selected node **Signals** to your functions, which act like event handlers. It is also used to manage the **Groups** to which your node belongs to. The groups can act like tags that can be used in scripting to check if the node belongs to a certain group to decide how to interact.

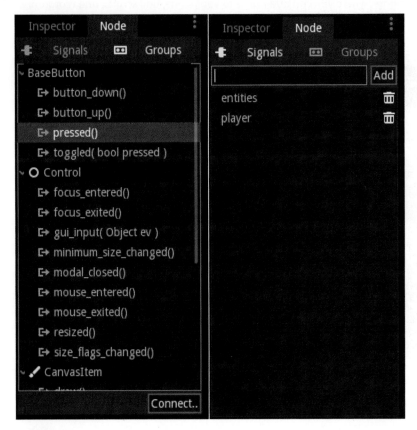

FIGURE 1.6
The Node dock.

Inspector

The Inspector dock (see Figure 1.7) is one of the most used docks, which is where you can edit the properties of the nodes and resources in the scene. The dock automatically shows the properties of a node when it is selected. It's a good place to look when you need pixel-perfect coordinates, and when making animations.

FIGURE 1.7
The Inspector dock.

Import Dock

The Import dock (see Figure 1.8) is the place to change your import settings for each file. Godot already has sensible defaults, but here you can change them to your specific needs. These settings can be changed when a file is selected on the FileSystem dock.

FIGURE 1.8
The Import dock.

Your First Scene

Now that you are introduced to the main editor interface, we will create a simple scene together.
This scene will contain an image and a simple button. We will also add a simple script to make the
image appear and disappear when the button is clicked.

Making a Simple Scene

To get your hands dirty, let's start using the editor to put together this simple scene.

1. On the Scene dock, click on the ➕ Add Node button.

2. You'll see the **Create New Node** dialog. Select the ◉ **Node2D**, which will be your root node. Notice how the viewport goes into the **2D** mode automatically. This contextual change is quite common inside the Godot editor.

3. Double click the Node2D you just created on the **Scene** dock and rename it to "MyFirstScene."

4. Click again on the ➕ **Add Node** button, but this time add a 😊 **Sprite** instead. You can leave the default name.

5. Drag the Godot **icon.png** from the FileSystem dock to the **Texture** property in the **Inspector**. This is the easiest way to set properties, which accepts a file as a value.

6. Select the **MyFirstScene** node again. This step is important so that the next node is added as a child of the root.

7. Add a 🆗 **Button** node now. This can also keep the default name.

8. In the **Inspector**, set the **Text** property of the node to "Click Me!"

9. Click and drag the Sprite until it is near the center of the screen. You can see the screen boundaries as a blue rectangle in the main viewport.

10. Move the Button so it is a bit below the Sprite. By now you'll have something like this:

FIGURE 1.9
Your first scene in the Godot Engine editor.

11. Click on the ![Play Edited Scene icon] **Play Edited Scene** button on the top right corner.

12. An alert will show up, saying you need to save the scene before playing. Select **Yes** and save it as "**MyFirstScene.tscn**", which is the default value.

13. The scene will automatically play. You can close the game window when you're done testing.

NOTE

Resource Path

When saving the scene, you may have noticed the "res://" path. This is your "Resource Root" and it points to the project folder. This path contains all resources exported to the final game, so anything outside your project folder can't be added to the game. This behavior ensures that your project is self-contained and avoids surprises when exporting the final game.

Also, note most of the time this path is not writeable. The export process usually creates a ".pck" file, which is a Godot-specific binary format that contains all your game files together and cannot be edited at runtime.

Adding a Script

You have likely noticed that the Scene button does nothing when clicked. That's the expected result since we haven't told it what to do. We'll fix it now with a little bit of scripting. While this might sound scary at first, programming is an essential part of game development so the sooner we start, the better.

To do this, select the root node on the **Scene** dock and click on the ![Add Script icon] **Add Script** button just above it. A dialog will appear (see Figure 1.10) where you can select the type of script you want and where to save it. In this case, we want a **GDScript** that inherits a Node2D (because that's the type of node receiving the script), not a built-in, and save this as "MyFirstScene.gd" on the root of the resource path.

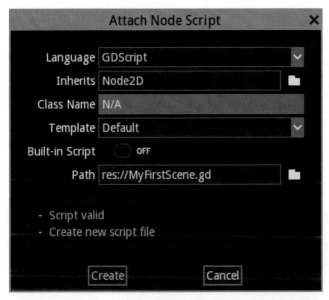

FIGURE 1.10
The Attach Node dialog. This is used both when creating new and
attaching existing scripts to your nodes.

After clicking on the **Create** button, the main viewport will automatically switch to the **Script** mode. The script you just created is already opened and filled with a default template. For our current purposes, you can delete everything in this file except for the first line.

Before doing any coding, we'll connect the Button's **pressed** signal to a new function using the Editor Interface. This will call the function whenever the Button is pressed. To do this you need to select the Button on the **Scene** dock, then click on the **Signals** part of the **Node** dock. You can see here the whole list of signals for a button. Click on the **pressed()** signal, and then on the **Connect** button below it. You'll see the **Connect Signal** dialog, which will be better explained in later Hours. For now, you can accept the defaults and click on the **Connect** button.

This will once again make the Script Editor appear, but now with a new function called `_on_Button_pressed()`. This function will be called whenever the Button is clicked. Now you can fill the whole script with the code in Listing 1.1.

LISTING 1.1   Simple Button Behavior

```
extends Node2D

func _on_Button_pressed():
    $Sprite.visible = not $Sprite.visible
```

This code is quite simple and what it does is simple to grasp: it sets the `visible` property of the node called `Sprite` to the opposite of its current value. This will make the Sprite toggle its visibility every time the function is called, which happens when the button is pressed. You can now play the scene again and click the button to see it in action.

TIP

Visual Scripting

Godot also has a visual scripting language. It is quite unique and, while not as powerful as GDScript, it can be used if you are not acquainted with programming and prefer a visual medium. Figure 1.11 shows how the button behavior code looks like when made in VisualScript.

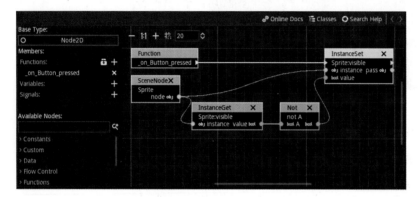

FIGURE 1.11
Simple Button behavior using Visual Scripting.

Setting Up a Main Scene

If you tried to run the project instead of just running the current scene, you would receive an error message saying that there's no main scene defined (see Figure 1.12). The main scene is the one that runs automatically when a game starts. For example, it can be used for the main menu or the initial credits animation.

FIGURE 1.12
Confirmation message asking to select a main scene before playing the project.

If you click on the **Select** button on this message, you'll see a file dialog where you can select a scene. For now, you only have one scene, so you can choose that one. Once it is confirmed, the project will play automatically with the scene you just selected. From now on, every time you run the project this scene will be played.

Project Settings

In Figure 1.12 you saw how you can change your main scene later in the **Project Settings**. This is an important place to check, because it provides a lot of options that you can change to tweak how your project is presented to the final user. You can open it from the **Project** menu, as shown in Figure 1.13.

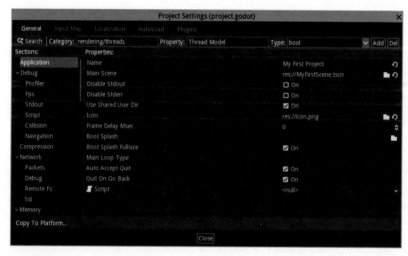

FIGURE 1.13
Godot Engine's project settings.

For instance, from there you can change the default resolution of the window and whether it runs full screen, and define the window title, as well as other presentation options. You can also make core tweaks such as default gravity settings and other physics options, as well as changing default graphics settings.

NOTE

Other Tabs in Project Settings

You have likely noticed that the Project Settings have a handful of tabs. The settings themselves are on the first **General** tab, but the others are quite useful as well. These will be covered more specifically in later hours.

▶ **General:** here are the options to tweak your game's presentation and behavior.

▶ **Input Map:** this is where you can map keys and gamepad buttons to actions. More on that in the hour about input.

▶ **Localization:** in this tab, you can import translation files and set the remapping of resources.

▶ **AutoLoad:** you can set up script and scene Singletons here, which are available in all scenes.

▶ **Plugins:** the editor plugins are listed here and can be activated and deactivated.

Summary

In this hour, you got started with the Godot Engine. You learned how to download and install Godot, saw the Project Manager interface, created your first project, and started the visual editor. Then you got yourself acquainted with the main editor interface and what each of the docks do. You learned how to create a simple scene using nodes and how to add scripts to them. You also learned about the project settings and how to set up the main scene.

Q&A

Q. Where is Godot Engine installed?

A. If you used the Windows installer, it'll be on your AppData folder. Otherwise, it remains where you left the executable.

Q. How can I go back to the Project Manager after opening a project?

A. You can click on the **Project** menu and select **Quit to Project List**.

Q. Can I set multiple scripts to the same node?

A. No, each node can have only one script attached to it.

Workshop

Answer the following questions to make sure you understood the content of this first hour.

Quiz

1. True or false: Godot Engine occupies a lot of space on the hard drive.

2. How do you import an existing project to the Project Manager?

3. Where can you set the properties of a selected node?

4. True or false: the first scene you make in a project is the main scene.

5. Where in the hard drive is the Resource Path?

Answers

1. False. Godot takes only about 30MB of your hard drive.

2. When in the Project Manager interface, click on the **Import** button.

3. On the **Inspector** dock.

4. False. You must explicitly select a scene as the main one.

5. It is in the same place as your project folder.

Exercises

Take your time to get used to the editor. The remaining book will refer to the concepts learned in this hour, so it's important to have a good understanding of them.

1. Create a new scene and add a Node2D as the root node.

2. Rename the root node to "MyTestScene" and save the scene with the default name.

3. Add a 😃 **Sprite** to the scene.

4. Using your operating system's file manager, copy an image to your project folder.

5. See how the new image appears to the **FileSystem** dock? Set that image as your Sprite texture.

6. Try to change the dimensions and rotation of the Sprite using the editor. The contextual toolbar at the top of the main viewport will help you with this.

7. Look at the inspector and see how the properties of the Sprite change as you alter it in the visual editor.

8. Use the toolbar's 🔒 **Lock** and 🔓 **Unlock** buttons. Notice how the padlocks appear in the viewport and Scene Dock to show the current lock status.

9. Select the image in the **FileSystem** dock. Now go to the **Import** dock and change the settings there. Click on the **Reimport** button to see the changes applied in the main viewport. Play a while with the settings.

10. Open the **Debug** menu and enable **Sync Scene Changes**.

11. Run your scene and, without closing the game window, make changes to your Sprite. Notice how the game window will update automatically to show the changes you are making in-editor.

12. Add a 🏷 **Label** node to your scene and set its **Text** property to anything you like. If you still have the game window open, you'll see how the new node also appears in the game window.

13. Close the game window and save your scene with the **Scene** menu or by pressing **Ctrl+S**

14. Open the **Project Settings** and set this new scene as the main one.

15. Play the project to see how the main scene changed.

HOUR 2
Scene System

What You'll Learn in This Hour:

▶ What Godot's Scene System entails

▶ What nodes are and how to use them

▶ How nodes and scenes relate to each other

▶ How resources are managed in Godot

▶ How to explore the possibilities of the scene system

One special part of Godot and what makes it different from other engines is its **Scene System**. Godot is based upon nodes and how they compose a scene. In this hour, you'll learn how this system works and what can be done with it. While this chapter may be more abstract, it is the foundation upon which Godot is built, and will be helpful to design and develop all of your games.

Nodes and Scenes

All Godot games are based on nodes and scenes. Nodes are atoms of game functionality, and are put together to make scenes. These scenes can then be combined to make bigger and more complex scenes. This is what you have to take into account when designing your games.

Node

A **Node** is the most fundamental element of the game-building process. It is a basic block of functionality that has a name, properties, and a special function. A node can be extended via inheritance in the OOP (object-oriented programming) sense, which is done inside the engine itself or via modules. For your game functionality, the node can be extended with a script to have custom and specific actions such as decreasing the life of the player when hit by a bullet.

When you click on the ✚ **Add Node** button of the Scene dock, you are greeted with a large list of nodes from which to choose. While it may seem daunting to learn what all these nodes do, you don't need to do it all at once. The nodes have descriptive names that are easy to remember and are organized by their inheritance tree: the nodes down the tree are specializations of their parent. Also in that dialog, you can either click a node to select it and see its description on the box below or simply hover your mouse cursor over any node to see a tooltip with the description.

There are three main types of nodes: ⊙ **Node2D**, ⊙ **Spatial**, and ⊙ **Control**. These are the bases for most of the node types and relates to their specific functions (see Figure 2.1). Node2D is the base for all nodes in 2D games, as Spatial is for all 3D nodes. There is some correspondence between 2D and 3D nodes, e.g., Camera (derived from Spatial) versus Camera2D (derived from Node2D). This relationship makes it easy to alternate between 2D and 3D games with maintained familiarity. The Control node is the base for all GUI, which can be used in both 2D and 3D games.

Every node can have a callback to process within the game loop. This makes sure, for instance, that the AnimationPlayer node has a chance to update the Animation each frame and a Particles node can process in the next batch. This also applies to custom scripts, so you can check if the user has pressed a button that'll move the player character.

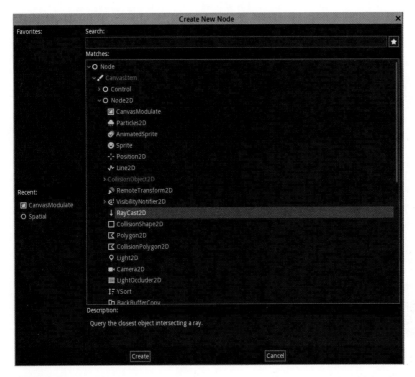

FIGURE 2.1
Create New Node dialog, which contains a list of all nodes you can add to a scene.

NOTE

Game Loop

A commonplace element in game development is the **game loop**. This is a code that gets executed every frame to update the game world, check user input, and draw the result to the screen. Godot has two types of game loops: **Idle** and **Fixed**. The Idle process is so called because every frame is drawn as fast as possible. The Fixed processing has a fixed timestep that is synchronized with the physics loop, with a default of 60 FPS (Frames Per Second).

Scene

A node by itself cannot do much. To explore its full potential, it needs to be combined with other nodes to expand functionality. That's why we make **Scenes**. A scene is nothing more than a node with other nodes as children, forming a tree structure. It is important to notice that the scene structure is formed by the fact that nodes can have multiple children but only a single parent.

A scene starts with one node (called the **root**), which can have any number of children and grandchildren (see Figure 2.2).

FIGURE 2.2
Scene Tree of Godot's Platformer 3D demo project

This tree structure guarantees how the nodes interface with its parent and children. Here's a breakdown of the tree properties:

▶ Nodes are processed in tree order. The root node will receive the process callback before its children.

▶ Nodes are drawn in tree order. The parents are drawn before the children, which means that children cover their parents (this does not apply to 3D nodes).

▶ Nodes inherit the transform of their parents. This means that if a node changes position, rotation, or scale, it'll be applied to all of its children. Children's transforms are relative to their parent.

Resources

Another special type of object inside Godot is the **Resource**. While nodes represent behaviors (physics interaction or UI controls, for example), Resources represent data. As an example, the **AnimationPlayer** node is responsible for playing and stopping Animations. To know what it needs to do, it needs the data that comes from the **Animation** Resource. An Animation contains all of the properties of nodes that need to be animated, and the AnimationPlayer reads this data to make the needed changes in the scene.

There are a lot of core Resource types in the engine, but you rarely need to create the manually. When you set the texture property of a Sprite, Godot creates a Resource from the PNG file that you set. The same happens when you create an Animation inside the AnimationPlayer inside the editor. Most of the time, Resources are created with specific contextual editors or by import plugins.

If you need to create a Resource manually, you can do so by clicking the **New Resource** button in the Inspector dock. A dialog much like the one you see when you add nodes will show up, but this one shows the Resource types instead. It is interesting to take a look at this list and see all types of Resources provided by Godot, but you rarely (if ever) need to create Resources this way. Resources can also be created in the Inspector property dropdown if the property requires a Resource type.

NOTE

Custom Nodes and Resources

It is possible to create your own node types by creating new editor plugins. Custom nodes and Resources appear in the dialog list, so they behave like core types. How to do this won't be covered in this book, but it can be found in Godot engine's official documentation.

Inspecting and Editing Resources

Resources can be edited in the Inspector-like nodes. While not all Resource types have meaning-ful exposed properties in the editor, some types greatly benefit from the Inspector. If a property requires a Resource, you can open it by clicking the property itself, and it'll open in the Inspector dock. You can go back to the previously edited object by pressing the ◀ **Back** button or by clicking the ⊙ **History** button.

Some Resource types have custom editors. For instance, if you create a ⚙ **Theme** Resource, the proper contextual editor will appear where you can edit the theme options. This happens if you click a property that contains a theme but also if you double-click the file in the FileSystem dock.

Resource Locations and Uniqueness

Resources in Godot can either be saved inside the scene file or as its own separate file. There are advantages and disadvantages in both workflows, and it's usually best decided case by case. In general, if you reuse the Resource across scenes, it is best to save as a separate file so it can be load in multiple places.

You need to understand that Resources are shared by default. If you duplicate a node in the tree, the Resources they use will be shared, and if you edit one, it'll affect all instances that use it. Usually, this behavior is desired (Godot ensures that the Resource is loaded only once from the disk, increasing performance), but if you want to have two different copies of the Resource, you need to make them unique. This can be done by clicking on the ⋮ vertical ellipsis besides the property on the Inspector and selecting 📋 **Make Unique** on the dropdown menu (see Figure 2.3). You can also make all sub-Resources of a node unique by selecting the corresponding option in the Inspector 🔧 **Tools** menu.

FIGURE 2.3
Resource dropdown menu
on the Inspector dock.

Combining Scenes

While a scene by itself can be quite powerful, it is easy to make it too big and difficult to maintain. A game is composed of many scenes. You don't need to see a scene as simply a "level" or an "area" of the game, but also as a collection of small composition blocks that can be combined into larger scenes. For instance, your player can be a scene that is then put into the larger level scene.

Inheriting Scenes

There are two ways in which a scene can be extended. They can be either Inherited or Instanced. Inheritance is a way to create derived scenes from a same base. You may have a default structure with nodes and properties set to a character. Then your player is a character that can benefit from the structure by tweaking a few values with an **Inherited Scene**. The enemy is also a character and can be inherited of the same scene. If for some reason the way characters are structured changes, you can simply change the base scene.

Inheritance works in scenes similar to how it works in general OOP. You have a base scene with some general structure and the child scene that inherits from it, specializing the structure by adding other nodes to the tree and changing the base properties. **Inheriting scenes is the same as instancing them as the root node for a new scene.**

You can create one by clicking on the **New Inherited Scene** option under the **Scene** menu. The editor will open a dialog where you can select the base scene.

Instancing Scenes

When you are designing your level, you need to put several enemies in place. These enemies all look and behave alike, so you can simply copy and paste the nodes to put them in various places. However, if later you need to change how they look, you'll need to find all the copies to change them. That's where **Scene Instancing** can help.

Instead of making your enemies directly in the level scene, you can create a new scene with just the enemy. You can customize it until you're satisfied, then make an instance of it in the level scene. An instance means there's a reference to another scene inside the tree. Since scenes always have a single root node, they can behave like a node, which you can place anywhere in the tree.

When you change the original scene on the disk, all instances will be updated to reflect the new values. Note that if you change a property of an instanced scene, it won't affect the original, and if the original ever changes, this property won't be updated. To revert the property to its original value, you need to click the 🔄 **Revert** button beside the property in the Inspector dock.

Instancing Scenes

There are four ways to instance a scene in the editor. Let's try each of them by following these steps:

1. Make a simple scene that can be instanced. It can contain just the root node. Save this scene as "**subscene.tscn**".

2. Create a new scene and add a 🔘 **Node** as the root.

3. Save the scene as "**main-scene.tscn**".

4. Click on the 🔗 **Instance Scene** button in the Scene dock.

5. In the file dialog that appears, select "**subscene.tscn**" and click on the **Open** button.

6. You can see on the Scene dock a new child node with a special 🎬 **Subscene** icon. This means this node comes from another scene.

7. Now locate the "**subscene.tscn**" in the FileSystem dock.

8. Drag the "**subscene.tscn**" file from the FileSystem dock and drop it over the root Node on the Scene dock. That's the second way to instance scenes.

9. Select the root Node in the Scene dock.

10. Drag the "**subscene.tscn**" file from the FileSystem to the main editor viewport. You can see a preview of how it'll look.

11. Drop the scene anywhere in the Viewport. It'll be placed there as a child of the selected node. This is the third way to instance a scene.

12. On the Scene dock, select the root Node.

13. Back on the FileSystem dock, right-click "**subscene3.tscn**" the file and select **Instance** on the menu that appears (see Figure 2.4). That is the last way to instance a scene in the editor.

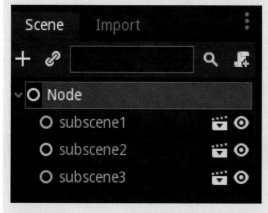

FIGURE 2.4
Instanced scenes shown in the tree.

TIP

When to Create a New Scene

It's tempting to start a new scene and add nodes until you're satisfied. But it's important to have a design idea before making the scenes of the game. You can think of each isolated component as a scene. A "Player Character" likely will be its own scene. The protagonist's house is bound to be its own scene, too, and maybe each piece of furniture is a scene, especially if they are reused in other houses.

Some game engines have a distinction between "scenes" and "prefabs." Godot does not make such a distinction. If you are used to make prefabs in other engines, make it a scene when using Godot. This makes the workflow much more flexible, and you can make design diagrams thinking about how the Scene Tree will be constructed by concrete objects.

Managing Subscenes

When you break down your game in small, single-function scenes, it's much easier to deal with the content. However, you need to know how to maintain the larger scenes that are composed of the smaller ones. This section shows a few tips on how to manage your scenes and ease the way you edit them.

Opening Instanced Subscenes

Sometimes, you need to tweak something in the original scene to reflect everywhere it's instanced. You don't need to fiddle around the file system to find it. You just need to click the **Open Subscene** button that appears beside the node in the Scene dock. When you click this icon, the original scene that was instanced will open in another tab inside the editor. If you make changes and save the subscene, then go back to the where it was instanced, the editor will update the view to reflect the changes.

Editing Subscene's Children

By default, only the root node of the instanced scene is shown. This helps keep the Scene dock clear of clutter and encapsulates the functionality of subscenes. However, sometimes you may want to change a property of a child of the subscene's root. This is possible if you enable the **Editable Children** option. You can do that by right-clicking the node in the Scene dock and enabling the option in the context menu.

Note that any property of the instanced that you edit will save in the main scene. So, if you change the original subscene later, the changes won't reflect in the main scene, because they were overridden there. This is the case even if you disable the Editable Children option later. You need to revert the properties that you don't want to override.

Unlinking an Inherited Scene

It may be the case that you edited the subscene so much that it's simply easier to remove the link to the original scene. Or you simply want to copy a subscene because the structure is similar, but it is unrelated to the original. In these cases, you can remove the instanced status of the subscene by clicking on the **Discard Instancing** option in the right-click context menu of the node.

When the instancing is discarded, the subscene tree will integrate in the main scene tree and become part of it. This is like making the subscene part of the main scene from the beginning.

Splitting a Scene

There are cases when you want to do the opposite: the scene has become too big and certain elements can be made into a subscene to be reused. Godot also offers the possibility to save a branch of the tree as a subscene. If you right-click the node in the Scene dock, you can select the **Save Branch as Scene** option. This will make a file dialog appear so you can save the subscene. After saving it, the branch will turn into an instanced scene right way.

NOTE

Cyclic Dependencies

Godot will detect and stop you from making cyclic dependencies. This means that if scene A instances scene B, which then instances scene C, Godot won't let you instance scene A inside scene C. Because A depends on B, which depends on C, adding A as a subscene will make the scenes themselves children, which is an undefined behavior.

Summary

In this hour, you were introduced to Godot's Scene System. You learned about Scenes, Nodes, and Resources. You saw how a Scene is composed as a tree of nodes and learned that nodes represent behaviors, while resources contain data. You learned how to split and join scenes to help you compose your game.

Q&A

Q. Can a node have more than one parent?

A. No, a node can have only one parent. This ensures the tree structure.

Q. What is best for performance: a big monolithic scene or a lot of instanced subscenes?

A. This depends on the project structure, but usually there's no noticeable performance impact on instancing subscenes. In fact, if these subscenes are reused, it's likely more performant to instance them.

Q. What happens if I delete a scene or resource from the disk that is used somewhere?

A. When you open the scene inside the editor, a dialog will appear so you can fix the missing dependencies. When deleting from the FileSystem dock, the editor will warn you if the file is used elsewhere.

Workshop

Here are a few questions for you to review the contents of this second hour.

Quiz

1. What is the fundamental element of a game?

2. True or False: Resources are shared between nodes by default.

3. How are subscenes indicated as such?

4. In which order are the nodes processed?

5. True or False: Resources are loaded only once from the disk.

Answers

1. The node is the base element to create games.

2. True. When a Node that contains a Resource is duplicated, or when the Resource is copied using the copy/paste function of the Inspector, the resources are shared by default unless explicitly made unique.

3. There's a special icon in the Scene dock indicating that the node is an instanced scene.

4. They're processed in tree order, and the parent is processed before its children.

5. True. If the game requests a resource that is already in its memory, Godot won't load it again from the disk.

Exercises

This hour is more conceptual than practical. You should take some time doing these exercises to help you visualize the concepts inside the editor and see how everything is affected.

1. Create a new scene and add a ⬤ **Node** as the root node.

2. Rename the root node "**MasterScene**" and save the scene as "**master-scene.tscn**".

3. Create another scene and add a 🙂 **Sprite** node.

4. Rename the node "**SubScene**" and save the scene as "**sub-scene.tscn**".

5. Instance the "sub-scene.tscn" inside the "main-scene.tscn".

6. Go to the "sub-scene.tscn" in editor and change the position of the only node there. Save the scene.

7. Go back to the "main-scene.tscn" and observe how the subscene is updated.

8. Change the position of the subscene inside the master scene and save it.

9. Go to the subscene in editor and once again change the position of the root. Save the scene.

10. When you go back to the master scene, notice how the Sprite's position isn't updated anymore.

11. Select the SubScene node on the master scene.

12. In the Inspector dock, find the Transform > Position property. Click on the 🔄 **Revert** button.

13. Observe how the node changes position to the place saved in the subscene.

HOUR 3
2D Graphics

What You'll Learn in This Hour:

▶ Peculiarities of the 2D graphics in Godot
▶ Making simple vector math operations
▶ Using 2D cameras
▶ Creating TileSets and TileMaps
▶ Making a parallax background effect

Godot Engine has dedicated tools to work on 2D games. **While many of the functions of the engine can be used the same way in 2D and 3D, some of the topics don't have a one-to-one comparison**. The 2D graphics pipeline is one of these examples. In 3D, you have a world to explore and position objects, but for 2D, you have only the screen plane to work with.

In this hour, you'll learn to deal with 2D graphics and how Godot treats the screen plane. You'll also see some of the specific tools for making 2D games, how they work, and how to use them.

Sprites and Draw Order

The basis of a 2D graphics engine is the Sprite. A **Sprite** is simply an image that can be drawn anywhere on the game screen. It can also be scaled, rotated, and flipped, which allows for a great number of visual effects. Before we get deep into how Sprites are used, let's first talk about the Viewport, which is where they are drawn.

Viewport Coordinates

The Viewport is a bit different than the Main Viewport in the editor, because now we're talking about how the game will look when it is running. You can consider the Viewport as a Cartesian plane where the (0,0) position is the top left corner and the Y axis goes downward, which is depicted in Figure 3.1. The Viewport itself can be scaled and stretched in the final game if the user can resize the window, but the coordinate system remains the same.

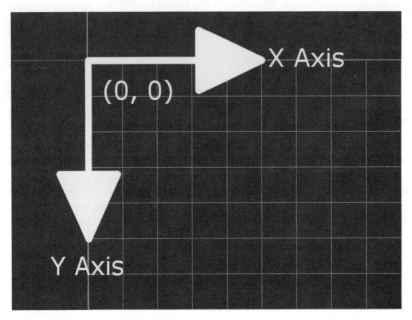

FIGURE 3.1
Godot 2D Coordinate System

Draw Order

Nodes are drawn in the tree order. This means that nodes higher in the hierarchy will be drawn first, and thus will be shown behind the bottom nodes. This is the reverse order of layers, which are usually drawn in image editing software. Figure 3.2 shows a sample of the draw order. If you want a node to be shown on top, it must be in the bottom of the tree. Note that the children of a node are drawn after it, but they appear behind the next sibling of such a node.

TIP

Remote Transform

Remember that the position and scale of a node is affected by its parent. Sometimes you want that to happen but also want that node drawn before other nodes above it in the tree. For this use, there's the ![icon] RemoteTransform2D node. You can add it as a child of the node, which applies the transform and targets the node you want to draw behind. Then you can leave the node higher in the tree and have it affected by another node's transform.

Note that you have some other options, such as setting the Z-index of the node (higher Z values are drawn on top) or enabling the **Show Behind Parent** property. But the latter option is limited, and the Z value is less performant than the tree order.

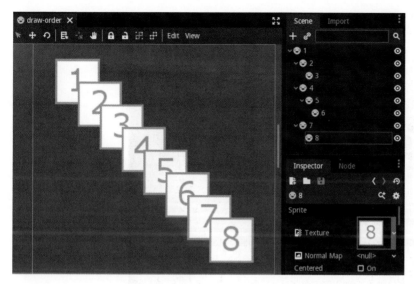

FIGURE 3.2
Visual example of the draw order. Notice how the Scene Tree dock shows the nodes in the same order they are drawn.

Sprites

The Sprite node is very useful for 2D games. It is just a single texture that you can rotate, scale, and position anywhere in the viewport. This node can be used for characters, props, HUDs, and any other thing that needs an image. Sprites are also great for spritesheet animations, since you can select a region of the image to show.

Sprite Regions

While the engine documentation explains every property, we'll see a couple of Sprites' abilities. One of them is the **Region** property. It allows you to show only a part of the texture in the game. This is very useful if you have a sheet image with many items and want to display a single one without slicing the image.

In the bottom panel, you can find a **Texture Region** editor (see Figure 3.3). This tool can be used to visually slice the image and select exactly the portion you want to show. Note that this tool is only available when a Sprite node is selected.

Frames

If you are making a spritesheet animation, selecting individual regions for each frame can soon become tedious. Godot has a tool to help in this task: the frames property of Sprite. You can set **Vframes** to the number of rows the spritesheet has and similarly the **Hframes** to the number of columns. Then you set the **Frame** property to the current frame of the sheet, remembering that

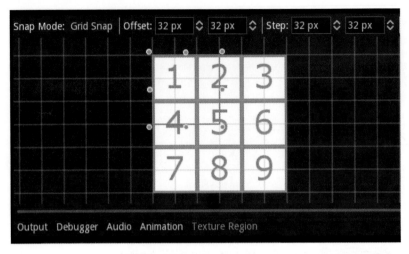

FIGURE 3.3
Texture Region editor tool.

it starts with zero. The number of frames is equal to the number of rows times the number of columns. The frames go from left to right and top to bottom (the same order as reading a text).

Vectors and Transforms

Let's take a pause from the engine tools and talk a bit about the theory and math of 2D graphics. While this may seem scary and difficult, this knowledge will make your game developer life much easier. By using vector math, you can avoid using trigonometry and angle calculations, and also use the built-in engine functions.

Vector

As stated before, the Viewport can be seen as a Cartesian plane. A **Vector** is usually described as an (x, y) pair that represents the horizontal and vertical distance from the axes, respectively (see Figure 3.4). The starting point (0, 0) is where the axes cross each other and is called the **origin**.

While vectors are used as a position, they can also be seen as a combination of **direction** and **magnitude**. If you imagine a vector as an arrow from the origin to the position it specifies, the direction is where the arrow is pointing and the magnitude is the length of the arrow.

To calculate the magnitude, you can use the Pythagorean Theorem. The length of the vector is the hypotenuse, while the x and y components are the sides. Thus, $||v|| = \sqrt{x^2 + y^2}$. However, Godot engine already provides a helper function to get the length of a vector: `var m = vector .length()`.

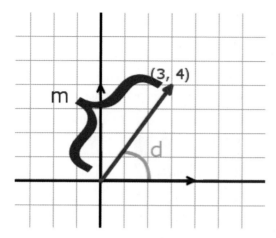

FIGURE 3.4
A vector in 2D space. The "m" represents the magnitude, which is the length of the vector.
The "d" is the angle of the horizontal axis, which is a visual way to represent direction.

Vector Operations

There are a few possible mathematical operations with vectors that are very useful to use in games. You can add, subtract, and multiply a vector with a scalar (that is, a regular number). There are also two vector-specific operations: dot product and cross product (see Figure 3.5).

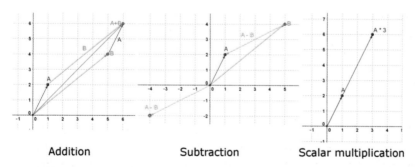

Addition   Subtraction   Scalar multiplication

FIGURE 3.5
Vector operations described visually with graphs.

▶ **Addition** is done component by component. (1, 2) + (3, 4) = (4, 6). Visually, addition is the same as starting the second vector in the end of the first one instead of the origin. If you see that as movement, it is the same as moving from the origin to the end of the first vector and then moving the distance of the second in its direction.

▶ **Subtraction** is done like addition. $(1, 2) - (3, 4) = (-2, -2)$. It is the same as a vector going from the second one to the first. This is useful for getting the distance between vectors.

▶ **Multiplication with a scalar** is the same as multiplying the scalar for each of the vector components. $3 \times (1, 2) = (3, 6)$. The resulting vector keeps the same direction but has the length multiplied by the other number. It's called a "scalar" because it scales the vector.

▶ **Dot product** is a kind of multiplication of vectors, and is defined as the sum of the products of the vector components. $(1, 2) \cdot (3, 4) = 1 \times 3 + 2 \times 4 = 11$. The result is a scalar, which is equal to the magnitude of both vectors multiplied by the cosine of the angle between them, or mathematically speaking: $a \cdot b = ||a|| \, ||b|| \cos \theta$. This can be used to get the angle between the vectors, though Godot has helper functions for that too. It is also useful to know on what side of the vector things are.

▶ **Cross product** is the other type of vector multiplication, and is only defined for three and seven dimensions, so it is not useful for 2D. The cross product of two vectors result in another vector, which is perpendicular to both. This will be better explained in the chapter about 3D graphics.

Unit vectors

A unit vector is a vector with magnitude of 1. These are very useful when used as direction only, since each can be multiplied by a scalar to change the magnitude. It is also useful to calculate the dot product of unit vectors, because the result value is always in the $[-1, 1]$ interval and it has a special meaning: if the vectors are parallel, the dot product is 1; if they are perpendicular, the dot product is 0; and if they have opposite direction, the dot product is -1.

The process of getting a unit vector from a regular vector is called **normalization**, and can be achieved by dividing each component by the vector magnitude. Godot also has a helper function for that: `var unit = vector.normalized()`.

Transforms

Another mathematical knowledge that is useful for games is how matrices can be used to transform objects. Each node resides in its local space and is affected by the transforms of its ancestor to determine its position in the global space. You can see that easily in Godot by adding a Sprite in the tree and another one as its child. Move the parent in the scene, then select the child and see its Position property in the Inspector dock: (0, 0). You can visually see that it is moving in the scene, but that's because the node is being affected by its parent transform.

The transform is a mix of translation (or position), rotation, and scale (see Listing 3.1). The translation is the distance between the origins of the global and local space. The rotation and scale could be represented as an angle and a vector, but it is described as two vectors: one describes the horizontal position (where the X axis of the node's local space is located), and the other represents the vertical axis. The three vectors are joined in a 3×2 matrix:

$$\text{transform} = \begin{bmatrix} X_x & X_y \\ Y_x & Y_y \\ O_x & O_y \end{bmatrix}$$

The first two rows are how the X and Y axis of the local space is transformed, and the last line is the translation. Godot has a Transform class to help you with those functions.

LISTING 3.1   Transform operations

```
var transform = Transform2D()
var x = transform.x # X axis vector
var y = transform.y # Y axis vector
var o = transform.o # Origin translation vector
```

The Power of Transforms

The main use of matrices is to store transform operations. If you multiply one transform matrix by another, the result is a matrix that combines both operations (see Listing 3.2). Note that order matters and while mathematically the last transform is applied first, Godot works in the reverse order. By default, a Transform is defined with the identity matrix $\begin{bmatrix} 1 & 0 \\ 0 & 1 \\ 0 & 0 \end{bmatrix}$. This means that no transform is made and the object keeps its default position, rotation, and scale.

For instance, you can get a simple scale matrix that will change the rotation of the node and combine it with another that changes the scale.

LISTING 3.2   Combining transforms

```
var rotate_matrix = Transform2D().rotated(deg2rad(90)) # rotate 90 degrees
var scale_matrix = Transform2D().scaled(Vector2(2, 2)) # scale twice in each axis
var translate_matrix = Transform2D().translated
var combined_matrix = translate_matrix * rotate_matrix * scale_matrix  # combine
the transforms in order
$my_node.transform *= combined   # apply the transform to a node
```

NOTE

Inverse Transform Matrices

Another interesting possibility made available by matrices is the ability to invert the transform. If you apply the inverse matrix, it is the same as reverting all the transformation. You can, for example, make a node ignore its ancestors' transform.

Note that the inverse transform only works if the matrix is orthonormalized (i.e., the vectors are normalized and orthogonal to each other); otherwise, you need to get the affine inverse to correctly apply the inverse transform. Godot provides both as helper functions.

Cameras

It is not uncommon for a game to have levels bigger than the window. In an RPG, the player usually has a large world to explore. That's where Cameras come in. Instead of moving the whole world to fit the viewport, you can simply add a Camera and make it follow the player.

The ▢ Camera2D is like every other node: you place it in the Scene Tree wherever you want it to be. It is commonly placed as a child of the character's root node so it follows the player around. The node itself is very simple. Here is a breakdown of its major properties:

- ▶ **Offset:** This changes the camera center. Instead of moving the camera's position, you can set the offset to make the camera scroll. It is very useful for making animations, such as a shake effect, and it's easily reset to the original place.

- ▶ **Anchor Mode:** This sets whether the follow node should be on center and respect margins (**Drag Center**) or if it remains fixed on the top left corner (**Fixed Top Left**).

- ▶ **Rotating:** This designates whether the Camera should rotate with the parent. If it rotates, you'll see the world rotating instead of the target node.

- ▶ **Current:** This sets the active camera. There can be only one current camera per viewport.

- ▶ **Zoom:** This changes the zoom of the view. Larger numbers make things seem further away.

- ▶ **Limits:** This limits how far the camera can go. It's useful for not letting the camera out of the level boundaries.

- ▶ **Drag Margins:** You can make the camera stay still if the parent is moving only inside the drag margins. It's also possible to enable individually for the horizontal or vertical axis.

- ▶ **Smoothing:** If enabled, the camera will have smooth transitions of speed instead of abruptly moving and stopping. You can also set the smoothing when reaching the camera's limits.

NOTE

Split Screens

Cameras are very useful when implementing split-screen games. You can have a camera for each player and make them render in different Viewport nodes. This feature is better explained in the chapter about Viewports.

TileMaps

Another common feature in 2D games is the TileMap. It allows you to make a set of tiles and use them to create the screens of your game. Not only does this reduce the amount of art you need, it also helps you quickly create large and varied levels. Godot has the ▦ **TileMap** node specifically for this purpose.

Making a TileSet

Before creating your game stages with TileMaps, you need first to create a ⊞ **TileSet** resource. Godot has a way for you to transform your source images into a resource that the engine can understand and use. You can either use a single image for your whole TileSet or split each tile into its individual file.

Create your TileSet

Grab your favorite tile set image(s) and learn how to make your own TileSet resource by following these steps:

1. Copy your tile set image(s) to the project.

2. Create a new scene and add a ◉ Node2D as the root.

3. Save the scene as "**tileset-source.tscn**".

4. Add a ☺ **Sprite** as a child of the root and rename it to match your tile.

5. Set the Sprite's texture as the image for your first tile.

6. If needed, set the Region property to match your tile.

7. If you need physics collisions, add a ▦ **StaticBody2D** as a child of the Sprite. You'll also need a ▪ **CollisionShape2D**, as seen in the chapter about physics.

8. Repeat steps 4 to 7 until all the tiles are added.

9. Save the scene.

10. Click on the menu **Scene -> Convert To -> TileSet**.

11. Save the file as "**tileset.res**". This is your TileSet resource!

TIP

Grid and Snapping

While you don't need to set the position of the Sprites in the scene to create the TileSet, it is nice to have all of them visible. In this task, you may find it difficult to position the tiles next to each other. This is where the grid and snapping functions can help.

In the toolbar on the main viewport, you'll see the **Edit** menu. There, you can enable the **Use Snap** and **Show Grid** options. The grid will likely not match your tile size by default, but you can configure it in the same menu by clicking on the **Configure Snap** option. Then you can set the Grid Step option to the same size as your tiles. It'll be much easier to organize your tile set in the scene.

Using TileMaps

Now that you have a TileSet resource ready, let's use it to make a game stage. Using a TileMap is very simple; you just need to add a ▦ **TileMap** node to the scene and set its ▦ **TileSet** property to the file you just created. You can do that by dragging from the FileSystem to the Inspector dock. You also need to set the **Cell Size** property to match the size of your tiles.

Once you select the TileMap node on your scene, the editor will change to show the palette of tiles in the left of the Main Viewport and show a grid to help you position your tiles. The process of composing a stage is simply selecting the tile you want on the list and clicking on the scene where you want it to appear. If you right-click on a place in the map, the tile is cleared.

There are a few contextual items on the toolbar for TileMap creation. Here's a breakdown of them:

- ▶ **Tile position:** The first item shows the current position of the mouse in tile coordinates. It also shows the name of the tile placed in the position. This is useful if you need mathematical precision when placing the tiles.

- ▶ ▦ **TileMap:** This menu has a few functions to edit the map. The next bullets will cover the items of this menu.

- ▶ **Bucket:** This option works similar to painting programs by filling an enclosed area with the same tile.

- ▶ **Pick Tile:** It's the same as the eyedropper function of painting programs. It allows you to select the tile under the cursor to become the active tile for painting.

- ▶ **Select:** This allows you to select a portion of the map.

- ▶ **Duplicate selection:** This makes a copy of the selection and lets you place it elsewhere in the map.

- ▶ **Erase selection:** This deletes the currently selected tiles.

- ▶ ▦ **Transpose:** This changes the rows of the tile into columns and vice versa. Visually, it's the same as rotating 90[dg] to the left and mirroring the image.

- ▶ ↔ **Mirror X:** Mirrors the tile in the horizontal axis.

- ▶ ↕ **Mirror Y:** Mirrors the tile in the vertical axis.

- ▶ ◯◖◗◗ **Rotate Buttons:** Rotate the tile by 0[dg], 90[dg], 180[dg], and 270[dg], respectively.

TIP

Third-party TileSet and TileMap Tools

There are several third-party tools to make TileSets and TileMaps, such as the Tiled Map Editor. While Godot does not support those out of the box, you can find plugins in the Asset Library. There are also plugins to split your tile set image automatically into a TileSet resource.

Other Projections

Orthogonal TileMaps are the most common type, so it is Godot's default mode. But it is also possible to make isometric and hexagonal maps.

For the Isometric mode, you need to change the TileMap mode from **Square** to **Isometric**. The editor will automatically change to show the tiles in the way you want. For Hexagonal mode, you can keep the mode on Square, but change **Half Offset** property to either **Offset Y** or **Offset X**, depending on the map orientation. This will make the grid look like a "brick wall," where the rows or columns have an offset in relation to the previous one.

You can also make a custom projection by selecting the **Custom** mode and changing the **Custom Transform** property to your own transform matrix.

ParallaxBackground

Another interesting and useful node is the ParallaxBackground. It allows you to easily make the parallax effect, in which distant objects seem to move more slowly than closer ones. This effect is common in side-scrolling games and gives another depth to the visual aspect of your game.

ParallaxBackground Node

The node itself is a helper for you to achieve the desired effect. Together with the ParallaxLayer node, this provides all the options for you to customize the parallax background. Let's break down its properties:

- ▶ **Offset:** This designates how much of the background is offset. This is set automatically if you have a Camera2D, but can otherwise be set with code or animations to make effects (such as clouds moving).

- ▶ **Base offset:** This sets the base value for the offset property of the children of ParrallaxLayer nodes.

- ▶ **Base scale:** This is the base scale value for the children of ParallaxLayer.

- ▶ **Limit begin/end:** This is the limit to where the background will scroll. The "limit begin" marks the top-left limit, while "limit end" sets the bottom-right limit. The background will stop scrolling as the camera reaches outside those limits.

- ▶ **Ignore camera zoom:** If enabled, the background will ignore the camera zoom property and will be drawn at its regular size.

ParallaxLayer Node

The ParallaxBackground works by having multiple ParallaxLayer nodes as its children (see Figure 3.6). Each layer works as a plane in a distant position. By having multiple layers, you can

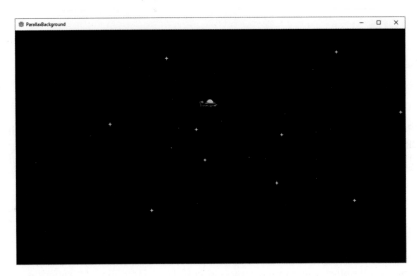

FIGURE 3.6
Parallax background sample

make each layer move at its own speed, giving the parallax effect you want. This node has only three properties:

▶ **Scale:** This is how much this layer moves relative to the background offset. Lower values make it go slowly, and it's used for further layers. You can set different scale values for each axis.

▶ **Offset:** This is the starting offset of this layer. This makes the layer start in a different position.

▶ **Mirroring:** This is the size of the layer frame. Once it passes the size defined here, the layer will start repeating. Note that if this property is less than the screen size, it may not work as intended.

TRY IT YOURSELF ▼

Make a ParallaxBackground

This effect is much more interesting when seeing it in practice. Follow these steps to make your own project:

1. Make a new project and add the images for the background, ship, and stars into its folder.

2. Create a new scene and add a ⬤ Node2D as the root.

3. Save the scene as "**parallax-background.tscn**".

4. Add a 😊 **Sprite** as a child of the root and name it "ship".

5. Set the Sprite's texture as the ship's image.

6. Add a 📷 **Camera2D** node as a child of the ship. Set it as **Current** using the Inspector dock.

7. Add a 🔳 **ParallaxBackground** node as a child of the root.

8. Add a 🔳 **ParallaxLayer** as child of the previous node. Set its **Scale** to (0.2, 0.2). This will be the back one.

9. Add a 😊 **Sprite** as a child of the layer and assign the background texture to it. Stretch it to fill the viewport.

10. Add the small stars as Sprites. You can do that easily by selecting the ParallaxLayer node and dragging the star image from the FileSystem dock to the viewport. They'll be added to the tree as sprites and children of the selected node.

11. Create another 🔳 **ParallaxLayer** as a child of the ParallaxBackground. Set the **Scale** to (0.5, 0.5). This will be a closer layer so it'll move faster.

12. Add the big stars as children of the last ParallaxLayer.

13. Add a new script to the **Ship** node with the code in Listing 3.3.

14. Save the scene and play it. You can move the ship using the arrow keys of your keyboard or the d-pad of a joystick. The parallax effect should be visible when you move it.

LISTING 3.3   Ship Movement

```
extends Sprite

export var speed = 500

func _process(delta):
    var direction = Vector2()
    if Input.is_action_pressed("ui_left"):
        direction.x = -1.0
    elif Input.is_action_pressed("ui_right"):
        direction.x = 1.0
    if Input.is_action_pressed("ui_up"):
        direction.y = -1.0
    elif Input.is_action_pressed("ui_down"):
        direction.y = 1.0

    var velocity = direction * speed * delta;
    position += velocity
```

Summary

In this hour, you gained a lot of knowledge about 2D graphics not only in Godot but in general. You learned how Sprites work and in which order nodes are drawn. You saw how vectors and matrices help deal with transformation of objects in the screen. You also learned how to use 2D cameras, tile maps, and the ParallaxBackground effect.

Q&A

Q. What are the other 2D nodes?

A. There are a lot of nodes for use in 2D: all the descendants of ⊙ **Node2D** and a few more. Some of them are covered in other chapters, but some are out of the scope of this book. You can learn about them in the engine documentation.

Q. Why there are some artifacts when I use a region of a spritesheet?

A. The filtering of textures may cause artifacts if the Sprites are close together. This can be fixed either by disabling the filter of the texture in the Import dock or enabling the **Filter Clip** property of the Sprite.

Q. Vector math seems too complicated. Do I really need to learn it?

A. While it's not essential, it'll make your game code much easier to make and cleaner, especially in complex movements. Without that, you'll have to rely on angles and trigonometry, which can become even more complicated.

Workshop

See if you can answer the following questions to test your knowledge.

Quiz

1. True or False: the children of a node are drawn before their parent.
2. How can you show only part of an image using a 😊 **Sprite** node?
3. What happens if you multiply two transforms?
4. Is it possible to multiply a vector by another?
5. What is the purpose of the 📷 **Camera2D** node?
6. True or False: Godot needs an external tool to deal with tile maps.
7. What does the **Scale** property of the ⬛ **ParallaxLayer** node do?

Answers

1. False. The parent nodes are drawn before their children.

2. Enable the **Region** property and set its **Rect** to the desired portion of the image.

3. You get a new transform that combines the effects of the two.

4. There are two ways to multiply vectors: the dot product and the cross product.

5. It serves to move around and show the level that is bigger than the window.

6. False. Godot has tools to make TileMaps inside the editor.

7. It changes how fast the layer moves in relation to the background offset.

Exercises

Here are few exercises to get yourself acquainted with 2D graphics.

1. Create a new scene with a **Sprite** as the root. Set its texture to some image.

2. Add another Sprite as its child, set its texture, and move it away from the start position.

3. Move the root node around and see how the child moves.

4. Add a **RemoteTransform2D** node as a child of the root and assign its **Remote Path** property to the other child of the root.

5. Move the RemoteTransform2D around (use the **Move** tool). See how the target Sprite moves around to follow it.

6. Save the scene and play it to see the results.

HOUR 4
Scripting

What You'll Learn in This Hour:

- ▶ The relationship of objects and scripts
- ▶ Basics of GDScript
- ▶ Signals and groups

Many games shine because of their unique or well-polished game mechanics. Most behaviors need manual programming, which can often be quite complex. Godot features a scripting system with which you can implement those systems, and it encourages you to apply many battle-tested patterns of software engineering.

This fourth hour will show you how to use **GDScript**, Godot's custom **scripting language**, to give nodes and objects custom behaviors. It shows how to create scripts, attach them to objects and nodes, and make them interface with other objects. We will see how you can use predefined and custom signals to decouple parts of your code and use groups to identify different objects that are related in your game code.

Node and Script Relationship

We learned about the Scene Tree and nodes in Hour 2, "Scene System." Now we will learn how to add your own code to these nodes using Godot's scripting interface.

We learned there are different node types, like Node2D or Control. These different types follow the model of **single inheritance**. That means every node type has a **parent type** from which it inherits all properties and behaviors. This is a common model in the world of **object-oriented programming**. The root type for things that can be part of the Scene Tree is Node. A simple node does nothing special; it's just the basic skeleton an object needs to be part of the Scene Tree.

Node2D inherits Node, so every Node2D can be used where a node could be used. Often, you'll find a notation like this:

```
Node2D < Node
```

That means Node2D inherits Node. Sprite inherits Node2D, so the inheritance order would look like this:

```
Sprite < Node2D < Node
```

You will find that notation in Godot documentation.

Node is not the end of the inheritance chain. The very root type for all node types (except core types) is **object. Everything inherits an object**, directly or indirectly. Because this is the base type, Godot uses this type as the starting point for the scripting system. Every object can have a script attached to it. A script is some kind of object that can give additional behaviors to its owner (see Figure 4.1).

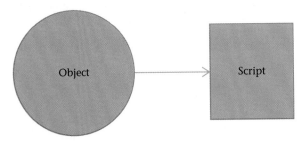

FIGURE 4.1
Object-script relationship.

The way your script can add behaviors to objects works as follows: the object gets asked to do task x. If the object has a script attached to it, it asks the script if it can do task x. If so, the script gets called to do said task (see Figure 4.2). If the object doesn't have a script attached, it sees if it can handle it on its own.

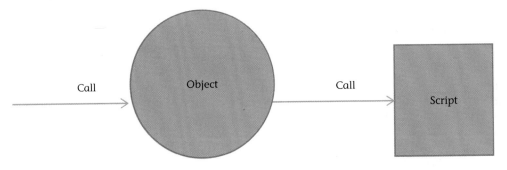

FIGURE 4.2
Method call delegated to a script.

Introduction to GDScript

The Godot engine features its own custom scripting language called GDScript. Godot supports other ways of scripting, like VisualScript, Mono/C#, and NativeScripts. GDScript is the most tightly integrated language of those listed above, as it was made specifically for Godot. Many people love it for its ability to quickly prototype games.

The Basics of GDScript

GDScript's syntax closely resembles that of Python. Every object has a type, and those types consist of class hierarchies. One GDScript file represents one "subclass." This means that everything you declare in the scope of the file (such as variables and functions) is part of the class definition, and it's not available globally to other files. Variables in this scope are called "**members**," and functions are called "**methods**." To use the code in a GDScript file, you need to set that script as the object script.

A GDScript file might look like the following in Listing 4.1:

LISTING 4.1   Sample GDScript File

```
# button_counter.gd
extends Node2D

signal count_updated(count)

# a variable to hold the number of times the button has been pressed
# since this is declared in the file scope it becomes a class member
var press_count = 0

# The maximum number of button presses allowed
const MAX_PRESSES = 42

# connect the "pressed" signal to a user defined method
func _ready():
    $Button.connect("pressed", self, "on_button_pressed")

# this gets called when Button gets pressed
func on_button_pressed():
    if press_count + 1 <= MAX_PRESSES:
        press_count += 1
        emit_signal("count_updated", press_count)
        $Button.text = str(press_count)
    else:
        $Button.text = "No more presses allowed."
```

TIP

Whitespace-sensitive Syntax

GDScript uses **whitespace** (space and tab character) to know which code belongs to which scope or block. This is similar to **Python** and many other languages, like **Haskell**, **CoffeeScript**, or **F#**. This technique is called **Offside-Rule**.

Other languages like C, C++, C#, Java, and many others use **Braces** to make that distinction.

Getting Started

To attach a script, use the Attach Node Script dialog, as shown in Figure 4.3.

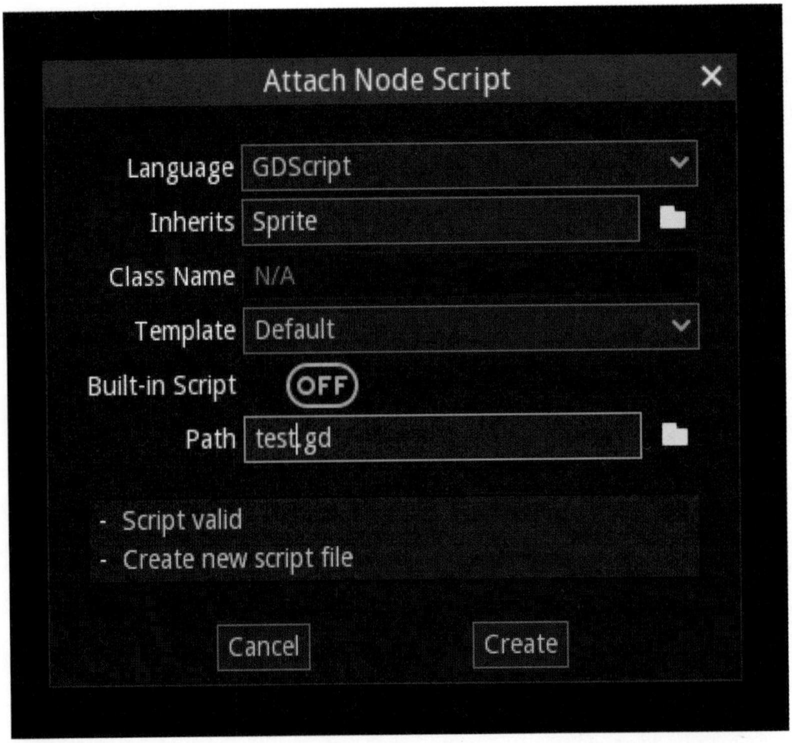

FIGURE 4.3
The Attach Node Script dialog.

Attaching a Script to a Node

The easiest way to add a Script to a node is to use the context menu in the scene dock:

1. In the **Scene dock**, click on a node to select it.

2. Click the **Attach Script** button.

3. The language should be set to **GDScript**.

4. Set a **Path** where the script should be saved.

5. Click the **Create** button.

Now the editor should show you the script that already contains some code to get you started. You can use the arrow keys to navigate around the text editor, type letters to insert them, and delete characters. All the common shortcuts and features are available.

TIP

Virtual Methods

Many node- and object-types have **Virtual Methods**, which a coder is supposed to **override**. By overriding a virtual method, you can give Godot an "entry point" to your custom code. A few of those virtual methods are presented here, but there are many more depending on the node-/object-type you're dealing with.

Life-cycle callbacks are special virtual methods that are conventionally prefixed with an **underscore**. They are called automatically by the engine when a certain event happens (such as when the node is added to the Scene Tree and when the user provides keyboard or joystick input).

_ready Method

When a node enters the Scene Tree, it first "sets up" all of its children. Then Godot tries to call a method named "_ready," which you can define in a script. This function takes no argument, and you can use it to set up an object or a default state for your script.

The famous "Hello World." program in GDScript might look like what is shown in Listing 4.2.

LISTING 4.2   Hello World Program

```
extends Node

func _ready():
    print("hello, world.")
```

If you modify the script to look like Listing 4.2 and press "Ctrl+S" to save the script, you can start the scene like you learned in Hour 1, "Introducing the Godot Engine," and see "hello, world." in the output tab on the bottom of the editor (see Figure 4.4).

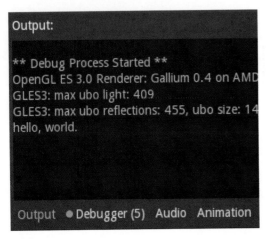

FIGURE 4.4
Output of the "Hello World" program from Listing 4.2.

Listing 4.2 shows the statement `print("hello, world.")`. That's the syntax to call methods and built-in functions. In this case, the script calls the print function with one argument. That one argument is a string (a string is text enclosed by double quotes).

_process Method and Using Input.is_action_pressed()

In the last chapter, Hour 3, "2D Graphics," we learned more about the Sprite node.

Every node has a method _process that a Script can override. The _process method gets called on every new frame drawn by Godot.

In this example, we will take a Sprite node and make it move left or right based on user input.

We set up our scene like this and set the `icon.png` that is included in every new project as the texture of that Sprite (Figure 4.5).

The _ready method did not take any arguments, but the _process method does take one argument, delta. It's the time in seconds since the last frame was drawn. This is particularly useful to implement frame rate-independent behaviors. We'll see how that works out in practice now. Listing 4.3 shows the GDScript file that's attached to the Sprite node.

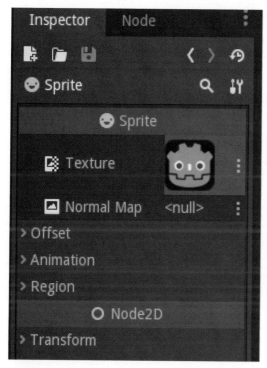

FIGURE 4.5
Scene and Sprite setup for the next example.

LISTING 4.3   Script Attached to the Sprite Node

```
extends Sprite

const MOVEMENT_SPEED = 50 # pixels per second

# notice that you can leave out _ready if you don't need it


func _process(delta):
    var input_direction = 0 # 0 is no movement, 1 is right, -1 is left

    if Input.is_action_pressed("ui_left"):
        input_direction = -1
    elif Input.is_action_pressed("ui_right"):
        input_direction = 1

    # now move the sprite around
    position.x += input_direction * MOVEMENT_SPEED * delta
```

Here you can see that `_process` takes one argument, which we called "delta."

We define a constant named movement_speed with the value 50. The value of a constant cannot be changed, and constants are only meant to give a name to constant values (to avoid the use of "magic numbers" in the code).

It also shows a few new concepts. The first is the declaration and initialization of a local variable using the `var name = expression` syntax.

This code is using "if" statements. It works just like many other languages; it executes some code based on the condition. If there's an `else` branch, the code under it gets executed when the condition is false. `elif` is just a short version of `else: if . . . .`

TIP

Input Singleton

We learned about the method call syntax when `_ready` was introduced. In the previous example, some method calls are prefixed by `Input`. This means they aren't methods on the current object (where this code executes), but in a **different class** or **object**. In this case, it's the **Input singleton**. We will learn more about singletons in Hour 6, "More Scripting," and more about Input in Hour 7, "Handling Input."

If one of those keys is pressed, we change the local variable that we created previously. Make sure to indent the code that should only be executed conditionally. The last line accesses the "position" property of the Sprite and increments the x component of that position. The position of a Node2D is a **Vector2**. A Vector2 is a core type and consists of two float components, **x** and **y**.

A Vector2 can be used to represent a **position** or a **direction**. In more complicated games, you can use vectors to perform linear algebra, which simplifies many tasks in game creation. When the "position" property of an object that inherits Node2D gets modified, the actual position in the scene will get changed.

So, this line moves the Sprite on the X axis in different directions depending on the input.

TIP

Complex Computations and _process

Try to avoid complex computations in `_process`. `_process` runs on every frame the engine renders; if `_process` is still busy following an algorithm, the engine won't be able to start working on the next frame.

This means if you have huge computations on every, or some, frames, the **frame rate will drop**.

_input and Basic Input Events

In the previous example, we used `Input.is_action_pressed(. . .)` in every frame to check if a key was pressed. Statistically speaking, it's much more common that a key is **not** pressed than that it is pressed. So, it might be wasteful to check for key presses all the time. That's what the `_input(event)` method is used for: it gets called whenever new events are created.

We won't go into too much detail here, because Hour 7 will talk about this in greater detail.

If we wanted to translate the above code to use `_input` instead of asking for key presses every frame, we could come up with the code in Listing 4.4.

LISTING 4.4   Shifting to use _input

```
extends Sprite

export var movement_speed = 50 # pixels per second

var input_direction = 0 # 0 is no movement, 1 is right, -1 is left

func _process(delta):
    # move the sprite
    position.x += input_direction * movement_speed * delta

func _input(event):

    # we test if the key was pressed. This will be one event
    # note that this method doesn't have the "just" word, because
    # events received in the _input callback happens only once per press
    if event.is_action_pressed("ui_left"):
        input_direction = -1
    elif event.is_action_pressed("ui_right"):
        input_direction = 1

    # we also test if the key was released, this is also just *one* event
    elif event.is_action_released("ui_left"):
        input_direction = 0
    elif event.is_action_released("ui_right"):
        input_direction = 0
```

The Sprite gets moved, but the user input only gets processed when it happens (but not all of the time).

Exporting Variables

Listing 4.4 uses a **member variable** called `movement_speed`. By prefixing the variable definition with **export**, this variable will show up as a property in the **Property Inspector**. An exported variable needs a proper **default value**, which will be shown in the Property Inspector.

That makes tweaking values a lot easier, and can be done by level designers or artists without having to go into the code to change values. If you use **scene instancing**, every instance will have its **own set** of exported variables—so you don't step on other people's toes!

Interfacing with Other Nodes

There are some methods that can be overridden so that Godot calls your code, but all of the previous code just acts on the node to which the script was attached! Bigger and more complex scenes require scripts to interface with other nodes in the scene.

To get a reference to a node inside the tree, you can use the `get_node` method. `get_node` is part of all nodes (since it needs access to the Scene Tree), and it takes a **path** relative to the current node that points to the node you want to reference (see Figure 4.6).

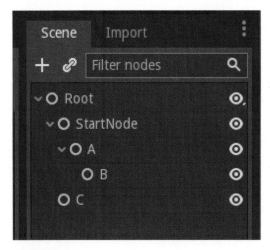

FIGURE 4.6
The scene setup for the `get_node` path example.

For example, to get a reference to the parent node, you'd use `var parent = get_node("..")`. As you can see, it's using **unix-style paths**. To access a child node called A, you would do `get_node("A")`, to get the child B of A, you would do `get_node("A/B")`, and to get the **sibling** node C, you would do `get_child("../C")`.

Listing 4.5 shows an example in which a script moves a child node instead of itself. Note the single project shown in Figure 4.7.

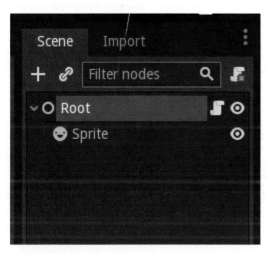

FIGURE 4.7
The Godot Project Manager with a single project.

The GDScript shown in Listing 4.5 moves the child node called "Sprite."

LISTING 4.5   Sprite Child Node

```
extends Node2D

const MOVEMENT_SPEED = 50 # pixels per second

var sprite_node

func _ready():
    sprite_node = get_node("Sprite")

func _process(delta):
    var input_direction = 0 # 0 is no movement, 1 is right, -1 is left

    if Input.is_action_pressed("ui_left"):
        input_direction = -1
    elif Input.is_action_pressed("ui_right"):
        input_direction = 1

    # notice that the child is moved here
    sprite_node.position.x += input_direction * MOVEMENT_SPEED * delta
```

Because `get_node` is such a common operation, there is an alternative syntax. It's `$Path` instead of `get_node("Path")`. Table 4.1 shows how these syntaxes relate.

TABLE 4.1 Alternative Syntaxes

get_node("A")	$A
get_node("A/B")	$A/B
get_node("A/space in name")	$"A/space in name"
get_node("..")	$ ".."
get_node(" ../C")	$ "../C"

Calling User-Defined Methods on Other Objects

In bigger scenes, it's really useful to call methods from scripts that are attached to other nodes. To show how that can be done, let's consider the following scene in Figure 4.8.

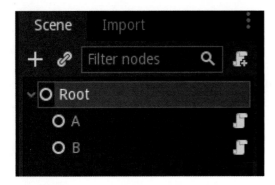

FIGURE 4.8
The script on "A" calls methods defined in the script on "B." See Listing 4.6.

LISTING 4.6 The Output

```
# expected output



B prints: This is a test.
B prints: Hello from A
```

Listing 4.7 shows the script on A.

LISTING 4.7   The A Script

```
# A.gd
extends Node

func _ready():
    $"../B".test_method("This is a test.")
    get_node("../B").test_method("Hello from A")
```

As expected, these calls go through the method defined in the script on B, shown in Listing 4.8.

LISTING 4.8   The B Script

```
# B.gd
extends Node

func test_method(arg):
    print("B prints: ", arg)
```

As you can see, calling functions when you know what to call is pretty straightforward, but sometimes you need to call methods on other objects, which you don't know about. This is done via signals, which is introduced in the next section.

Signals and Groups

Let's now take a look at signals and groups.

Signals

Signals and **groups** are two mechanisms to reduce **coupling** in game code. Signals are an implementation of the **observer design pattern**. The base concept is that an object notifies other objects that are interested in some actions (see Figure 4.9). The coder doesn't know when and where these actions might be of interest, so it's not possible to just hard-code these connections to other objects. That's where the concept of signals helps.

An object can emit multiple possible signals. When a signal is emitted, all the "listeners" (or observers) will get notified (or more specifically, a method gets called). It can also be seen as providing a callback to the object that is emitting the signal.

This means there are two sides a signal: emitting it and somebody "listening."

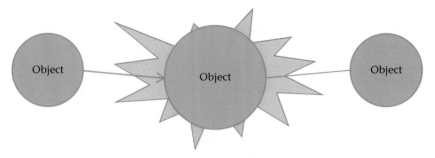

FIGURE 4.9
An object emits signals; other objects connect to those signals.

Reacting to Signals

One simple example is detecting if a Button was pressed (see Figure 4.10 and Listing 4.9).

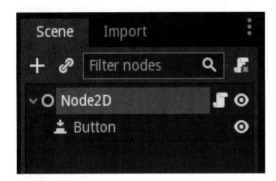

FIGURE 4.10
GDScript code that connects a method to a signal on the child node "Button."

LISTING 4.9   GDScript Detecting if a Button Was Pressed

```
extends Node2D

func _on_Button_pressed():
    print("Button got pressed")

func _ready():
    $Button.connect("pressed", self, "_on_Button_pressed")
```

To "listen" to a signal (or provide a callback), the signal needs to be **connected** to a method of an object. connect expects the name of the signal as the first argument, the object to which to connect the signal as the second argument, and the name of the method on that object as the third argument. The fourth argument of this method is optional, and it expects an array of **bindings**, which will be sent as additional parameters to the connected methods. This can be useful if you connect multiple signals to the same method (like one that handles the pressing of many buttons), because you can add an extra parameter to identify the sender.

Instead of connecting the method to a signal in code, we can use the Godot Editor to do the same thing (Figure 4.11).

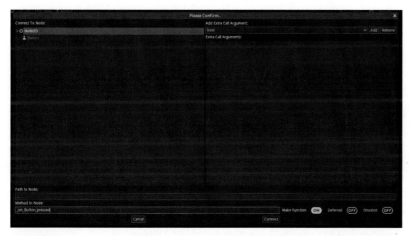

FIGURE 4.11
The Godot Editor provides the functionality to connect signals via a graphical user interface.

TRY IT YOURSELF ▼

Connecting a Method to a Signal

To connect a method of an object to a signal on another object, you can use the editor:

1. In the **Scene dock**, click a node to select it.

2. In the **Node dock**, click **Signals**.

3. **Double-click** the signal to which you want to connect a method.

4. A new **Dialog Window** will pop up.

5. **Select the object** in the Scene Tree **on the left** that you want to connect to the signal.

6. Enter the **name of the method** that will react to the signal.

7. Click the **Connect** button.

It is possible to connect a signal to a method defined on an object other than `self`.

```
$VisibilityNotifier2D.connect("exit_screen", some_bullet, "queue_free")
```

Sometimes, connecting signals to built-in methods, like "queue_free," can be a real timesaver. This code will cause a "bullet" object to be automatically destroyed after it leaves the screen thanks to the VisibilityNotifier2D Node.

Emitting Signals and Defining Custom Signals

In the previous section, we showed how to connect and react to signals. In a game project, it often is advantageous to define your own signals to reduce coupling between objects.

One example is to use signals in order to perform some action **after** another action was performed. The "key_collected" animation on the Player shouldn't play before the "chest_opened" animation on the Chest has finished. Signals are also very useful for managing scene changes, achievement systems, game-progress systems, and many more things to reduce complexity in the code base.

There are two ways to define a custom signal in GDScript: using the `signal` keyword and using `Object.add_user_signal()`. The most preferred way is to use the signal keyword, as it will enable the editor to connect methods to user-defined signals just like they do to built-in signals.

To define a signal in a script, you need to write the "signal signature" so the editor knows about it and can offer functionality like auto-completion.

Here is an example of the syntax used to define a custom signal in GDScript:

```
extends Node

signal test_signal(some_argument, another_argument)
```

Signals can pass arguments to all the methods connected to them; these arguments' names are written comma-separated in between the parentheses of the signal declaration.

You can find the user-defined signals in the same place as the built-in signals, in the Node dock under Signals (See Figure 4.12).

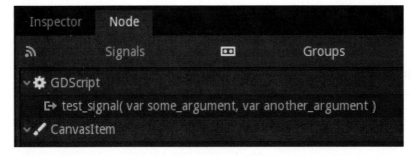

FIGURE 4.12
User-defined signals will show up in the Node dock.

To emit a signal, the method `Object.emit_signal(signal_name, arguments)` is used. By calling this method, all the methods connected to that signal will be called too.

Listing 4.10 is pseudo code showing how custom signals can be used and emitted.

LISTING 4.10   Pseudo Code Using Custom Signals

```
extends KinematicBody2D


# user defined signal
signal jumped()


# more code . . .


func _ready():
    self.connect("jumped", self, "_on_jumped")
    # more code . . .


func _input(event):

    # more code . . .

    if event.is_action_pressed("jump") and can_jump():
        velocity.y = -JUMP_VELOCITY
        emit_signal("jumped")

    # more code . . .


func _on_jumped():
    $SamplePlayer2D.play("jump_sound")
    jump_count += 1
```

Groups

Groups are a way to group objects together. An object can be checked for "membership" in a group, which makes groups useful to distinguish different types or game objects (for example, "bullet hits enemy" and "bullet hits ally").

There are two ways to add an object to a group. It can be done in the **Node dock** in the editor or done in code.

To add an object to a group using the editor, the Node dock needs to be used. It has a category, "Groups," in which all the current user-defined groups are visible and editable (Figure 4.13).

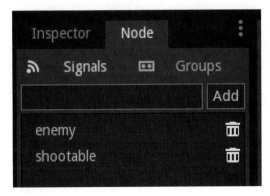

FIGURE 4.13
The Groups tab in the Node dock showing a few groups added to a node.

▼ TRY IT YOURSELF

Adding a Node to Group

To add a node to a group, follow the following steps:

1. In the **Scene dock**, click a node to select it.

2. In the **Node dock**, click **Groups**.

3. **Enter the name** of the group.

4. Click the **Add** button.

To remove a node from a group, click the **Icon** next to the group name.

Adding an object to a group via code is really straightforward. It is done using the `Object.add_to_group()` method, which takes the name of the group as the only argument.

```
object.add_to_group("shootable")
```

A classic example is to detect if enemies entered a certain area of the map or if the hero got hit by a bullet (or a flying cat).

There's also a method in the Scene Tree that allows you to call a method in every member of a group. This is like the reverse of signals: instead of emitting for anyone who's observing it, this will broadcast the information to everyone in the group. You can use this by calling `get_tree().call_group("group_name", "method_name")`. Additional arguments will be sent as parameters for the methods. Note that this can generate script errors if some members of the group don't have the specified method.

To show how groups can be effectively used, the next example makes use of the Area2D node, which hasn't been introduced yet. To use it correctly, PhysicsBodies have to be set up and CollisionShapes need to be created. This will get explained in greater detail in Hour 8, "Physics System," about the Physics System in Godot. But a vague understanding should be enough to read the example.

An area can be used to detect if PhysicsBodies (or other areas) have entered (or "collided") a certain area. In this example, the Area2D is a child of a Player node, is used to detect bullets from either allies or non-allies, and emits appropriate signals.

Listing 4.11 shows example code about signals that can be used to allow for easier composition with other mechanisms, like achievement or statistic systems.

LISTING 4.11   Achievement Systems

```
extends KinematicBody2D # Player

signal shot(damage)
signal shot_by_friendly(ally)

signal died()


var health = 250.0


func _on_Area_entered(object):

    if object.is_in_group("bullet"):
        # we got hit by a bullet

        # note: all objects of type bullet have a damage property
        emit_signal("shot", object.damage)

        if object.owner.is_in_group("ally"):
            # we got shot by one of our allies

            emit_signal("shot_by_friendly", object.owner)

        health -= object.damage

        if health < 0:
            emit_signal("died")
```

```
        # destroy the bullet
        object.queue_free()

func _ready():
    $Area2D.connect("area_entered", self, "_on_Area_entered")

    self.connect("died", self, "on_death")
    self.connect("shot", self, "on_shot")

func on_died():
    # implement dying here
    self.queue_free()

func on_shot(damage):
    $SamplePlayer2D.play("hit_sound")
```

Summary

In this chapter, you learned how Scripts can be used to add custom code to an object, how to **create** scripts, and how to overwrite the virtual methods `_ready`, `_process`, and `_input` to set up your object and interface with user input.

You also learned about signals and groups, which can be used to notify objects interested in some of the actions your nodes can perform. You saw how groups can be used to differentiate nodes and objects in certain groups, making it easy to implement different behaviors depending on the type of group the current object is dealing with.

This was just a basic introduction to some of the concepts. In Hour 6, we discover more concepts facilitated in Godot to make scripting easier. But GDScript is a fully fledged language, and there's more to it than what would fit in one or two chapters, so always be on the lookout to learn more about it!

Q&A

Q. What happens if you emit a signal with the wrong number of arguments?

A. Godot will show an error that the arguments don't match.

Q. Is get_node an expensive operation?

A. It depends on the complexity and length of the path. But try to avoid using get_node in _process and save a reference in a variable instead if you can.

Q. Can an object connect to the same signal multiple times?

A. Yes, it's useful sometimes to trigger different actions when one signal gets emitted. However, if you connect the same signal to the same object and method, the engine will output an error.

Q. Is there a limit on how many groups to which an object can be part?

A. Practically no. Of course, there are some limits, like memory constraints, but for the everyday needs of game developers, it will never become a problem.

Workshop

Answer the following questions to make sure you understand the content of this hour.

Quiz

1. What type does every class type inherit from?

2. Can every object be part of the Scene Tree?

3. If your game runs at 60 frames per second, how often will _process be called?

4. If your game runs at 60 frames per second, how often will _input get called?

5. What is the difference between `const` and `var`?

Answers

1. Every class type directly or indirectly inherits from the Object class.

2. No; only objects of Node type can be part of the Scene Tree.

3. On every frame, so every 1/60 seconds = 16 ms.

4. _input only gets called when there are input events to process, so it's independent from the frame rate.

5. `var` variables can be mutated, while `const` values can't be changed, as they are immutable.

Exercises

Try to make a button that spawns Sprites that fall down and increase a counter when they leave the screen:

1. Place a Button and a Label Node in the scene.

2. Create a new scene containing only the Sprite, and save it in the project folder with the name "sprite.tscn".

3. Connect a method to the Button's "pressed" signal. By calling `load("res://sprite.tscn").instance()`, you get a reference to the node representing the scene.

4. Add the Sprite node to the scene by using `add_child`.

5. Add a script to the Sprite scene. It should move the Sprite down (Tip: postion.y =+ speed * delta) and emit a custom signal when position.y
is greater than a certain value. Then use `queue_free()` to delete the Sprite.

6. Connect a method to the custom signal on all of the spawned Sprites. If it's emitted, increase a counter.

7. To show the number in the label, you can use `$Label.text = str(counter)`.

HOUR 5
Game 1: Space Shooter

What You'll Learn in This Hour:

▶ Creating a 2D pixel art game from scratch

▶ Using the Timer, Area2D, and CollisionShape2D nodes for gameplay

▶ Using the AnimatedSprite, CanvasLayer, and Label nodes for graphics and UI

▶ Handling basic input and signals to drive game logic

▶ In-game generation of instances through script

In this hour, you will use what you learned in the previous hours to create an actual game. It will be a simple 2D, top-down, side-scrolling, shoot-'em-up type of game where you control a spaceship and shoot at incoming asteroids. The game will keep track of the number of asteroids you have shot down and end when an asteroid collides with your ship. In the process of making the game, you will learn some concepts we only talked about briefly or haven't mentioned yet, like input, project settings, animated Sprites, timers, areas, and UI. Don't worry though; we will explain them as we go, and later chapters will cover them in more depth.

Concept and Design

The spaceship is controlled with the arrow keys and can shoot lasers by pressing the spacebar. Asteroids spawn at random locations outside the screen and fly toward the spaceship from right to left. When the spaceship hits an asteroid with its laser, the asteroid explodes and the player scores a point. If an asteroid manages to touch the spaceship, both explode and the game is over. The game (see Figure 5-1) can be restarted by pressing the enter key, and can be exited at any time by pressing the escape key.

We will model the interactions of the spaceship, the laser shots, and the asteroids using **Area2D** nodes and signals, which we briefly mentioned at the end of Hour 4. We will also make a simple UI (user interface) showing the current score using Godot's UI nodes.

We will make the ship move on a static screen with a non-moving camera, simulating the movement of the ship through space by an infinitely scrolling background and asteroids that move in and out of the screen from right to left. The advantage of this method over an actually moving

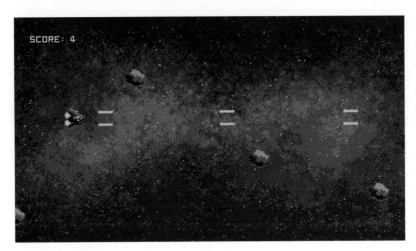

FIGURE 5.1
Screenshot of the finished space shooter game.

spaceship is that we do not need to create huge horizontal levels, which can be difficult to manage. We can also more flexibly and precisely time and randomize the appearance of asteroids. If
you want to extend the game with enemy ships, power-ups, and bosses, you can spawn them in an
easier and timed fashion by using the static screen method.

Game Components as Scenes

Even a simple game like we are going to make has a lot of complexity and interaction between
different game parts. To tackle this complexity, we can use many of Godot's helpful concepts to
manage our game components. We can build our spaceship, the asteroids, and the laser shots as
separate scenes that communicate indirectly through signals with each other. This allows us to
work on each part in isolation. We will create the scenes shown in Table 5.1.

TABLE 5.1   Scenes Needed for the Game

Scene	Description
player	The player scene consists of an 🔲 **Area2D** and a ⬛ **CollisionShape2D** node used to detect collisions with asteroids, an 👾 **AnimatedSprite** node representing the spaceship on screen, and a **Timer** node that is used to limit the shooting rate of the player. A player script is attached to the root node of the player scene that contains the movement, the shooting, and destruction logic of the spaceship.
shot	This scene represents a laser shot of the spaceship and consists, similarly to the player scene, of an **Area2D, CollisionShape2D,** and **AnimatedSprite** node. Its attached script handles collisions with asteroids and moves the shot forward every frame.

Scene	Description
asteroid	The asteroid scene also consists of an **Area2D**, a **CollisionShape2D**, and an **AnimatedSprite**. The asteroid's script handles collision with the player and the laser shots, as well as moving the asteroid forward every frame.
explosion	Consisting of a **Sprite** and a **Timer** node, the explosion scene is instanced into the game when an asteroid or the spaceship is destroyed. The **Timer** node makes sure that the explosion is only shown briefly.
stage	The stage scene is our main scene, which contains instances of all of the above scenes. Additionally, it contains UI text for the score, the "game over" message, and an infinitely scrolling background **Sprite**. The stage scene root has a script attached that spawns new asteroids periodically, detects if an asteroid is destroyed, and updates the score accordingly. It also detects if the spaceship crashed into an asteroid and shows the "game over" message.

Making the Scenes

Before we start creating the actual scenes described above, we'll want to make some changes to the project configuration. As this will be a proper 2D pixel art-styled game, we want those pixels to look nice and crisp on most run-of-the-mill 16:9 displays. A pixel art game is most commonly rendered with a low internal resolution, then stretched full-screen onto the display. For this, it is wise to choose an internal game resolution with a 16:9 aspect ratio, which shares an integer scaling factor with common resolutions like 1080p and 720p. We need to do this to prevent pixel squashing and stretching for most display configurations when running the game in full screen. For this example project, we'll choose an internal game resolution of **320x180** pixels, because it nicely divides the resolutions 1920x1080 and 1280x720.

Luckily for us, Godot is built with this common 2D use-case in mind, and we can just make the following changes in the **Display > Window** section of project settings. It can be found in the main menu under **Project > Project Settings.**

In addition to setting the **Width** and **Height** properties to 320 and 180, respectively, we also set the **Test Width** and **Test Height** properties to 720p. The purpose of these is to get a bigger window resolution when testing the game in the editor, as 320x180 is pretty small on a modern 1080p desktop resolution.

If you want to test how the game looks in full-screen mode, tick the box beside the property **Fullscreen**. However, we recommend debugging scripts in windowed mode with the **Resizable** property enabled, as this is much more convenient, especially on a multi-monitor setup.

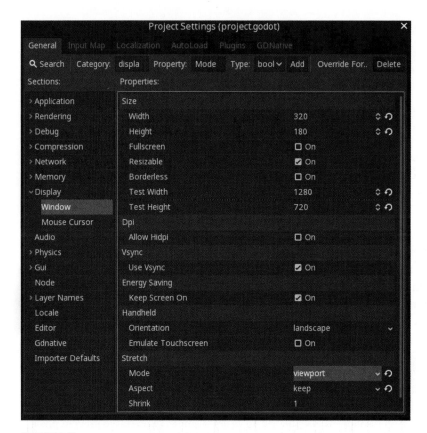

FIGURE 5.2
Display –> Window section of the project settings. Note the 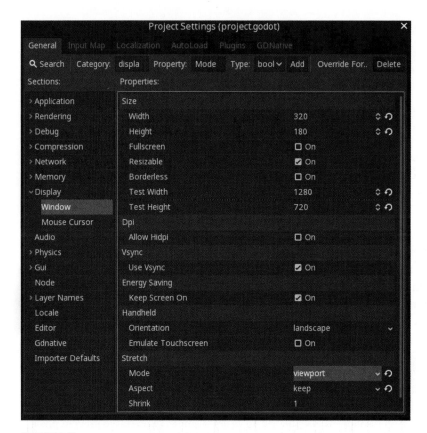 symbol indicates a changed property.

To tell Godot that we want to stretch our game to the screen size while maintaining the aspect ratio, we need to modify the properties **Mode** and **Aspect** in the **Stretch** section. To maintain the aspect ratio, we can simply choose **keep**, which causes Godot to **not** disproportionally stretch our game (and therefore distort it) if the aspect ratio of our game and the aspect ratio of the display resolution differ. To stretch our game to the screen, we have two options to select in the **Mode** property: **2D** and **viewport**.

The **2D** mode renders the game at the current desktop resolution while stretching it to fit the screen. The **viewport** mode renders the game precisely at the specified resolution in the **Width** and **Height** properties into an off-screen image, then stretches that image to full screen. This might superficially sound very similar, but it has very different implications on the look and feel of the game. We encourage you to play with these modes after you finish making the game to get a better feel for it. To simulate a more retro look and feel, we will go with **viewport** mode for now.

With these preliminaries done, we will create the actual scenes needed for the game in the next section. If you get stuck at any point in this hour, feel free to take a look at the example project in the accompanied "Godot-Hour5" folder.

Creating the Player, Asteroid, Shot, and Explosion scenes

For the player, we need to make a new scene and create an ▣ **Area2D** node as the root node. We will name it "player" and add it to the "player" group. Take a look at the **previous hour** if you need a refresher of how to add nodes to a group. As was briefly mentioned in the **previous hour**, an **Area2D** node, among other things, detects overlaps with other **Area2D** nodes and fires a signal on detection. We will use this fact to check for overlaps between the spaceship, the laser shots, and the asteroids, and differentiate between them using group names.

Before we can detect anything, however, we need to add a ▣ **CollisionShape2D** node, on which the collision detection will be based upon, to our **Area2D** as a child node. Rename the **CollisonShape2D** node "hit_zone" and create a circle-shaped collision by clicking on <**null**> beside the **Shape** property in the Inspector and choosing ⬤ **New CircleShape2D**. After that, we can change the radius of the circle shape to 6 pixels by clicking on <**CircleShape2D**> beside the **Shape** property in the Inspector.

FIGURE 5.3
Creating shapes in the CollisionShape2D node.

When we create the player script later, we'll need to connect the **area_entered** signal of **Area2D** to the script. For now, we are finished with the **Area2D** and **CollisionShape2D** nodes.

We can now add an 🤖 **AnimatedSprite** node as a child node of "player" and call it "sprite." The **AnimatedSprite** node is similar to the 🙂 **Sprite** node you already encountered, with the difference that you can assign multiple images to the **AnimatedSprite**, which will play in a sequence at a predefined frame rate. There are other more flexible ways to animate Sprites in Godot beside the **AnimatedSprite** node, as you will see in Hour 10, "Animation." As we want to keep it simple for now, we just use **AnimatedSprite** to get the job done.

We are now ready to create our first simple animation. First, locate the "sprites" folder, which contains all the needed Sprites for this hour, in the accompanying "Godot-Hour5" folder and copy it into your Godot project folder using your OS's file explorer. In the **AnimatedSprite** Inspector, click on the <**null**> beside the Frames property, then click on **New SpriteFrames**. Click again on the new <**SpriteFrames**> to open the **Animation Frames Editor** at the bottom of the editor.

FIGURE 5.4
Inspector and Animation Frames window of the AnimatedSprite node.

Note that Godot created a default animation for us, so we only need to add some Sprite frames. Let's do this by clicking on the 🗁 button left of the **Paste** button. This opens a file dialog where we can navigate to our "sprites" folder, then select and open both "player1.png" and "player2.png" by holding the shift key.

You might notice that the Sprite frames we inserted are not crispy at all. You might say, "But you promised me crispy pixels some paragraphs earlier! Why did we need to do all this setting up with screen resolution, if we still get blurry Sprites?" The problem has to do with how Godot handles importing textures, or in our case, the "player1.png" and "player2.png" images. We have to tell Godot that we want to use the images as pixel art Sprites, instead of the default smoothed textures Godot automatically imports.

To do this, navigate to the "sprites" folder in the editor's **FileSystem** dock and double-click on "player1.png". On the top-right side of the editor screen, click on the **Import** tab, which is beside the **scene** tab. You will see a lot of options, which you can ignore for now, as Godot provides us with a convenient preset for pixel art. By clicking on the **Preset** button, selecting the **2D Pixel** preset and clicking on **Reimport** below, Godot will reload the image with pixel art-friendly settings.

If you repeat the previous paragraph for "player2.png" and then navigate back to our **AnimatedSprite** node, you should see nice and crispy Sprites like in the right side of **Figure 5.5**.

Now you might ask if you need to do this process for every Sprite you put into your project. The answer is, gladly, no. After changing to a desired preset, you can choose **Set as Default for 'Texture'** after clicking on the **Preset** button. This applies your preset for every future image you bring into the project.

For images you already put into the project (like the ones in our "sprites" folder), you can just delete all the files in it that have an **.import** file extension using your operating system's file explorer. These are metafiles where import settings for the corresponding image are stored. Godot will regenerate those files for each image automatically using your preset, so everything should now look crisp. For more information on importing images, check out Hour 14, "Project Management."

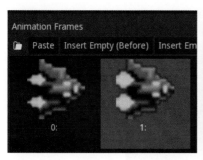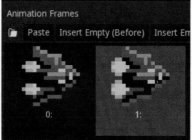

FIGURE 5.5
Left: Blurry Sprites we don't want. **Right:** Crispy Sprites we do want.

FIGURE 5.6
FileSystem and Import docks in the editor.

To see the final animation, check the box beside the **Playing** property in the **Inspector** of the **AnimatedSprite** node. You should now see the spaceship's exhaust animating in the editor.

The last thing we need to do before we are finished with the node creation part of the spaceship is add a **Timer** node as a child node of "player," which we will name "reload_timer." It will be used later in the script to limit our spaceship's fire rate. **Timer** nodes in Godot are used to create timed events by firing a **timeout** signal on a timeout. By default, a **Timer** will restart after a timeout. As we want to restart our timer by ourselves, we set it to **One Shot** in the **Inspector**. While we are at it, let us change the **Wait Time** to 0.2. This will cause our ship to "reload" for 200 milliseconds after firing. We can later fine-tune this value when we write the actual player script.

FIGURE 5.7
Inspector showing the "reload_timer" Timer node.

▼ TRY IT YOURSELF

Creating the Asteroid Scene

To create the asteroid scene, we need to repeat almost the same steps as when we created the player scene.

1. Create an ▣ **Area2D** node as the root, call it "asteroid," and put it in the "asteroid" group.

2. Create a ▣ **CollisionShape2D** node called "hit_zone" as child of "asteroid" and add a ◎ **CircleShape2D** with **Radius** 6 to it.

3. Create an ☻ **AnimatedSprite** node called "sprite" as a child of "asteroid," add the "asteroid1.png" and "asteroid2.png" frames to it, and make sure to check the **Playing** property.

4. Set the **Speed (FPS)** property of the **AnimatedSprite** to 3 (see Figure 5.4).

Creating the Shot Scene

To create the laser shot scene, we need to repeat similar steps to the ones above.

1. Create an ▣ **Area2D** node as the root, call it "shot," and put it in the "shot" group.

2. Create a ▣ **CollisionShape2D** node called "damage_zone" as a child of "shot" and add a ▢ **RectangleShape2D** with **Extends** (8, 4) to it.

3. Create an ☻ **AnimatedSprite** node called "sprite" as a child of "shot," add the "shot1.png" and "shot2.png" frames to it, and make sure to check the **Playing** property.

4. Set the **Speed (FPS)** property of the **AnimatedSprite** to 10 (see Figure 5.4).

Note the "damage_zone" of the shot scene uses a  **RectangleShape2D** instead of a **CircleShape2D**. By using a rectangular shape, we can model the Sprite shape of the laser shot much better than a circle would. Also note the shot scene does not have any **Timer** nodes like the player or asteroid scene, as it does not need any.

TRY IT YOURSELF ▼

Creating the Explosion Scene

To create the explosion scene, we just need to:

1. Create a Sprite node as the root, call it "explosion," and assign to it the "explosion.png" image.

2. Create a Timer node called "queue_free_timer" as a child of "explosion" and set it to **One Shot** and **Autostart**. Set the **Wait Time** of the **Timer** to 0.1.

3. Connect the **timeout** signal of the **Timer** to the **queue_free** function of the "explosion" node. See Hour 4 if you need a reminder on how to connect signals.

What you accomplished above is a scene that, when instantiated, frees itself (disappears) after 100 milliseconds. The enabled **Autostart** property of the "queue_free_timer" causes the **Timer** to start running as soon as it is instantiated in the game. And when the **Timer** timeouts, it frees its parent, causing the whole scene to disappear from the game. When placed into the game, it creates the illusion of a short explosion.

You can test this by running the scene by itself using the button in the top right corner of the editor. Note that you may need to temporarily increase the **Wait Time** of the **Timer** to compensate for the startup delay of the game.

If you followed all the previous steps, you should get the following Scene Trees for the player, asteroid, shot, and explosion scenes:

FIGURE 5.8
Scene Trees of the player, asteroid, shot, and explosion scenes.

Creating the Stage Scene

▼ TRY IT YOURSELF

Creating the Stage Scene (Part 1)

To create the first part of the stage scene, we need to:

1. Create a ⬤ Node2D node as the root and call it "stage."

2. Create a ⧗ Timer node called "spawn_timer" as a child of "stage" and set it to **Autostart**.

3. Create a ☻ Sprite node called "background" as a child of "stage" and assign to it the "background.png" image.

4. Lock the **Sprite** with the 🔒 button from the toolbar, like we learned in Hour 1, so we won't accidentally select it in the editor due to its size.

5. Open the **Offset** fold in the **Inspector** of the **Sprite** and disable the **Centered** property so that the **Sprite** now aligns with the top left corner of the **Viewport**.

6. Instantiate your player scene as a child node of "stage." Please take a look at Hour 2 if you need a refresher on how to instantiate a scene in the editor.

You should now see something similar to Figure 5.9 in your editor, except for the score and "game over" text, which we are going to create next.

FIGURE 5.9
Editor view and Scene Tree of the stage scene.

You encountered Godot's UI elements briefly in Hour 1, and we will go into details about them in Hour 9, "GUI." In this hour, we will use UI elements to show the player's score and a "game over" text, though we will also see how to use custom fonts to match the in-game text to your game's particular art style.

To make sure our on-screen text is always on top of all other in-game elements, it's a good practice to place it into its own **CanvasLayer** node. A **CanvasLayer** node separates all its child nodes into a new canvas layer defined by the **Layer** property in the **Inspector**. Note that we have already used the **ParallaxBackground** in Hour 3, which is also a type of canvas layer, and we'll go more into the details about canvas layers in Hour 21, "Viewports and Canvas."

Creating the Stage Scene (Part 2)

To create the score in the stage scene, we need to:

1. Create a ▨ **CanvasLayer** node called "ui" as a child of "stage."

2. Create a ◀ **Label** node called "score" as a child of "ui," enable its **Uppercase** property in the **Inspector,** and set its **Text** to "score: 0."

To make the score text look like the one in Figure 5.9, we need to:

1. Scroll down in the **Inspector** of the **Label** node until you see the **Custom Fonts** and **Custom Colors** folders, and open both.

2. For the **Font Color** and **Font Color Shadow** properties in the **Custom Colors** folder, pick some nice colors of your choice or insert the hex-codes **6fffbb** (cyan) and **2f1f47** (dark purple), respectively.

3. Use your OS's file explorer to locate the "fonts" folder in the accompanying "Godot-Hour5" folder and copy the "hour5.ttf" font into your project folder.

4. In the **Font** property of the **Custom Fonts** folder, create a **New DynamicFont** and open it in the **Inspector** (similar to how you did before with collision shapes).

5. In the **Font** folder, click on **<null>** beside the **Font Data** property, select **Load,** and choose the "hour5.ttf" font.

6. Finally, move the "score" **Label** to the top-left corner of the screen (or any place you like).

▼ To make a game over text like in Figure 5.9, we need to:

1. Duplicate our "score" 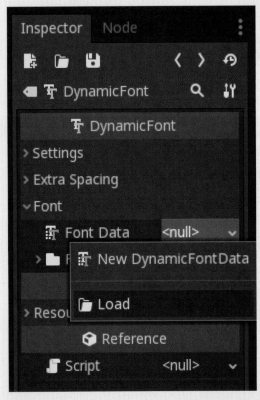 Label, rename it "retry," and set its **Align** property to **Center**.

2. Change its **Text** to "game over" **<linebreak>**, then type: "-press the enter key to retry-"

3. Move the "retry" **Label** to the center of the viewport boundaries, like in Figure 5.9.

FIGURE 5.10
Loading a TrueType font as a Dynamic font. For more information on importing fonts, check out Hour 14, "Project Management."

Note that we enabled the **Uppercase** property of the **Label,** because our provided TrueType font "hour5.ttf" only supports uppercase letters. Feel free to use your own fonts if you like to support lowercase letters and various symbols like exclamation marks or parentheses.

The last thing to do is hide the "game over" message by clicking on the 🎯 icon next to the "retry" **Label**. We will later make it reappear using the stage script when the spaceship is destroyed.

This concludes the creation of the stage scene.

Scripts and Input

In this section, we will write the scripts to make the game actually playable.

Creating the Player, Asteroid, and Shot Scripts

Let us jump right to creating and attaching a player script called "player.gd" for the root node of the player scene just like you learned in the previous hour. You can delete the **_ready** function and the comments, as we won't need them. To get some basic ship movement going, let's write a script similar to the movement script we wrote in the previous hour, shown in Listing 5.1.

LISTING 5.1   Basic Ship Movement with the Arrow Keys—player.gd

```
extends Area2D
const MOVE_SPEED = 150.0

func _process(delta):
    var input_dir = Vector2()
    if Input.is_key_pressed(KEY_UP):
        input_dir.y -= 1.0
    if Input.is_key_pressed(KEY_DOWN):
        input_dir.y += 1.0
    if Input.is_key_pressed(KEY_LEFT):
        input_dir.x -= 1.0
    if Input.is_key_pressed(KEY_RIGHT):
        input_dir.x += 1.0

    position += (delta * MOVE_SPEED) * input_dir
```

The above script first defines a move speed for the ship (in pixels per second), then in every frame asks the **Input** class if any of the arrow keys are pressed. If one of the arrow keys is pressed, the corresponding axis direction in the **Vector2 input_dir** is added. Finally, we add the input direction multiplied by a fraction of the ship's move speed to the position. Note that we multiply with delta here to ensure a frame rate-independent movement of the ship.

Note also that the axis directions are the same as in Figure 3.1 of Hour 3, and that pressing two opposing directions like left and right at the same time sets the corresponding axis to zero, which is what we want to happen.

In Hour 7, "Handling Input," we will see more sophisticated ways to handle input like defining **input actions** and using the gamepad and keyboard interchangeably. For now, the keyboard with some hard-coded keys is enough to get our simple game started.

▼ TRY IT YOURSELF

Tweaking the Speed

You can play-test directly by pressing in the top-right corner ▶ and controlling the ship with the arrow keys on your keyboard. Note that Godot might ask you to select a main scene; if so, select the stage scene you created in the last section. Play around with different values of MOVE_SPEED and choose one that feels comfortable.

While play-testing your game, you may have noticed that the spaceship can freely move out of the screen. We want to prevent this by extending our script shown in Listing 5.2.

LISTING 5.2   Ship Movement Constrained to Screen—player.gd

```
. . .
const SCREEN_WIDTH = 320
const SCREEN_HEIGHT = 180

func _process(delta):
    . . .
    if position.x < 0.0:
     position.x = 0.0
    elif position.x > SCREEN_WIDTH:
     position.x = SCREEN_WIDTH
    if position.y < 0.0:
     position.y = 0.0
    elif position.y > SCREEN_HEIGHT:
     position.y = SCREEN_HEIGHT
```

You may remember that at the beginning of this hour, we set our game resolution to 320×180. Those are the exact numbers as in the SCREEN_WIDTH and SCREEN_HEIGHT constants. We use them to check if the ship moved past the screen borders and set it back to the screen border.

When play-testing, you may notice that the ship still moves halfway off the edge of the screen. This is because the spaceship's position vector represents its exact center, so the ship is allowed to move past the screen until its center hits the edge. If you would like to fix this, you can add some pixel constant to the **if**-statements (see the **exercises** at the end of this hour).

With the movement done, let's allow the ship to shoot some laser shots. Let's first create a "shot.gd" script for the root node of the shot scene (Listing 5.3).

LISTING 5.3   Laser Shot Movement—shot.gd

```
extends Area2D
const SCREEN_WIDTH = 320
const MOVE_SPEED = 500.0

func _process(delta):
    position += Vector2(MOVE_SPEED * delta, 0.0)
    if position.x >= SCREEN_WIDTH + 8:
        queue_free()
```

The above script allows the laser shot to move horizontally to the right by a certain amount per frame. If the shot moves beyond the screen, we delete the shot from the game by calling the node's **queue_free** function. This function makes sure the shot is deleted from memory **after** it has finished all of its processing in the current frame.

To do the actual shooting, we'll want to spawn laser shots at the spaceship's position when the player presses the spacebar. For this, the player script needs to know about the shot scene and instantiate it into the stage. We can get the shot scene with **preload** ("res://path_to_your_shot_scene/shot.tscn") and save it into a variable for later instantiation.

To place a laser shot into the game, use the **instance** function on the loaded shot scene and add the instance into the stage scene's root with the **add_child** function. To get the stage scene's root, we can use the **get_parent** function, because our spaceship instance is a child node of the stage's scene root (see Figure 5.9). We set the **position** of the instance to be the same as the ship's **position** to make it appear as if the laser is coming out of the ship. Let's extend our player script to let the ship shoot lasers (Listing 5.4).

LISTING 5.4   Spawning Laser Shots on Keypress—player.gd

```
...
var shot_scene = preload("res://scenes/shot.tscn")

func _process(delta):
    ...
    if Input.is_key_pressed(KEY_SPACE):
        var stage_node = get_parent()

        var shot_instance = shot_scene.instance()
        shot_instance.position = position
        stage_node.add_child(shot_instance)
```

When play-testing this, you will notice the ship fires lasers way too fast. We need to limit the fire rate somehow. Luckily, we already planned for that by providing a "reload_timer" to the player scene. Connect the "reload_timer" node's **timeout** signal to our spaceship's script (it should automatically create the **_on_reload_timer_timeout** function for you).

We next create a Boolean variable called **can_shoot**, set it initially to true, and conditionally check it before shooting. After shooting, we set it to false and start the "reload_timer," When the "reload_timer" timeouts, it sets the **can_shoot** variable back to true so that the ship can shoot again. For all this to work, we need to make the following modifications to the player script:

LISTING 5.5   Limiting Fire-Rate—player.gd

```
...
var can_shoot = true

func _process(delta):
    ...

    if Input.is_key_pressed(KEY_SPACE) and can_shoot:
        ...
        can_shoot = false
        get_node("reload_timer").start()

func _on_reload_timer_timeout():
    can_shoot = true
```

There is now a noticeable fire-rate reduction when the game runs. You can tweak the reload time by modifying the **Wait Time** property in the **Inspector** of the "reload timer."

▼ TRY IT YOURSELF

Shooting Two Lasers at the Same Time

You may now look at the finished game's screenshot in **Figure 5.1** and complain that there are two laser shots firing from the ship, while our ship is firing only one. To fix this, you can reuse these lines from Listing 5.4 to create a second shot instance and then place both at (position + Vector2(9, −5)) and (position + Vector2(9, 5)) respectively.

```
var shot_instance = shot_scene.instance()
shot_instance.position = position
stage_node.add_child(shot_instance)
```

Now that the ship can shoot lasers, we need some asteroids to shoot at. Instantiate some asteroid scenes in the stage scene by dragging the "asteroid.tscn" scene you created from the **FileSystem** dock into the editor viewport. Now shooting or flying into the asteroids will have no effect, because we did not write the needed scripts for it. Let's change that by making the asteroids fly toward the spaceship and explode by either getting hit by the spaceship or a laser shot. Create an empty script for the root node and add an empty **_process()** function. Connect its **area_entered** signal to the **_on_asteroid_area_entered** function of your asteroid script like you learned in the previous hour. Your asteroid script should now look something like what is shown in Listing 5.6.

LISTING 5.6   Empty Asteroid Script—asteroid.gd

```
extends Area2D

func _process(delta):
    pass

func _on_asteroid_area_entered(area):
    pass # replace with function body
```

When the collision shape of a laser shot overlaps with the collision shot of your asteroid, the **_on_asteroid_area_entered** function is called. You can test this by putting a **breakpoint** keyword into the function body. The game will then halt at the moment a laser shot or the spaceship touches an asteroid.

To add the needed functionality, extend the asteroid script as shown in Listing 5.7.

LISTING 5.7   Asteroids Flying Toward the Spaceship and Exploding on Impact—asteroid.gd

```
extends Area2D

var explosion_scene = preload("res://scenes/explosion.tscn")

var move_speed = 100.0
var score_emitted = false

signal score

func _process(delta):
    position -= Vector2(move_speed * delta, 0.0)
    if position.x <= -100:
        queue_free()
```

```
func _on_asteroid_area_entered(area):
    if area.is_in_group("shot") or area.is_in_group("player"):
        if not score_emitted:
            score_emitted = true
            emit_signal("score")
            queue_free()

            var stage_node = get_parent()
            var explosion_instance = explosion_scene.instance()
            explosion_instance.position = position
            stage_node.add_child(explosion_instance)
```

This might seem like quite a lot at first, but we can mostly break things down into parts we have already seen before. For example, you may recognize the content of the **_process()** function is almost the same as the laser movement code from Listing 5.3, only going in the opposite direction. You also might recognize the last block in the listing. This spawns the explosion scene into the game at the position of the asteroid. We have seen this in Listing 5.4, where we spawned laser shot scenes from the player script.

Remember that we assigned the root nodes of the player, shot, and asteroid scenes to groups of their respective names? At the beginning of the **_on_asteroid_area_entered** function, we check whether the area that overlaps with our asteroid is a laser shot or the spaceship by verifying group names. We briefly saw this concept at the end of the previous hour, and use it to prevent the collision of asteroids with other asteroids.

Next, check if the **score_emitted** Boolean is false, set it to true, emit the **score** signal, and call **queue_free**. The **score** signal will later be used in the stage script to track the score. But why do we need the additional **score_emitted** Boolean if we free the asteroid anyway? This is to prevent the emitting of the **score** signal more than once. This can happen when two shots hit the asteroid in the same frame. As we hinted before, **queue_free** does not immediately delete the asteroid. It instead waits **after** the asteroid finished all its processing in the current frame, including all the calls to the **_on_asteroid_area_entered** function that are needed.

When play-testing, you should now see the asteroids you placed into the stage flying at you. Shooting at or flying into asteroids will destroy them. But you will also notice that the laser shots, as well as the spaceship, will keep on flying after colliding with an asteroid. We are going to change that next.

Note that the **destroyed** signal in the player script and the **score** signal in the asteroid script are used by the stage script that we will create in the next section.

Finishing the Player and Shot Scripts

To finish the shot script, you need to:

1. Connect the **area_entered** signal of the "shot" node to its shot script, just like you did with the asteroid script. You can just use the default suggested **_on_shot_area_entered** function.

2. Modify the function body of the **_on_shot_area_entered** function so that **queue_free** is called when the shot collides with an area in the group **asteroid**.

To finish the player script, you need to:

1. Connect the **area_entered** signal of the "player" node to its player script, just like you did above. You can again use the default suggested **_on_player_area_entered** function.

2. Create a new signal called **destroyed** in the player script.

3. Modify the function body of the **_on_ player _area_entered** function so that when the space-ship collides with an area in the group **asteroid**:

   ▶ **queue_free** is called

   ▶ an explosion scene is spawned just like in the asteroid script

   ▶ the **destroyed** signal you created in the previous step is emitted

Creating the Stage and Background Scripts

When play-testing, you should now have working gameplay. The asteroids fly toward your spaceship. and you can shoot them. The laser shots and asteroids disappear on collision, and the asteroids spawn an explosion. If the spaceship touches an asteroid, both explode. Now the problem is that the score is not tracked by the "score" **Label**, and we run out of asteroids quickly. Also, we cannot restart the game after colliding with an asteroid, and the "game over" message is nowhere to be found.

Let's focus first on the player's interaction with the game and UI by creating the following script shown in Listing 5.8 for the root node of the stage scene.

LISTING 5.8 Input and UI of the Stage—stage.gd

```
extends node2D
var is_game_over = false

func _ready():
    get_node("player").connect("destroyed", self, "_on_player_destroyed")
```

```
func _input(event):
    if Input.is_key_pressed(KEY_ESCAPE):
        get_tree().quit()
    if is_game_over and Input.is_key_pressed(KEY_ENTER):
        get_tree().change_scene("res://stage.tscn")

func _on_player_destroyed():
    get_node("ui/retry").show()
    is_game_over = true
```

This connects the **destroyed** signal of the spaceship to our custom **_on_player_destroyed** function as soon as the stage loads. We have seen in the previous hour this is an alternative to connecting to signals by using the editor. As soon as the spaceship is destroyed, it makes our "game over" message visible and enables pressing the enter key to restart the game.

Restarting the game works by using the **change_scene** function and passing our current scene as a parameter. Note that you can pass the path to any scene into the function, so level changes can also be done with it. The **change_scene** function is a method of the **Scene Tree**, which you can retrieve by calling the **get_tree** function. We also use it here a second time in conjunction with the **quit** function to let the player quit the game by pressing the escape key.

To create periodically spawning asteroids, we first connect the **timeout** signal of the stage scene's "spawn_timer" node to our stage script. When the timer timeouts, we spawn an instance of the asteroid scene at a random location outside our screen. While we are at it, we can connect to the **score** signal of each spawned asteroid to update our score. For this, we do the following modifications to our stage script in Listing 5.9.

LISTING 5.9   Spawning Asteroids and Tracking the Score—stage.gd

```
...
var asteroid = preload("res://scenes/asteroid.tscn")
const SCREEN_WIDTH = 320
const SCREEN_HEIGHT = 180
var score = 0

func _ready():
    ...
    get_node("spawn_timer").connect("timeout", self, "_on_spawn_timer_timeout")

...
func _on_spawn_timer_timeout():
    var asteroid_instance = asteroid.instance()
    asteroid_instance.position = Vector2(SCREEN_WIDTH + 8, rand_range
(0, SCREEN_HEIGHT))
    asteroid_instance.connect("score", self, "_on_player_score")
    add_child(asteroid_instance)
```

```
func _on_player_score():
    score += 1
    get_node("ui/score").text = "Score: " + str(score)
```

Note the usage of the built-in **rand_range (min, max)** function. It returns a random floating point value between the min and max, which is in our case the top and bottom of our screen.

Also note that when changing scenes, everything, including the score we accumulated, is reset. Please look at Hour 12, "File System," if you want to know how to save a game's progress persistently to disk and reload it when needed.

When play-testing, you will notice everything now works as it should. But something feels off. Right! The background is still static. Let's change that by creating the following script for the "background" **Sprite** in the stage scene, as seen in Listing 5.10.

LISTING 5.10   Infinitely Scrolling Background—background.gd

```
extends Sprite
const SCREEN_WIDTH = 320
var scroll_speed = 30.0

func _process(delta):
    position += Vector2(-scroll_speed * delta, 0.0)

    if position.x <= -SCREEN_WIDTH:
        position.x += SCREEN_WIDTH
```

The above code works very similarly to the movement code in the asteroid script, with the exception that it repositions the background Sprite one screen-width to the right if it moved past one screen-width to the left. This creates the illusion of an infinitely scrolling background.

Summary

In this hour, you created a simple but complete 2D pixel art game from scratch! You learned to work with the **Area2D** nodes, as well as the **AnimatedSprites** and **Timer** nodes. You also learned how to work with scenes that interact with each other in a game context, and how to structure those scenes to keep them decoupled from each other by using signals. You have hopefully seen the usefulness of instancing scenes from code, as it allows a dynamic game flow. You will revisit many of the concepts shown here and in greater detail in later hours.

Q&A

Q. Why do we even need to queue_free everything? Can't we just hide nodes?

A. You could, of course, just do that. But then Godot has to keep all those objects in memory and possibly has to still do the **_process**() function on every object on every frame, even if we do not need them anymore. This can be very bad for performance and memory consumption.

Q. Why do I get the same asteroid pattern every time I start the game?

A. Because Godot uses a default seed for its random number generator. If you want a different pattern each time the game starts, you can reseed the random number generator by placing the **randomize**() function into the **_ready**() function of the stage script (you may need to create a _ready() function first).

Q. Why do we connect the destroy and timeout signals in the stage script by code?

A. There is no particular reason other than to show that this is possible. You could connect them by using the editor. The **score** signals of the asteroids, however, cannot be connected by using the editor, because the asteroids do not exist in the stage scene until they are spawned in-game.

Q. What is the number 8 doing in the if-statement of the _process() functions in the asteroid and shot scripts?

A. The dimensions of the shot Sprite and the asteroid Sprite are both 16x16 pixels, respectively. If we ask for position.x >= SCREEN_WIDTH + 8, we mean that the x position of the Sprite should be greater than the screen width plus half its Sprite-width in pixels. As the Sprite position is normally its centerpoint, we mean, "Is the Sprite now out of our screen boundary?"

Workshop

Answer the following questions to make sure you understood the content of this hour.

Quiz

1. What does the **One Shot** property of a **Timer** node do?

2. How can we prevent our pixel art from getting blurry?

3. What are the steps needed to spawn another scene into a scene by script?

4. What does **queue_free** do and when?

5. How does the "score" **Label** in the stage scene know when it needs to update its score?

Answers

1. It lets the Timer stop after a timeout. Without the property, the **Timer** would restart again.

2. We need to turn off the filter property in the import dock or use the **2D Pixel** preset.

3. We need to **preload** the scene, instantiate it with **instance**, set its position, and then add it as a child to the parent scene using **add_child**.

4. The **queue_free** function deletes a node from memory and therefore removes it from the game. It does this after the node has finished all its processing, including all input and signals that need to be processed.

5. The "score" **Label** is updated by the stage script. The stage script connects to the **score** signal of an asteroid when it gets spawned into the game. As soon as the asteroid is destroyed, it emits its **score** signal, which causes the stage to increment its internal **score** variable and write it to the "score" **Label**.

Exercises

1. Make it so that the spaceship's Sprite does not move past the screen border anymore by adding a margin of 8 pixels or more to the code of **Listing 5.2**.

2. Create a dynamic difficulty that depends on the score by adding the value of the **score** variable to **asteroid_instance.move_speed** in the **_on_spawn_timer_timeout** function of **Listing 5.9**.

3. Spawn asteroids faster with time by multiplying the **wait_time** variable of the "spawn_timer" node in the **_on_spawn_timer_timeout** function of Listing 5.9 with 0.99. By multiplying itself by 0.99, the **wait_time** will decrease slowly without becoming a negative (like it would by just subtracting a fixed time).

4. Assign a new game icon to the project by overwriting icon.png in the root folder of the project with the "icon.png" provided in the accompanied "Godot-Hour5" folder.

5. Try getting a score over 300!

HOUR 6
More Scripting

What You'll Learn in This Hour:

► Using Godot's notification system

► Singletons in Godot's API

► Creating custom autoloads/singletons

► Editor tools

► Interfacing with other Godot scripting languages

In Hour 4, "Scripting," you learned about the basics of scripting in Godot using GDScript, and in Hour 5, "Game 1: Space Shooter," you designed and implementing a space shooter game. By now, you should have some experience and familiarity with GDScript. GDScript and Godot have a lot more to offer, so it's time to expand that field of knowledge even more.

In this hour, you'll learn about Godot's notification system, a way to pass "messages" to certain objects and nodes. We will also explore the world of singletons and autoloads, the latter of which provides a way to define custom singletons. Godot's Editor is very flexible, and lets you run scripts to make changes to scenes using code. The ability to have multiple languages in one project brings up the question of how these languages should interact. This will be covered in this section.

Notifications

Godot has a notification system through which objects can send messages to other objects. Notifications are used to guide the initialization and deletion of objects, and to receive events not available through the input singleton or the InputEvent system. The notification system is a low-level system that's usually not used very often in script code, but sometimes you need control over more things not exposed to script-exposed classes.

A "notification" is just a number (see Listing 6.1). That number usually corresponds to a constant defined somewhere else (unless you send your own notification that does not represent a constant).

LISTING 6.1   Sample Notification

```
extends Node

func _notification(what):
    if what == MainLoop.NOTIFICATION_WM_FOCUS_IN:
        print("Welcome back!")
    elif what == MainLoop.NOTIFICATION_WM_FOCUS_OUT:
        print("Bye, have a great time!")
    elif what == NOTIFICATION_PREDELETE:
        destructor()

func destructor():
    print("This object is about to be deleted.")
    # cleanup here
```

The methods `_ready`, `_process`, and many others are implemented using notifications. You will see how later in this section.

Sending Notifications

To send a notification to an object, the method `Object.notification(int what, bool reverse=false)` is used.

The `what` argument is the notification to send. The `reverse` argument specifies the order in which those notifications are processed. Every class has the option to handle a notification; sometimes, it's necessary for the parent classes to process it after the children have processed it. Usually, you never need to specify that argument, as the default value causes the desired behavior in most cases.

`Object.notification()` only operates on one object, but since many things center around Scene Tree in Godot, every node has a method, `Node.propagate_notification(int what)`, that will "hand" the notification down the tree. It will first call `_notification` on the node itself, then on all the children.

Receiving Notifications

In the introduction to this section, you saw a small example that used `_notification`. The `_notification` method receives all notifications sent to an object.

The following GDScript code prints the value (number) of every notification received:

```
extends Node

func _notification(what):
    print("got notification: ", what)
```

The `what` parameter is the number that represents the notification. Usually, `if` or `match` statements are used to branch execution based on that argument. In the next subsection, we'll see some common notifications and how to use them effectively.

Commonly Used Notifications

In-Editor Documentation

If you Ctrl+Left click on a class name, the editor help will open. You can see all the notifications defined by that class on those pages in the code editor.

Object Notifications

As mentioned in Listing 6.1, **NOTIFICATION_PREDELETE** is useful in implementing a destructor-like functionality. This notification gets sent just before the object gets deleted. Listing 6.2 is an example script that shows one possible usage of **NOTIFICATION_PREDELETE**.

LISTING 6.2   Sample Notification

```
extends Object

# open files, log into network or something else...

func _notification(what):
    if what == NOTIFICATION_PREDELETE:
        print("I'm about to be deleted!")
        some_file.close()
        networking.unregister(self)
```

There's also **NOTIFICATION_POSTINITIALIZE**, but it's not usable from scripts, because at that point in time, the script has not yet been attached to the object. For initialization, use `_init` or, in case of nodes, `_ready`.

Node Notifications

As we know, a node is something that can be part of a tree, so the node class defines many notifications that have to do with the Scene Tree.

- ▶ **NOTIFICATION_ENTER_TREE:** Gets sent when the node enters the tree. It means the children have not yet been added and the node has entered the tree on its own. It's advisable to override the `_enter_tree` method instead.

- ▶ **NOTIFICATION_EXIT_TREE:** Gets sent when the node is about to leave the tree. You should override the `_exit_tree` method instead.

▶ **NOTIFICATION_MOVED_IN_PARENT:** Gets sent when the node gets moved using the `Node.move_child` method.

▶ **NOTIFICATION_READY:** Gets sent when the node enters the tree and all the children get initialized as well. You should override `_ready` instead.

▶ **NOTIFICATION_FIXED_PROCESS:** When `set_fixed_process(true)` is called (or a `_fixed_process` method is present), this notification gets sent every "fixed process frame." It's similar to `_process`, but it's not running as fast as the frame rate. Instead, it's running as fast as the physics engine simulates the world. The `delta` time can be acquired with the `Node.get_fixed_process_delta_time` method.

▶ **NOTIFICATION_PROCESS:** This notification gets sent for every frame the engine processes (when `set_process(true)` was called or a `_process` method is present). The `delta` parameter can be acquired with the `Node.get_process_delta_time` method. You should override the `_process` method instead of using notifications.

▶ **NOTIFICATION_PARENTED:** Gets sent when the node gets assigned a parent node.

▶ **NOTIFICATION_UNPARENTED:** Gets sent when the node's parent gets removed (it no longer has a parent, but it still exists).

▶ **NOTIFICATION_PAUSED:** Gets sent when the node processing is paused (using `get_tree().set_pause(true)`). It stops the node from running `_process`, `_fixed_process`, and the `_input` methods.

▶ **NOTIFICATION_UNPAUSED:** Like **NOTIFICATION_PAUSED**, but gets called again when the node gets unpaused.

▶ **NOTIFICATION_INSTANCED:** Gets sent when a scene gets instanced and all the nodes in it are created.

▶ **NOTIFICATION_TRANSLATION_CHANGED:** Gets sent when the selected language in a game gets changed (by using `TranslationServer.set_locale`). This gets used to update all the texts that can be localized.

Main Loop Notifications

A Main Loop is an object that defines how an application runs in Godot. In the case of games, it's the Scene Tree (which inherits the Main Loop). The Scene Tree includes the tree of nodes. It also decides when to quit the game, and it receives some unique notifications concerning window focus.

▶ **NOTIFICATION_WM_MOUSE_ENTER:** Gets sent when the mouse cursor enters the window.

▶ **NOTIFICATION_WM_MOUSE_EXIT:** Gets sent when the mouse cursor leaves the window.

▶ **NOTIFICATION_WM_FOCUS_IN:** Gets sent when the window gains focus. This happens when the window is out of focus and gains focus by a user clicking into the window or by using a key combination (commonly alt+tab) or the taskbar.

▶ **NOTIFICATION_WM_FOCUS_OUT:** Gets sent when the window loses focus. Can be used to open a menu or pause the game to save resources whenever the player doesn't have the game window active.

▶ **NOTIFICATION_WM_QUIT_REQUEST:** Gets sent when the game should close. By default, the game simply closes, but this notification gets sent anyway. If the game should not close automatically, `get_tree().set_auto_accept_quit(false)` should be used. This way, the game does not close and can, for example, display a "Saving?" dialog. To close the game manually, `get_tree().quit()` must be used.

These are the most commonly used notifications, but of course, there are many other notification types.

In composition with `Node.propagate_notification`, it can be useful to pass custom notifications down the node tree, but be careful to not "shadow" an existing notification. Usually, it's better to use groups with `SceneTree.call_group`. You can also use the `Node.propagate_call` method to call a method on all nodes in a branch.

Singletons and Autoloads

This section covers singletons, a commonly used design pattern, and autoloads, which are nodes loaded at startup that remain loaded during an app's runtime. Both are important to understand and use in Godot.

Singletons

One of the most popular and commonly used design patterns in object-oriented programming is the **singleton** pattern. The singleton pattern ensures that there is only one object (sometimes called the *instance*) of a certain class. This is desired when you need a globally accessible state or don't want programmers to create their own instances of that type. Often, this object is accessed through a **class-method** (meaning it doesn't require an object to call) that returns a reference to that object.

In Godot's codebase (which is in C++), you'll often see code like this:

```
OS::get_singleton()->print("Hello World");

Input::get_singleton()->is_action_pressed("ui_accept");

Engine::get_singleton()->get_frames_per_second();
```

You can see that a method `get_singleton` gets called. It's the method that returns a reference to the only instance of that class.

In Hour 4, the `Input` singleton was used to check if events had been pressed. There are many more singletons in Godot that can be used in GDScript and other scripting languages.

Because GDScript was made to make scripting as easy and straightforward as possible, it has a simplified syntax for accessing singletons. Instead of calling a method to access the singleton, GDScript knows which singletons exist, and lets you access them by writing the name of the class as if it were the object.

Let's take a look at a comparison of singleton usage in C++ (Godot source code) and GDScript.

Here is the C++ code:

```
// C++
Input::get_singleton()->is_action_pressed("ui_accept")
```

And here is the GDScript:

```
# GDScript
Input.is_action_pressed("ui_accept")
```

Commonly Used Singletons

Here is a list of commonly used singletons:

ResourceLoader: Has methods for loading resources from the file system. `ResourceLoader.load_interactive` can be used to load resources without blocking the main thread.

OS: Has methods for using operating system functions, such as setting and getting the contents clipboard, starting new processes, and changing window properties (full screen, title, size).

Engine: Has methods for getting information about some properties of the running engine, such as `get_frames_per_second()`, `get_version_info()`, `get_target_fps()`, and `get_frames_drawn()`.

ClassDB: This class has all the information about Godot classes you can use in any scripting language. It can be used to create instances of classes you only know at runtime, for example, after prompting the user what to do. This can be done using `ClassDB.instance(class_name)`, where class_name is a string (that can be computed at runtime). It also has methods for querying information about classes, such as `class_get_method_list`, `class_get_signal_list`, and `get_inheriters_from_class`.

ProjectSettings: Can be used to set and get values from **Project Settings**. Using `get` and `set`, it is the programmatic counterpart to the Project Settings window in the editor, and is useful for changing settings in an in-game menu. The `save` method saves the changes to the project configuration file.

InputMap: The programmatic counterpart to the **Input Map** tab in the Project Settings window; `add_action` and `action_add_event` are the most commonly used methods with this singleton. They add a new input action to the input map (which can be checked with `Input.is_action_pressed`), and add an event to an action. Thus, when an event known to that action occurs, InputMap knows which event triggers which action. An "event" refers to an input event like a key press or a joystick button, which gets mapped to an action.

Performance: Can be used to get information about various processes in the engine, such as the number of draw calls used in the last frame, how many objects currently exist, how many nodes exist, how much memory is currently used, and much more. This information can be queried using the `get_monitor` method, which takes one of the many constants that this class defines as the argument.

Input: Used to get information about all kinds of user input methods, this is easily the most-used singleton in Godot. There are methods for getting joystick, gyroscope, and magnetometer states, and for controlling gamepad vibration and user-defined input events. There's more about these singletons in Hour 7, "Handling Input."

AutoLoad

Having global objects accessible from everywhere can be really useful, so it would be a shame if the same wasn't possible for objects with scripts attached to them. Godot's answer to that is **AutoLoad**. An autoload is a node that gets loaded at startup and stays loaded for the entire runtime of the application/game.

Autoloads can also be scenes loaded from a path to a scene file. This means the scene can be created from the editor and have a scene tree (multiple nodes), and a root of a specialized type (not just a Node).

An autoload is always located in the scene tree as a child of the root node (see Listing 6.3). The node itself is a simple **Node** node (because the autoload is there for its custom behavior, not the node behavior). The name of the node is the name of the autoload. So, an autoload named "GlobalGameState" would be located in `/root/GlobalGameState`.

LISTING 6.3   Sample Autoload Code

```
extends Node

var coins_collected = 0

func coin_collected():
    coins_collected += 1

func save_state():
    # write the state into a file

func read_state():
    # read the state from a file
```

To create an autoload, you have to create a script that extends the **Node** and saves it somewhere in the project directory. Because Godot loads all the autoloads, it needs to know which scripts are supposed to be used under which name. This can be done in the Project Settings window in the AutoLoad tab. Once you provide a name and the path to the script, the autoload will be loaded on start-up (see Figure 6.1).

FIGURE 6.1
Autoloading a script in the AutoLoad tab.

When that is done, you can use the autoload from every script (see Listing 6.4), just like engine singletons.

LISTING 6.4   Autoloading from Every Script

```
extends KinematicBody2D

# player variables here

func _on_Area_entered(area):
    if area.is_in_group("coin"):
        # collected a coin.

        GameState.coin_collected()

        emit_signal("coin_collected")
```

TIP

Autoload Location

Because autoloads are just nodes in the tree, you can access them with `get_node` too! The previous code also works when `$"/root/GameState .coin_collected()"` is used.

Editor Tools

Scripts in Godot can operate in a so-called "tool" mode. The tool mode lets the script run in the editor instead of just when you run the scene.

NOTE

It's All a Game

The Godot editor itself is an application built using Godot. It's the reason Godot has so many control nodes—the editor uses all those UI elements. Because the editor is just a "game," it can run scripts too.

There are two common ways to use tool mode scripts: creating an **EditorPlugin** or an **EditorScript**. While editor plugins comprise a huge topic, editor scripts are a lot easier to get into and grasp. Both share a common interface, so learning about using EditorScript will also help when trying to write an editor plugin.

If a script inherits from EditorScript, it can run in the editor, make changes to the current scene, and perform other actions that the editor can do, such as importing files or saving scenes and resources.

One use of an editor script is to let it make changes to your scene that are tedious to make by hand. For example, it can be used for procedurally generating levels, which then get an "upgrade" by the designers and artists. So, it's nice to have a basic framework with which to work and have those levels generated automatically.

To showcase that functionality, we will add a circle of Sprite nodes to the current scene. The script can also be modified to help you create beautiful images (see Listing 6.5).

LISTING 6.5   Adding Sprite Nodes to the Scene

```
tool
extends EditorScript

var texture = preload("res://icon.png")

var origin = Vector2(500, 250)
var radius = 200

var num_sprites = 20

func _run():

    for i in range(num_sprites):

        var node = Sprite.new()
        node.texture = texture

        node.set_name("sprite" + str(i))

        get_scene().add_child(node)
        node.set_owner(get_scene())

        node.scale = Vector2(0.5, 0.5)

        node.position = origin + Vector2(radius, 0).rotated((2 * PI) / num_sprites * i)
```

Figure 6.2 shows how you can use EditorScript.

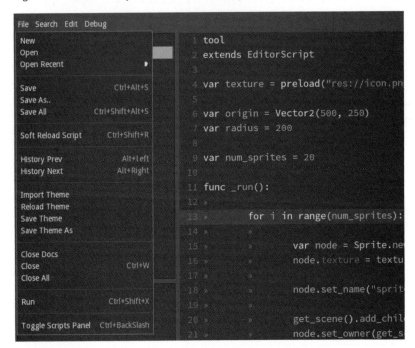

FIGURE 6.2
Running EditorScript and seeing the change in the scene.

In Figure 6.3, you can see the output from successfully running the script in Figure 6.2.

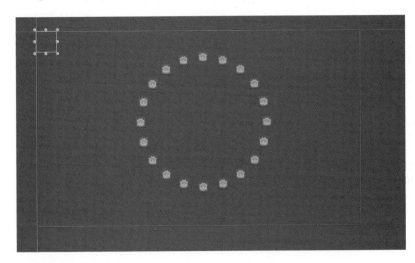

FIGURE 6.3
The successful outcome from the script shown in Figure 6.2.

Every script that gets executed in the editor must have the `tool` keyword at the top of the file.

As you can see, the script must inherit EditorScript to access the editor functionality. The `_run` method gets called when the script runs in the editor (see the Q&A section later for more). The `_run` method is special to EditorScript, so it can't be used in any arbitrary script (well, it can, but it won't be called unless you call it manually).

Because the editor is an application in Godot, it uses the Scene Tree. And because the editor has its own Scene Tree, the autoloads configured in Project Settings aren't loaded, so you can't use them in tool scripts.

The `get_scene` method returns a reference to the root node of the current scene. This reference can be used to add new child nodes to the scene. The editor script creates new Sprite nodes, adds them as children, and sets the position so that they are all positioned in a way to estimate the shape of a circle.

TIP

Adding Nodes to the Scene

The previous editor script adds new nodes to the scene by using the `add_child` method. This adds the children to the tree, but the current scene doesn't know about it; the children are just living in the editor, and the scene doesn't care about them much. To let the scene know about those children so they don't just hang around and get removed, the method `set_owner` needs to be used after the call to `add_child`. Then the new child nodes will show up in the Scene tab.

The "owner" of a node indicates that the node belongs to the scene being edited, so it should be saved and shown in the Tree tab. Similarly, when a subscene is instantiated inside the scene being edited, the owner of all the nodes of the subscene will be the root of the subscene, and not the root of the scene being edited. That's how the editor knows not to save those nodes when the scene is saved.

EditorInterface

EditorScript has access to the editor interface through the `get_editor_interface` method. Godot's EditorInterface has many useful methods for interacting with the editor. Here are a few methods that you might find useful:

▶ **get_editor_settings:** Similar to `ProjectSettings`, this can be used to access and change the editor settings with code.

▶ **get_editor_viewport:** Returns a reference to the viewport in the editor. This can be used to draw custom things on the viewport.

▶ **get_open_scenes:** Returns an array of paths to scenes that are currently opened inside the editor.

▶ **open_scene_from_path:** Used to open scenes like a user does when he uses the UI "Scene→Open Scene."

▶ **save_scene** and **save_scene_as:** Used to save modified scenes to a disk. This could be used in an editor plugin that automatically saves all scenes in a certain interval.

Interfacing with Other Godot Scripting Languages

Godot's internal architecture allows for multiple scripting languages and systems to co-exist in a project and even communicate with one another.

The way the system works influences how GDScript works internally. It's especially easy to call methods defined in other scripting languages, because it's specifically made for Godot.

The uniform way to call methods on an object is to use `Object.call` or `Object.callv`. This will work in all languages, no matter from which language you're calling.

The way GDScript's calling mechanism works is exactly the same. If you type `some_object.some_method(a, b)`, internally it performs `some_object.callv("some_method", [a, b])`. The same syntax can be used across all languages, as shown here and illustrated in Figure 6.4.

```
extends Node
func _ready():
    $"../VSNode".a_visual_script_method()
```

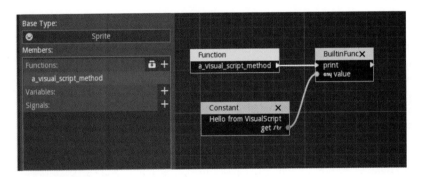

FIGURE 6.4
A GDScript calling a method on a VisualScript.

Different languages might have different ways of calling `callv`, but that's what it all comes down to. Alternatively, `Variant.call` can be used. This also automatically handles methods of core types, such as `String.length`. As long as a language binding exposes these methods, it can call into any other scripting language used in Godot.

Summary

In this hour, you learned more about singletons and their usage in Godot. You also saw how to make your own singletons by creating autoloads, which are available in every script. Because the editor is built using Godot itself, it's possible to script inside of it, which helps bring procedural generation and many other things right to the editor and to scenes you're working on. Godot's object system allows different scripting languages to interoperate seamlessly; you know how to call back and forth between languages.

Q&A

Q. **What is the difference between autoloads and in-engine singletons?**

A. Autoloads are user-defined nodes that are children of the `/root/` node. Singletons are C++ classes that are made available to the scripting system.

Q. **How can you change project settings from within a game?**

A. The `ProjectSettings` singleton can be used to set and get settings. They can be updated by using `ProjectSettings.get("setting/name")` and `ProjectSettings.set("setting/name", new_value)`.

Q. **How can a script run inside the editor?**

A. Scripts can be in "tool" mode, which enables them to run inside the editor. The tool mode gets activated by writing the "tool" keyword at the top of the GDScript file. Other scripting languages might have a different mechanism to activate tool mode.

Workshop

Answer the following questions to make sure you understood the content of this hour.

Quiz

1. What method needs to be defined to receive notifications?
2. What notification gets sent when the current object is about to be destroyed?
3. How do you access an autoload's method `test` when the autoload's name is `MyAutoLoad`?
4. What singleton can be used to query information about the game's performance?
5. How do you run an editor script inside the editor?

Answers

1. The `_notification` method.
2. The `NOTIFICATION_PREDELETE` notification.
3. The call would be `MyAutoLoad.test()`.
4. The `Performance` singleton, but some methods on the `Engine` singleton are useful too.
5. Select the script to run in ScriptEditor, then click "run" in the "file" menu (or Ctrl+Shift+X).

Exercises

Editor scripts can be really useful. Try to get more familiar with them by letting one automatically generate scenes for different enemy types:

1. Create an editor script by using the "new" entry in the "file" menu inside the ScriptEditor. Name it however you want, but it needs to inherit EditorScript, and it needs to be in tool mode.

2. Define an array of names for the enemy scenes. This can be done with `var enemies = ["enemy_name_0", "enemy_name_1", ... ]`. You can iterate over all the elements with `for entry in enemies:`, where entry will be the name of the currently iterated element.

3. For each element, create a node with the name of the enemy (with `set_name`). You can get creative here. Create a Sprite and use the "modulate" property to tint the texture. You can also add timers or other nodes—don't be afraid to explore some nodes you haven't seen yet.

4. Create a scene with the `PackedScene` class. To create a PackedScene object, use `PackedScene.new()`. To use the recently created node as the root node for the scene, you have to use the `pack(Node node)` method on the PackedScene object.

5. Save the scene by using ResourceSaver singleton's method `save` with the file path as the first argument and the scene as the second argument.

Handling Input

What You'll Learn in This Hour:

▶ How nodes receive inputs from player

▶ Querying for inputs from Input singleton

▶ Making your game responsive to player's input

▶ What Action is and its importance in custom input mapping

▶ Simulating player's action using InputEventAction

Input management is among the most important topics when it comes to game development. Input is what differentiates other kinds of entertainment and video games. A game would be very boring if players could not control their characters. Godot engine takes care of difficult tasks, such as getting raw data from devices, and provides an easy interface for game developers. It has a very interesting way of integrating user inputs with its node system. The engine also provides various helpers to make input handling easier.

In this hour, you'll learn how to manage user input and make your game respond to it. We'll first look at how a node receives inputs from a player. Then we will move on to InputEvent class, a class that contains information that needs to properly respond to inputs. After that, we will do some coding in GDScript. Then we will take a look at the InputMap singleton and how it can help when players want to choose how they want to control the game. Finally, we'll get to know InputEventAction, a special subclass of InputEvent that can simulate player action.

Input Basics

Before we get into more in-depth topics about responding to inputs and managing them, it is important that you know how to acquire those inputs in context of the node system of Godot engine.

Getting User Input

There are two ways to get user input:

1. Having a function called every time when the user makes a change. (Using _input)

   This is mostly useful when the input of interest involves changes to the input device; for example, choosing button press or release, mouse move or click, and screen touch or drag. You might want to get the input this way when dealing with user interface or game actions, such as attacking, shooting, using an item, etc.

2. Querying the device. (Using Input singleton)

   This is useful when you want to know if a specific button is being pressed at the time. You might want to do this every frame (in _process callback) to make the player character move when a player holds a button down.

Most game inputs will fall into either one of the previous cases. When you have to respond to an input, it can be helpful to first ask yourself into which category the input falls.

NOTE

Limitation of Querying the Device

Some input events cannot be reliably received by querying the device, as the event ends as soon as it happens. Mouse-wheel scrolling is one example. Also, there is no method to query touch-screen events through the Input singleton yet.

Callbacks

Node has several callbacks (virtual functions) that can be used to manage inputs. Even when ignoring those not related to inputs, there is still quite a lot of them, and this can be confusing to new developers. However, most of the time, you don't really need more than the following two callback functions.

Input Function

_input is a virtual function of a generic Node type that is called every time there is a change involving input devices. The node lowest in the hierarchy is called first (see Listing 7.1).

LISTING 7.1   Input Function

```
func _input(event):
```

`event` is an object derived from the InputEvent class containing information related to the received input. When a node responds to the input, it should call `get_tree().set_input_as _handled()` to prevent other nodes from responding to it again.

If `_input` is present in the script, that node will automatically get input callbacks. To manually start or stop getting input callback, use the function shown in Listing 7.2.

LISTING 7.2   Function to Manually Start or Stop Getting Input Callback

```
set_process_input(enable)
```

Set `enable` to `false` to stop getting callback. Setting it to `true` will resubscribe the node to receive input events.

Unhandled Input Function

`_unhandled_input` is similar to `_input` and is also a virtual function of a generic Node type. However, it is called in every node in the tree when an input event passed to `_input` is not marked as handled (Listing 7.3).

LISTING 7.3   Unhandled Input Function

```
func _unhandled_input(event):
```

`event` is the same object of the InputEvent class containing information related to the received input. This function is called when the previous input is not handled by any node. It can be disabled and re-enabled the same way as `_input`. See Listing 7.4.

LISTING 7.4   Function to Manually Start or Stop Getting Unhandled Input Callback

```
set_process_unhandled_input(enable)
```

Similar to _input, setting `enable` to `false` stops the node from getting callback. Setting it to `true` will resubscribe the node to receive unhandled input events.

For a simple game, you can use either _input or _unhandled_input, but for more complex games, it is suggested you put actual game controls, such as character movement, in the _unhandled_input function and leave `_input` to nodes that receive specific events to handle them first. This includes advancing message dialog and setting them as handled. That's one way to prevent your player character from moving away while there's a message displayed on screen.

NOTE

Nodes with Special Input Handling

There are several nodes that have additional methods for input handling. To name a few:

▶ **Viewport** node can check for mouse position inside itself.

▶ **CollisionObject** and its 2D counterpart, **CollisionObject2D**, can receive input events through **Camera**. You can click on objects directly this way.

▶ **Control** node also has a callback similar to those discussed previously:
   `_gui_input(event)`.

This function is a bit different from previous functions, since it is local to Control. It is only called when it has the focus or the input happens within its boundary. You only have to use this function when making your own control, as Godot engine provides an easier-to-use signal system. The Control node and GUI are further discussed in Hour 9, "User Interface."

Input Singleton

`Input` is a singleton that manages inputs at global level. It is ideal for querying if a specific button is pressed, setting cursor position, capturing the cursor inside a game window, and containing input settings that affect the whole game. Listing 7.5 shows some of the helper functions.

LISTING 7.5   Input Singleton Helper Functions

```
Input.is_key_pressed(scancode)
Input.is_mouse_button_pressed(button)
Input.is_joy_button_pressed(device, button)
```

What you should put between the parentheses can be found in the **@Global Scope** section of Godot Engine API Documentations. Keyboard buttons are prefixed with KEY_. For example, KEY_ESCAPE for escape (esc) key, KEY_RETURN for enter key, KEY_M for letter 'M' key, etc. Mouse buttons are prefixed with "BUTTON_". Examples include BUTTON_LEFT and BUTTON_WHEEL_DOWN.

InputEvent Class

`InputEvent` is a class that contains information about user input. As you may have noticed from the previous topic, it is given to callback functions as an only parameter, so it is very important that you thoroughly understand this class.

Subclasses

`InputEvent` itself has very limited uses. Most important are the subclasses that derive from this class. Listing 7.6 shows the hierarchy of subclasses derived from `InputEvent`.

LISTING 7.6   Subclasses of InputEvent Class

```
InputEvent
    InputEventAction
    InputEventJoypadButton        - for joystick or gamepad button.
    InputEventJoypadMotion        - for joystick hat movement.
    InputEventScreenDrag          - for swiping on a touch screen.
    InputEventScreenTouch         - for tapping on a touch screen.
    InputEventWithModifiers
        InputEventKey             - for keyboard buttons.
        InputEventMouse
            InputEventMouseButton - for mouse buttons and mouse wheel scroll.
            InputEventMouseMotion - for mouse movement.
```

The `InputEventAction` class simplifies user inputs to game actions, such as "move player character forward." We will discuss more about this class later. The `InputEventWithModifiers` class, like its parent, has almost no uses on its own. Derived classes can be checked for usage of modifier keys, such as control (ctrl) keys, alternate (alt) or meta keys, and shift keys. The `InputEventMouse` class also has very little use on its own. Derived classes are events generated by the mouse. This means that the cursor position associated with events is available for you to use. This might seem like a lot, but we will take a look at each one individually in subsequent topics.

Keyboard and Joystick Input

Let's start coding some GDScript to better visualize what we have learned so far and how it can be applied in game development with Godot engine. We are going to handle basic keyboard and joystick inputs.

Keyboard Input

Create a new node of any type (this example will use generic Node type), so attach a GDScript to it. It doesn't matter if the script is built in or not. Type the script (you can omit the code comments) in Listing 7.7.

LISTING 7.7   Basic Keyboard Input Handling Script

```
extends Node

# _input callback will be called when a keyboard button is pressed or released.
func _input(event):
    # The event of interest is keyboard event, which is of class `InputEventKey`.
    if event is InputEventKey:
        # Display the word "Echo" at the end of the line if this event is an echo
        var is_echo = "Echo" if event.echo else ""
```

```
    if event.pressed:
            # When the player holds a button down, display "Key pressed", scancode
and whether it's an echo
            prints("Key pressed", event.scancode, is_echo)
    else:
            # Same as above, but display "Key released" when the key is released
            prints("Key released", event.scancode, is_echo)
```

Save the script and the scene. Try running the game. Try pressing a key button, then release it. Try pressing several ones simultaneously. See how the texts are printed to console by your inputs. The number following the "Key pressed" or "Key released" text is the same value as defined in @ **Global Scope**. For example, number 16777217 stands for KEY_ESCAPE. It can be very difficult for developers to debug the game when keys are represented as numbers. For this, OS singleton has a function that converts a scancode into human-readable text (Listing 7.8).

LISTING 7.8   Function to Convert Scancode into Human-Readable Text

```
OS.get_scancode_string(scancode)
```

Try using this function with the previous code. Now you are able to see the name of the pressed key in text.

Try holding a key down for a bit. You may notice that when you hold a key down, text repeatedly prints to the output with the word "echo" at the end of the line. This is the result of event.echo. It signifies that the InputEventKey is repeated automatically. You may also notice there is a fixed delay before this happens. This may remind you of a similar behavior in a text editor. When you hold a key down and wait a bit, the letter begins repeating as if you manually typed it very fast. Although it is useful when you make your own text input control, this behavior is rarely used in games. The player character should walk normally as the player holds the walk key down. We don't need to simulate the button being pressed repeatedly. To prevent echoes from being processed as normal inputs, simply create another condition for it, like what is shown in Listing 7.9.

LISTING 7.9   Prevent Echoes from Being Processed as Normal Inputs

```
if event is InputEventKey && !event.echo:
```

Let's try handling "keyboard button holding" using Input singleton (Listing 7.10).

LISTING 7.10   Using Input Singleton Inside Process Callback to Handle Keyboard Button Holding

```
extends Node

func _process(delta):
    # KEY_SPACE is an alias for 32, a scancode for spacebar
    if Input.is_key_pressed(KEY_SPACE):
        print("Holding spacebar")
```

Try pressing and releasing the spacebar. You'll notice that it outputs "Holding spacebar" not only the moment you press or release it, but every frame that you hold it down. This is very useful when you want to check if, for example, a character should move in this frame or not. With Using _process, you will have access to the delta variable. This variable tells how much time has passed since the last frame, and it varies each frame. It's very important to take this variable into account to keep the movement speed constant. Also, unlike previous handling with echo, there is no delay between the button pressing and function calling.

At this point, you should be able to tell the differences between using _input and Input singleton.

Moving a Sprite with Keyboard

Printing texts is boring, so let's try controlling a Sprite using GDScript with knowledge from the previous topic. Create a new node of type Sprite and set its texture. You can use the default robot icon. Attach the following GDScript shown in Listing 7.11.

LISTING 7.11   Controlling a Sprite Node

```
extends Sprite

export var SPEED = 100

func _process(delta):
    var direction = Vector2(0, 0)
    if Input.is_key_pressed(KEY_UP):
        direction.y -= 1
    if Input.is_key_pressed(KEY_DOWN):
        direction.y += 1
    if Input.is_key_pressed(KEY_LEFT):
        direction.x -= 1
    if Input.is_key_pressed(KEY_RIGHT):
        direction.x += 1
    direction = direction.normalized() # To make sure diagonal movements will be in
the same speed
    direction *= SPEED * delta          # Multiply by speed (pixels per second) and
the time passed (seconds)
    translate(direction)                # Move the Sprite by the direction vector
```

Try running the game and using directional keys to move the Sprite.

Joystick Input

Now let's continue handling joystick input. Godot engine abstracts gamepad and joystick layout so that the same script can work with different controller brands.You'll need a game controller to test your code. Edit your script into the code shown in Listing 7.12, save it, and try running the game.

LISTING 7.12   Basic Joystick Input Handling Script

```
extends Node

func _input(event):
    if event is InputEventJoypadButton:
        # print the button index
        prints("Button:", str(event.button_index))
```

Try pressing all joystick or gamepad buttons. Take note of the button index of directional keys. You will need them in the upcoming exercise.

Again, the human-readable button index values can be found in **@Global Scope** section of the documentations. It is prefixed by "JOY_BUTTON_".

Moving a Sprite with Joystick: Exercise

Let's try controlling a Sprite using the joystick the same way we did with the keyboard. Create a new node type of Sprite and set its texture. Attach the following GDScript shown in Listing 7.13. Be sure to fill in the blanks with the button index you get from the previous step.

LISTING 7.13   Controlling a Sprite Node Using Joystick: Exercise

```
extends Sprite

const SPEED = 100
var device_index = 0

func _ready():
Input.connect("joy_connection_changed", self, "joy_connect")

func joy_connect(index, connect):
    # When a joystick is detected, keep the device index in a variable
    if connect:
        device_index = index
```

```
func _process(delta):
var direction = Vector2(0, 0)
# Query Input singleton with the device index
if Input.is_joy_button_pressed(device_index, _____): # UP
        direction.y -= 1
if Input.is_joy_button_pressed(device_index, _____): # DOWN
        direction.y += 1
if Input.is_joy_button_pressed(device_index, _____): # LEFT
        direction.x -= 1
if Input.is_joy_button_pressed(device_index, _____): # RIGHT
        direction.x += 1
direction = direction.normalized() # To make sure diagonal movements will be in the
same speed
direction *= SPEED * delta          # Multiply by speed (pixels per second) and the
time passed (seconds)
    translate(direction)                    # Move the Sprite by the direction vector
```

Try running the game and use directional keys of the joystick to move the Sprite. Did you get all the button indices correctly? If your Sprite did not go where you expected, try switching the button index around.

Mouse and Touch Input

A large portion of gamers may prefer to use game controllers to play, but for some genres, such as first-person shooters (FPS), the mouse is also a viable option due to its precision. Games on mobile devices can make use of touch screen if the device has one. We'll learn how to respond to inputs from such devices.

Mouse Input

Similar to keyboard and joystick input, mouse inputs can be handled by following the code in Listing 7.14, which is using _input callback.

LISTING 7.14   Basic Mouse Input Handling Script Using Input Callback

```
func _input(event):
    if event is InputEventMouseButton && event.pressed:
        prints("Button", event.button_index, "is pressed at", str(event.position))
    if event is InputEventMouseMotion:
        prints("Mouse moved to", str(event.position))
```

The following code in Listing 7.15 uses Input Singleton:

LISTING 7.15   Basic Mouse Input Handling Script Using Input Singleton

```
func _process(delta):
    if Input.is_mouse_button_pressed(BUTTON_LEFT):
        prints("Holding left mouse button at", get_tree().get_root()
.get_mouse_position())
```

Moving a Sprite with Mouse

Let's do the same as we did in the previous topic. Create a new Sprite node, set its texture, and attach the script shown in Listing 7.16.

LISTING 7.16   Controlling a Sprite Node Using Mouse

```
extends Sprite

func _input(event):
    if event is InputEventMouseMotion:
        position = event.position
```

Try moving the mouse cursor inside the game window. The Sprite is now stuck to the cursor.

Touch Input

Touch input events can be handled like that shown in Listing 7.17:

LISTING 7.17   Basic Mouse Input Handling Script Using Input Callback

```
func _input(event):
    if event is InputEventScreenTouch && event.pressed:
        prints("Screen touch at", str(event.position))
    if event is InputEventScreenDrag:
        prints("Screen drag at", str(event.position))
```

If you do not possess a device with a touch screen or you prefer to test the game in the desktop, go to Project > Project Settings > General > Display-Window > Handheld > Emulate Touchscreen and turn this option on.

Moving a Sprite with Touchscreen

Let's finish this topic with the same example. Again, create a new Sprite node, set a texture to it, and attach the script shown in Listing 7.18.

LISTING 7.18   Controlling a Sprite Node Using Touchscreen

```
extends Sprite

func _input(event):
    if event is InputEventScreenTouch:
        position = event.position
```

The Sprite should now go wherever you tap.

Input Mapping

It is generally more beneficial to use Action and Input Mapping instead of defining individual keys in the script so that it can be easily ported to various platforms with minimal change to code. Most of the time, players are going to play your game with default controls given to them, but it would be nice to give them the opportunity to edit the controls so they can get into your game more easily and comfortably. However, in other engines or frameworks, this can be a burden to developers. Not only do they have to keep a list of user-defined controls, the game must be saved and reloaded each time it is launched. To help developers focus on more important things, Godot engine provides easy interfaces for this task, **Action** and **Input Map**.

Action

Action is basically a group of input events that achieve the same task. It can be named to reflect what it does in the game. For example, "move_up" Action has both KEY_W and KEY_UP in it. When a player presses either the 'W' key or up arrow key, Input.is_action_pressed("move_up") will return to true. You can check for this condition and make the player character move as a result.

Listing 7.19 uses Using _input.

LISTING 7.19   Handling Input Defined in Action Using Input Callback

```
func _input(event):
    if event.is_action("move_up"):
        if event.pressed:
            print("start walking")
        else:
            print("stop walking")
```

Using Input singleton is shown in Listing 7.20.

LISTING 7.20   Handling Input Defined in Action Using Input Singleton

```
func _process(delta):
    if Input.is_action_pressed("move_up"):
        print("walk")
```

This way, you don't have to check each individual key for a matching event. You also don't have to worry about user-mapped control. As long as it is in an Action, you can refer to it by the Action's name.

Modifying Actions in your game can be done prior to running the game using **Input Map** in the Project Settings or while in-game using **InputMap** singleton.

The Input Map of your project is accessible from the top-left menu bar. Choose Project > Project Settings > Input Map. Here, you'll find several default Actions that you can use, such as `ui_accept`, `ui_cancel`, etc. These default Actions cannot be deleted, as they are used by Control and its derivatives. You can add your own Action by typing the name in the text box and pressing a button that says "Add." The newly created Action will appear at the bottom of the list. You may add an event to it by pressing the ╋ button next to the Action's name on the right. Choose the type (Key, Joy Button, Joy Axis, or Mouse Button) to configure the button. Finally, press the "OK" or "Add" button. Editing or deleting an event from an Action can be done by pressing the ✎ icon or the 🗑 icon, respectively.

InputMap Singleton

Input Map is a user interface provided by the editor. The engine will pass all Actions in the Input Map to the **InputMap** singleton and automatically add them before the game starts. It is actually the **InputMap** singleton that does the job behind the scenes.

InputMap singleton keeps a list of Actions and events associated with each of them. Here you can add an Action, add an event to an Action, and check if an event matches an Action. It is very useful when you want to save or load user-defined controls. You can get Action and event lists by calling Listing 7.21.

LISTING 7.21   Functions to Get List of Actions and Events in InputMap

```
for action in InputMap.get_actions():
    var list = InputMap.get_action_list(action)
```

Then you can serialize the output to a configuration file by a method that works best for your game.

InputEventAction

InputEventAction is a special subclass of InputEvent. Unlike other subclasses of InputEvent that represent changes in status of input devices, it represents an Action. It can be used to simulate player actions. For example, a game has "move_up" Action, associated to KEY_UP, defined in the Input Map. You want to simulate this Action as part of auto-move function. You may achieve this by using Listing 7.22.

LISTING 7.22   Using InputEventAction

```
var action_move_up = InputEventAction.new()

func _ready():
    action_move_up.action = "move_up"
    action_move_up.pressed = true

func auto_move():
    Input.parse_input_event(action_move_up) # Input.action_press("move_up") also
works

func _process(delta):
    if Input.is_action_pressed("move_up"):
        move(Vector2(0, -1) * delta)
```

From the previous code, if auto_move is called, action_move_up is processed as if the player generated it. Since this action is a "pressed" action as defined by action_move_up.pressed = true, the game continues as if the button is held down indefinitely. You can pass another "release" Action to stop imaginary button holding or use Input.action_release("move_up").

NOTE

Devices Can't Create InputEventAction

InputEventAction will never be created by input devices. It can only be created via scripting or in the Inspector dock.

Summary

In this hour, you learned the differences between using _input and Input singleton to acquire player inputs. You learned how to respond to these inputs by using various properties of InputEvent. You were able to apply it with the Sprite node movement. You also learned about Action and InputMap and how they can be used in place of naming buttons. Finally, you learned about InputEventAction and saw one example of how it can be used.

Q&A

Q. Which is better: child nodes have their own _input function or only the parent node has _input function and manages it for its children?

A. There is no solution that works for every project. Both have their pros and cons. For reference, Godot engine codebase in C++ has some forms. One could say that it is easier to maintain, because there is only one _input function and the relationship with its children can be relatively easy to guess just by looking through the code. The downside is that the children depend on their parent and cannot work on their own. Generally, if you want your node to work on its own, put `_input` function in it, but if this functionality is not the case, you can do it either way.

Workshop

Answer the following questions to make sure you understood the content of this hour.

Quiz

1. Given `event is InputEventMouse` is `true`, `event is InputEvent` will be `true` or `false`?

2. If you want to call a function every time the player scrolls a mouse wheel, what callback functions would be the most appropriate place to check for input: `_ready`, `_process`, `_input`, or `_tree_exited`?

3. Regarding the following GDScript of a node inside the Scene Tree (Listing 7.23), how many lines of the text "Godot" would be printed if you type in the game window, one letter at a time, "g," "o," "d," "o," and "t," then release all keyboard buttons?

LISTING 7.23   Quiz 3: GDScript of a Node Inside Scene Tree

```
extends Node

func _input(e):
    if e is InputEventKey && !e.echo:
        print("Godot")
```

4. Regarding the following GDScript of a node inside the Scene Tree (Listing 7.24), what would be printed to the output console if, after "READY" is printed:

   1. The left mouse button is clicked?

   2. The mouse cursor is moved inside the game window?

   3. The "Escape" key is held down?

   4. The letter "M" key is held down?

   5. The "Enter" key is released?

LISTING 7.24   Quiz 4: GDScript of a Node Inside Scene Tree

```
extends Node

var event = Sprite.new()

func _ready():
    set_process_unhandled_input(false)
    if Input.is_mouse_button_pressed(BUTTON_LEFT):
        print("Left")
    print("READY")

func _process(dt):
    if event is InputEventMouseMotion:
        print(event.position.x)
    if Input.is_key_pressed(KEY_ESCAPE):
        print("Quit")

func _input(e):
    if e is InputEventKey && !e.pressed:
        print("Key")
    elif e.is_action("ui_accept"):
        print("Enter")

func _unhandled_input(e):
    if e is InputEventKey:
        print("Unhandled Key")
```

5. Regarding the same GDScript in problem number 4, with the `set_process_unhandled_input(false)` line removed, what is the function you would call to prevent "Unhandled Key" from being printed when "Key" or "Enter" is printed because of the same InputEvent?

Answers

1. `true`. InputEventMouse is one of the subclasses of InputEvent.

2. `_input`. Mouse-wheel scrolling cannot be reliably detected by querying Input singleton.

3. Ten lines—one for pressing and one for releasing, times five.

4.

   1. Nothing; the input event is queried once before "READY" is printed and is never checked for again.

   2. Nothing; "Left" is never printed because "event" is Sprite, not InputEventMouseMotion.

   3. "Quit"; every frame as long as you hold it down.

   4. Nothing; "Key" will print once you release it.

5. "Key"; it is not "Enter" at the releasing moment because the event matches the first condition.

"Unhandled Key" is never printed because of `set_process_unhandled_input(false)`.

5. `get_tree().set_input_as_handled()`

Exercises

Try to execute the following exercises to get more acquainted with input handling in Godot engine:

1. Remake "Moving the Sprite using Keyboard" example to make use of Actions.

2. Add a WASD control scheme to the "Moving the Sprite using Keyboard" example. (The "W," "A," "S," and "D" keys are up, left, down, and right, respectively.)

3. Add joystick directional buttons to the "Moving the Sprite using Keyboard" example. Your example should support both keyboard and joystick controlling like most games.

HOUR 8
Physics System

What You'll Learn in This Hour:

► Creating bodies that interact with each other
► Understanding the different types of bodies
► Using areas to detect presence and alter gravity
► Making use of the navigation tools

This hour will guide you through Godot's physics system. You'll learn how to create entities that interact with each other, respect gravity, and behave like real physical objects. You'll see how to make special areas that can detect the presence of objects and change the gravity in the section. Finally, you'll see how to use the navigation system to make entities walk around the game while avoiding obstacles.

Bodies and Shapes

Godot physics is primarily based on bodies and shapes. Bodies represent the physical entities that interact with one another, and shapes describe the space they occupy. By creating bodies and assigning shapes to them, you can tell objects how to behave in the game.

Physics Bodies

As will be seen in detail later (see Table 8.1), there are different types of physics bodies. They have 2D and 3D variants that behave alike, which makes the transition between them quite easy. Usually, the body is the root of the game object, since the physics engine can move the children together because of the inherited transform.

TABLE 8.1   Types of Physics Bodies

Type	Description
Static	An object that does not move in the game but interacts with other objects.
Rigid	An object that interacts with the physics engine and is affected by it.
Kinematic	Objects that aren't affected directly by physics but need to move and detect collisions.
Vehicle (3D only)	Road-traveling vehicles.

Collision Shapes

Collision shapes define the area of the object inside the physics engine. This ensures flexibility to define a hitbox that doesn't exactly match the shape of the visible object. It makes it possible, for instance, to make a hidden passage that looks like a wall, or to have a complex shape for the visible entity while keeping a simple shape on the physics side for better performance.

TIP

Shape Visibility

By default, collision shapes are only visible inside the editor. If you need to show them in-game to help you debug something, you can enable the Visible Collision Shapes option in the Debug menu (see Figure 8.1). This option affects the project in the editor, but won't be enabled in the exported game.

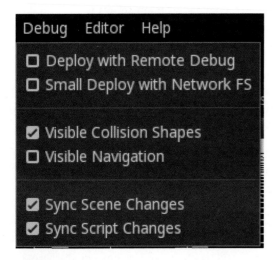

FIGURE 8.1
Debug menu. You can enable a few debugging features to help you find problems in the game.

To define a collision shape, you need to create a ⬤ **CollisionShape** or a ▣ **CollisionShape2D** node, depending on the type of game you are creating. This node must be a direct child to a physics body node. Then you need to set up the **Shape** property using the inspector. There are different types of shapes you can create in 2D and 3D. You should pick one that best suits the interaction you are expecting. Consult the engine documentation to learn about the various types of shapes.

In general, you don't need to be pixel perfect when defining collision shapes. Simpler shapes are better for performance, and likely won't be noticed by the final player. For instance, a ▮ **CapsuleShape** works great for characters, both in 2D and 3D. It is also possible to use multiple collision nodes for a single body, which makes Godot use the union of the shapes.

NOTE

Transforming Collision Shapes

Changing the dimensions and extents of collision shapes is quite natural, but you should be careful when changing the scale property. Negative and non-uniform scaling tend to cause issues with the physics, and the shapes don't respond as they should. You should avoid this kind of scaling, and instead change the parameters of the shapes themselves to adjust their size.

Meshes and Polygons

Simple shapes are great for performance, but sometimes they aren't good enough. For better fine-tuning of hitboxes, Godot provides the ▮ **CollisionPolygon** and ▮ **CollisionPolygon2D**. These nodes enable the ability to draw custom polygons using the editor tools.

For 3D, Godot has a tool to create collision shapes based on a mesh. Simply select the ▮ **MeshInstance** node with the desired shape, select the ▮ **Mesh** menu on the toolbar, and click on the desired option. You can create a trimesh for concave structures or a convex shape for a simpler mesh. It's also possible to create a navigation mesh from this menu.

TRY IT YOURSELF ▼

Making a Polygon Shape

Follow these steps to draw your own polygonal collision shape (see Figure 8.2):

1. Create a new scene and add a ▮ **Node2D** as the root.
2. Add a ▮ **RigidBody2D**.
3. Create a ▮ **CollisionPolygon2D** as a child of the RigidBody2D.
4. Click on the ▮ **Create Polygon** tool.
5. Click a few times to add points to your polygon.
6. Once you're done, you can click on the first point to close the polygon, or right-click to make it auto-close.
7. Select the ▮ **Edit Polygon** tool.

8. Move the points around to change the polygon shape. You can hold the `Ctrl` key while clicking on a segment to add a new point. To delete a point, just click it with the right mouse button.

9. Change the polygon until you're satisfied. There's nothing else that needs to be done; your polygon is ready.

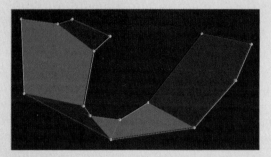

FIGURE 8.2
A polygonal collision shape. The colored areas show the convex decomposition of the shape.

TIP

Disabling Shapes

Godot offers you the ability to disable collision shapes. You can do that by checking the **Disabled** property of the shape in the inspector. Disabling shapes can be useful for changing the hitbox when the character pose changes (like ducking). Instead of transforming the shape with animation, you can enable some shapes and disable others. It can also be useful for testing; you can have multiple shapes on the node during the development process, but not all of them are being used.

One-Way Collision

An interesting property of collision shapes is the **One-Way Collision** option (FIgure 8.3). It is very useful in platform games, as you can create floating platforms that the player character can both stand on and jump through from a lower platform.

This effect is enabled by checking the property in the inspector. If you need some other direction, just rotate the shape. The Godot official platformer demo makes use of this property, so you can check it if you need a reference.

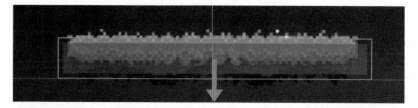

FIGURE 8.3
The one-way collision indication on a platform. You can see this in the official Godot platformer demo.

Types of Physics Bodies

As stated earlier, Godot has a few different types of bodies. Each has a specific function and acts in a certain way. Choosing the right type for the action you want can be tricky sometimes, but Godot makes it very easy to change the type of node if needed. Since 2D and 3D types are very much alike, they will be grouped together.

Static Body

This is the go-to body type for non-moving shapes. However, some moving structures might be better represented as ▣ StaticBodies, such as moving platforms and the pad of a breakout game. In general, a static body should be used if the object should act like a stop for other bodies but not be moved itself by the physics engine.

Static bodies do not increase the processor usage, since they don't need to actively check for collisions (instead, the moving bodies will make such checks). This means you can add many of them without worrying too much about performance (see Table 8.2).

TABLE 8.2   Static Body Properties

Property	Description
Friction	The amount of friction on the body's surface, on a scale from 0 to 1.
Bounce	How much other objects will bounce when coming in contact with the body.
Constant Linear Velocity	Simulates a motion for the body, which affects how other objects interact with it. This does not make the body move.
Constant Angular Velocity	Simulates a rotation of the body, affecting other physics objects that touch it.

Rigid Body

On the other hand, if you want an object to be fully controlled by the physics engine, 🌐 **RigidBody** is a good choice. This type of body has a mass, respects gravity and inertia, and can be pushed by other objects. It is generally used to simulate real-world physics.

Rigid bodies keep a linear, angular velocity. This means they'll keep moving in a certain direction and maintain their momentum. They'll also rotate when affected by other forces and keep rotating unless stopped by friction or another force (see Table 8.3).

NOTE

Rigid versus Soft Body

The concept of a rigid body contrasts with that of a soft body. A soft body can be deformed by physics (just like a basketball will deform when contacting the ground). Usually, such effects pass unnoticed if the material is elastic, so the use of rigid bodies is more efficient. Godot's engine does not support soft bodies, but, as it's still evolving, it very likely will soon.

TABLE 8.3 Rigid Body Properties

Property	Description
Mode	How the body will behave. "Rigid" is the default mode, as it is fully integrated with physics. "Static" mode does not move at all, "character" avoids rotation, and "kinematic" acts like a kinematic body.
Mass and Weight	Dictates how the body will interact with gravity and how much force it will have upon other objects.
Gravity Scale	How much the body will be affected by gravity.
Custom Integrator	Disables the internal integrator. With the exception of collisions, only your code on `_integrate_forces()` will move the object.
Continuous CD	Enables the continuous collision detection. Fast objects, such as ones that would pass beyond the wall in a single frame, will be detected. The 2D version also has options to use "ray" or "shape" for this kind of detection.
Contact Monitor/ Reporting	If contact monitoring is enabled, the body will emit signals when it detects a collision. The "contacts reported" property dictates how many object contacts will be detected at once.
Sleeping/Can Sleep	A body that does not move for some time will "sleep," i.e., it won't actively detect collisions, but will awaken if it comes into collision with another object. This property can stop that behavior.
Axis Lock (3D only)	Fixes the rotation of the body caused from other forces to a single axis.

Custom Integrator

One of the special capabilities of RigidBody is the custom integrator function. This allows you to complement or even replace the way the body moves, and can be useful for advanced and custom physics properties.

This is achieved by overriding the `_integrate_forces()` method in a script. The method receives a `Physics2DDirectBodyState` object, which can be used to probe and change the forces acting on the body.

TIP

Applying Impulses

RigidBody has a method called `apply_impulse()`. With it, you can shift the body as if some thrust were applied, making it change movement based on its mass and shape. You can imagine it as a bat hitting a baseball or a cue pushing a billiard ball.

Kinematic Body

This is a special type of physics body. A ![icon] **KinematicBody** can detect collisions and be moved via code, but isn't affect by other objects. It won't fall because of gravity or move around when hit by another object. This property makes it very useful for platformer characters that respect their own laws of physics.

While a dynamic character (i.e., one implemented with ![icon] **RigidBody**) is more seamlessly integrated with the physics engine, it's hard to predict its movement. A kinematic character is guaranteed to go from one non-colliding state to another, so it is more easily controlled via code.

TIP

Platformer Demo

Godot provides a collection of demo projects to show off many of its features. There are both 2D and 3D platformer game demos that makes use of the ![icon] **KinematicBody** functionality in addition to a 2D demo with a dynamic character. While the demos are not extensively documented, they are quite simple, and can serve as a reference. Make sure to check them if you have doubts.

Moving a Kinematic Body

Since this type of body does not move on its own, it's necessary to use scripting to achieve movement. Most of the time, you'll make use of the `move_and_slide()` method. This changes the object's position while respecting collisions and surface sliding, so movement is fluid and the object doesn't stick to walls or floors. You just need to feed the movement vector, and the body will follow it. Note that this is the speed, in units per second, that the object moves (for 2D, the unit is pixels). Therefore, you should not multiply by `delta` to calculate the change in position, since it's done by the method itself. This method receives other optional parameters as well, so check the engine documentation to learn what they can do. The following listing (Listing 8.1) shows an example of a 🏃 KinematicBody2D movement function.

LISTING 8.1   KinematicBody2D Movement Example

```
extends KinematicBody2D

# The speed in pixels per second
export (float) var speed = 100.0

# Run this function in a synchrony with physics processing
func _physics_process(delta):
    # Calculate the direction vector based on input
    var direction = Vector2()
    if Input.is_action_pressed("ui_left"):
        direction.x = -1
    elif Input.is_action_pressed("ui_right"):
        direction.x = 1
    if Input.is_action_pressed("ui_up"):
        direction.y = -1
    elif Input.is_action_pressed("ui_down"):
        direction.y = 1

    # Normalize the movement vector and modulate by the speed
    var movement = direction.normalized() * speed

    # Move the body based on the calculated speed and direction
    move_and_slide(movement)
```

This script can be applied directly to a 🏃 KinematicBody2D node. It checks the input to fill a `direction` vector. This vector is normalized to make it unit length and avoid faster movement in diagonals. When multiplied by `speed`, it makes a vector pointing in the same direction, but with `speed` as magnitude. Then we feed the result to the `move_and_slide()` function, making the body move while checking collisions and avoiding getting stuck to surfaces.

TIP

Collision Layers and Masks

Sometimes, you need to avoid certain types of collisions (e.g., avoiding bullets shot by enemies colliding into the enemies themselves). While it's possible to set exceptions, it may be a daunting task to set every pair. This is where layers and masks come into play.

A collision layer is a property of the collision object (body or area) that states the object type. You can set up names for the layers in Project Settings to help in this categorization. The collision mask states the type of object with which the body will collide. These are defined as flags, so any object can be in multiple layers and have multiple masks.

If you have object A on layer 1 with mask 2, it will not collide with objects of its own category, but will collide with all other objects on layer 2. If object B is on layer 3 with mask 1 and 2, it'll also collide with object A and objects on layer 2, but not with itself.

This is a topic that confuses a lot of Godot users, but it's easier if you imagine layers as categories or types of objects, and masks as collision targets.

Areas and Presence Detection

Besides physical movement simulation, sometimes you need to detect the presence of an object in a place, be it to activate a trap, trigger a cutscene, or engage a teleportation. Godot provides the 🔲 Area and 🔲 Area2D nodes to make this process easier.

These nodes are also responsible for enabling area effects, such as a gravity override (as we'll see later in this chapter), and audio alteration (as will be presented in Hour 19).

Area Monitoring

The 🔲 Area node has a monitoring property that is enabled by default. This property is responsible for detecting the presence of bodies and other areas inside the area. If it gets disabled, it will stop reporting overlaps and won't send signals.

There are eight signals responsible for warning when other objects enter or exit the area. Some are for bodies, others are for area overlaps. You can use these to detect and trigger an action when the objects start or stop overlapping.

You can also use the `get_overlapping_areas()` and `get_overlapping_bodies()` methods to list all the current overlapping objects. This can be useful if the action is triggered by a button press when in the area, not when the overlap starts. Both methods need the monitoring property enabled. Other areas must have the monitorable property enabled to be detected.

Gravity Override

Another interesting function of Areas is the ability to change the gravity in a certain location. This can be enabled by changing the Space Override property. It has a few possible values, but essentially, it can be summed up with "replace" and "combine".

Replacing will ignore all areas with a lower priority (as defined in another property) and simply replace the gravity by its current values. Combining will add the effects to the areas already calculated, following the priority order.

NOTE

Linear and Angular Damping

Areas can also replace/combine the linear and angular damping properties. These properties dictate how much the area will lessen the linear and angular momentum of the bodies passing through it. This also depends on the Space Override property being turned on.

Rigid bodies have similar damping properties, but the properties only affect the bodies themselves, like when air resistance is applied to an object.

Ray Casting

The idea of ray casting is creating a line—for example, shooting a limited-range laser and seeing if it hits something. This can also be used to check the line of sight. Though usually limited to a line, it's also possible to cast custom shapes, so you can use a cone for sight detection instead of a simple line.

There are mainly two ways to cast rays in Godot: by using the ⬇ RayCast or ⬇ RayCast2D nodes, or by calling the physics server directly in the code. The first method is great for simple casting, since it can be seen in editor and can be checked anytime. The other method is more advanced but also more flexible, and is easier for instant ad hoc ray casting, as well as shape casting.

RayCast Nodes

⬇ RayCast and ⬇ RayCast2D (see Figure 8.4) are very simple nodes. They simply cast a ray in the appointed direction and return the result every frame. You can make use of them by calling the `is_colliding()` and `get_collider()` methods, besides the other query methods.

TIP

Collision Exceptions

Like every other collision object, it's possible to set up exceptions to ray-casting effects so that if the ray hits a target marked as an exception, it will ignore it and look for the next.

This makes it easier to use the ray-casting nodes, because you don't need to worry about where the ray starts. For instance, if you're using it to determine the line of sight for a character, you can add the character body as an exception so the ray doesn't collide with it, allowing you to overlap them in Editor without issues.

Exceptions can only be added via scripting (by calling the `add_exception()` method), so you need some script attached to use this functionality.

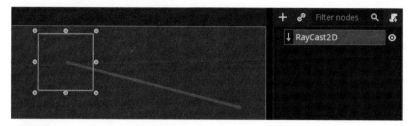

FIGURE 8.4
RayCast2D node as shown in Godot Editor.

Ray Casting via Scripting

A more complex but flexible setup uses scripts to cast a ray (or shape) and directly query its results. This involves accessing the space state. The basic way of doing this is to access the world from the object:

```
# For 2D
var space_state = get_world_2d().get_direct_space_state()
# For 3D
var space_state = get_world().get_direct_space_state()
```

This returns a `Physics2DDirectSpaceState` object, which can cast rays and shapes, among other capabilities. With it, you can use the `intersect_ray()` method to ray cast.

The `intersect_ray()` method receives a few arguments, but the most important are the first and second, which are mandatory. They set the start and end of the ray shape using the global space. The result of the method is a dictionary containing the collision data. If the result is empty, it means no collision happened. The returned dictionary structure is described in Table 8.4.

TABLE 8.4   Resultant Dictionary from an Intersect Ray Query

Key	Description
position	The global–space position where the collision happened.
normal	The normal of the plane where the ray collided.
shape	Index of the shape of the body with which it collided.
metadata	Metadata of the collided shape. This is not the regular object metadata, but the one set with the physics server methods.
collider_id	ID of the object that stopped the ray.
collider	The collided object itself.
rid	The RID of the collided object. This special type of object can be used as a reference to the object when dealing with the physics server directly.

Navigation and Path Finding

An interesting characteristic of some game types is the ability for movement of NPCs and other computer-controlled entities. It is used quite a lot in RPG and RTS games, and can be used for racing games too. This section will show how to use Godot tools to make precompiled movements and find dynamic paths in the game world.

Following Predefined Paths

A couple of nodes can be joined to make an object follow a predefined path (see Figure 8.5): ⚡ **Path** and ⚡ **PathFollow** (along with their 2D counterparts, ⚡ **Path2D** and ⚡ **PathFollow2D**). With them, you can draw a path in Editor and make it change the transform of the child nodes.

The ⚡ **Path** node is responsible in making the path itself. When selected, it shows a set of tools with which you can draw the curve inside Editor. This is a Bezier curve, and can be open or closed; you just need to set up the points and adjust their curvature with the pivots.

To make something go along the path, you need the ⚡ **PathFollow** node, which must be a direct child of a ⚡ **Path** node. This makes all the direct children conform to the path by changing their translations and rotations (see Table 8.5).

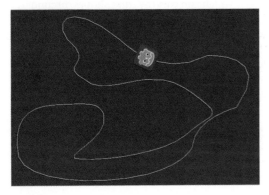

FIGURE 8.5
The Godot icon following a drawn path.

TABLE 8.5   PathFollow Properties

Property	Description
Offset	Offsets, in an absolute number, the child object in the path.
Unit Offset	Does the same as Offset, but considers a scale from 0 to 1.
H/V Offset	Changes the offset in relation to the path on the horizontal and vertical axes, respectively.
Rotation Mode	Selects the axes on which the node can be rotated when following the path. For 2D, you can only enable or disable the rotation.
Cubic Interp	Enables cubic interpolation when calculating the route between the points. If disabled, a linear interpolation is used.
Loop	Makes the excess value in offset act as a return to the beginning of the path.
Lookahead	Determines how many units the player can look ahead when interpolating the path. A greater value increases the accuracy but decreases the performance.

Basic Path Finding

You won't always know the exact trajectory beforehand. In an open-world game, you need to calculate the actual path during runtime, because the start and end points change all the time. Godot has the ▲ Navigation and ▲ Navigation2D nodes to help with this task.

To make use of this functionality, you need first to add a ▲ Navigation node. It has no restriction as to where it is on the tree, since it doesn't do more than provide the special path-finding methods. Then you need a ▧ NavigationMeshInstance (or ▧ NavigationPolygonInstance for 2D) as a direct child. This node is responsible for providing the navigable areas in the world. After this is set up, you need to call the methods from the ▲ Navigation node to calculate paths when needed and apply the translation to the moving objects. Note that Physics Bodies in the scene won't act as obstacles, so you need to craft your polygons and meshes in a way that they don't overlap with the places where a path isn't possible.

TIP

Generating Navigation Meshes

While the Godot editor makes it easy to draw navigation polygons for 2D, it does not provide a way to edit a 3D navigation mesh, since this would require advanced modeling functions. Instead, the easiest way to make this is to import from your 3D modeling software.

You can generate a ▧ NavigationMeshInstance from a ▧ MeshInstance quite easily. Just select MeshInstance and click on "Create Navigation Mesh" from the toolbar on the ▧ Mesh menu. Then move the resulting node to be a child of a ▲ Navigation.

▼ TRY IT YOURSELF

Simple Path Finding

Let's create a simple 2D scene to test the path-finding functions:

1. Create a new scene and add a ⬤ **Node2D** as the root.

2. Add a ◣ **Navigation2D**.

3. Create a ◪ **NavigationPolygonInstance** as a child of the Navigation2D.

4. Using the inspector, assign a new ◪ **NavigationPolygon** to the **Navpoly** property.

5. Click on the ◨ **Create Polygon** tool.

6. Click around to create a general outline for our map. This is very similar to how we created collision polygons in the last exercise. Click on the initial point again to close the polygon.

7. Click again on the ◨ **Create Polygon** tool.

8. Make a polygon inside the main one to create holes. Those will serve as walls in our map.

9. Repeat steps 7 and 8 to make multiple holes.

10. Add a script to the ◣ **Navigation2D** node with the following code:

```
extends Navigation2D

var start_point = Vector2()
var end_point = Vector2()
var path = []

func _input(event):
    if event is InputEventMouseButton and event.pressed:
        if event.button_index == BUTTON_LEFT:
            start_point = event.position
        elif event.button_index == BUTTON_RIGHT:
            end_point = event.position

func _process(delta):
    path = get_simple_path(start_point, end_point, false)
    update()

func _draw():
    for point in path:
        draw_circle(point, 10, Color(1, 1, 1))
    draw_polyline(path, Color(1, 0, 0), 3.0, true)
```

11. Enable the **Visible Navigation** option in the **Debug** menu. This will let you see the polygon in the running game.

12. Run the scene. Left-click to define the starting point and right-click to set the ending point. A line will be drawn with the path, with circles marking the calculated points (see Figure 8.6).

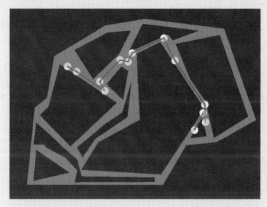

FIGURE 8.6
Running this exercise. The white circles show the path points, while the red line follows the path.

NOTE

A* (A-STAR)

A common algorithm used to solve paths within a graph of predefined points and connections is the A* (pronounced "a star"). It is widely used in games, especially in those that rely on a grid for movement, such as RTS and tactical RPGs. While it would be possible to write the algorithm with a script, Godot provides a dedicated class to help you leverage this path-finding tool with the native code performance of the engine core.

For details on how to use this functionality, consult the engine reference for the AStar class.

Summary

In this hour, you saw a major overview of the Godot physics engine. You learned about possible collision shapes, then got a description of the basic types of bodies available. You learned how to cast rays via nodes and via scripting. Finally, you learned the custom navigation and path-finding tools offered by Godot Engine.

Q&A

Q. **Why isn't Continuous Collision Detection (CD) always on?**

A. While Continuous CD can increase accuracy, it also degrades performance. It should only be turned on for fast-moving objects.

Q. **Why do rigid bodies sleep?**

A. When a body comes to a total rest, it's unlikely that it will hit anything, unless the world is changed by forces other than physics. Since it will move only if hit by something else, the other object will detect the collision and wake the rigid body. A sleeping body does not use computer resources, so you can have a scene with lots of objects and have it run better if most objects are sleeping.

Q. **What's the main difference between a rigid body and a kinematic body?**

A. A rigid body will be moved by the physics engine, i.e., it will be pushed by other objects hitting it and by gravity. A kinematic body will stay in place no matter how many objects hit it, and will only be moved by scripting.

Workshop

Try to answer the following questions to better memorize the contents of this hour.

Quiz

1. What are the main three types of bodies?

2. True or False: Collision shape nodes must be a direct child of the body.

3. True or False: It's OK to scale collision shapes.

4. How can you override the gravity of a certain spot in space?

5. Is it possible to make an object repeat the same predefined path indefinitely?

Answers

1. KinematicBody, StaticBody, and RigidBody.

2. True. The CollsionShape must be a direct child to assign a shape to the body.

3. False. Non-uniform scales can cause inaccuracies in the physics engine.

4. You can use the Area node with the Space Override property turned on.

5. Yes. The PathFollow node has a loop property that can be used for this purpose.

Exercises

Try to reproduce this scene to get an experience of the Godot physics engine.

1. Create a new scene and add a  Node2D as the root. Save the scene.

2. Make a ▦ StaticBody2D. Add a rectangular collision shape and move it to the bottom of the scene, like a floor.

3. Add a 🌐 RigidBody2D as a child to the root. Make a circular collision shape and position it over the floor.

4. Make sure to enable visible collision shapes in the debug menu.

5. Save the scene and play it. Observe the circular body falling to the floor.

6. Duplicate the 🌐 RigidBody2D four times and stack them in Editor, like in Figure 8.7:

FIGURE 8.7
A stack of circular rigid bodies. This is a way to see
how they interact when falling over each other.

7. Play the scene again to notice the movement of the balls.

8. Add a 🧍 KinematicBody2D to the scene. Make a capsule shape for it.

9. Create a script for the 🧍 KinematicBody2D and paste the code from Listing 8.1.

10. Play the scene. Use the arrow keys of your keyboard to move the capsule. Note how it moves and interacts with the other bodies.

11. Move the bodies in the scene around and test different configurations. Check the 🧍 KinematicBody2D and change the speed in Inspector. See how everything behaves.

HOUR 9
User Interface

What You'll Learn in This Hour:

▶ Displaying text inside the game window

▶ Important Control nodes properties and signals

▶ Using Containers to help create an interface

▶ Using GDScript to make an interactive interface

▶ Applying a Theme to your controls

As a game developer, communicating with players is almost unavoidable, whether you need to tell the players how many lives they have currently, how many items they possess, what have storytellers been saying to them, where they are, where should they go next, and so on. The same could be said for players. They need to tell the game what weapon they would like to use, which difficulty level they prefer, etc. This communication happens as soon as the game is launched and is done through the user interface.

In this hour, you'll learn how to use nodes designed specifically for user interface, Control. We will start with one of the most basic Control nodes, Label, by using it to display text on screen. Then, we get to know some useful properties of Control nodes. We'll also introduce you to Control nodes that are frequently used. Next, you'll learn about Container nodes and experiment with building a complex interface with them. You'll also learn how to make great interfaces using Theme. If you can't find a specific Control ready to be used right out-of-the-box, you can make your own basic Control.

Control

Control is a node inherited from CanvasItem, which means that it can be drawn in 2D. You might remember another class that also inherits from CanvasItem: Node2D. The main difference between these two is Control has a rectangular boundary (rect) that contains and sometimes crops its content, while Node2D has no such boundary. This is one of the most common concepts that confuses starters because these differences might not be obvious. Control sizing is relative to the parent's boundary, similar to Node2D, which inherits the parent's transform.

Basic Control Nodes: Label and ColorRect

Let's begin by creating a Label. It's a simple Control that displays text inside a game window. Creating a Label is done the same way you create other nodes. Label directly inherits from Control (see Figure 9.1).

FIGURE 9.1
A newly created Label node.

When you're done adding the Label, give it some text so that you can visualize it better. This can be done in the Inspector (see Figure 9-2).

FIGURE 9.2
Editing text property of a label using the Inspector.

If you want to add text that spans multiple lines, click the paragraph button next to the text box. A dialog with a larger text area will appear (Figure 9.3).

FIGURE 9.3
A label with text.

When a Control is selected, it is highlighted by its boundary (see Figure 9.3). You can drag any pink dot to resize the Control. However, you may notice you cannot resize the Label to be smaller than the space occupied by text. This is the absolute minimum size of a Control. Controls will never have a smaller size than this value. Minimum size varies by Control and its content. For Labels that don't clip text, their minimum size are the area where the text resides.

Let's add another Control node as a background of Label. Create a new ColorRect as a child of Label (see Figure 9.4). A white-colored rectangle should overlap where the Label is. Set its color property to be whatever you like, preferably not the same as Label's text color because we are going to make it a background. Then, go to the CanvasItem section and check the **show_behind_parent** property, which does exactly what it says. Our Label should visually be on top of the ColorRect now.

FIGURE 9.4
Show behind parent property makes a Label visible on top of a ColorRect.

We will make this ColorRect's boundary match that of the Label. Select ColorRect node, go to the 2D Editor toolbar, look for "Anchor," click it, and choose "Full Rect and Fit Parent" at the bottom (see Figure 9.5).

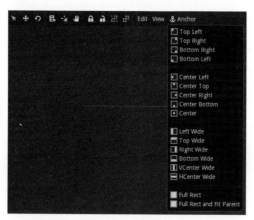

FIGURE 9.5
"Full Rect and Fit Parent" inside the Anchor menu.

The ColorRect should be the Label's background now (see Figure 9.6).

FIGURE 9.6
A Label with ColorRect background.

Properties of Control

We will use the previous Label to introduce you some of the important properties of Control. This is applicable to almost every Control node. To follow along, select a Label node and look at the Inspector. Scroll down a bit until the Control section is visible (see Figure 9.7).

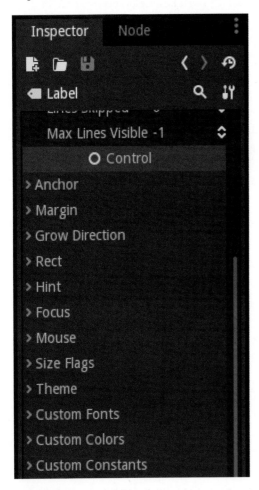

FIGURE 9.7
"Control" section in the Inspector.

We will take a look at each one in the following sections.

Anchor and Margin

Anchor and Margin both have four subitems: Left, Top, Right, and Bottom. They are related and affect each other. Let's look at Margin first (Figure 9.8).

Margin is a distance in pixels relative to the parent's boundary. Currently, our Label has Left and Top set to zero. Try changing Left to 15 and Top to 30 and then look at the difference.

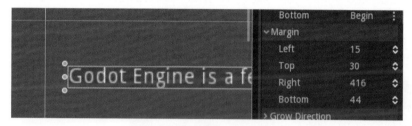

FIGURE 9.8
Effect of Margin property to a Control.

You will see the position has changed according to the Margin value. From Figure 9.8, Label is moved 15 pixels to the right and 30 pixels lower. If you set Margin to be a negative value, it will move the Control the other direction.

Anchor affects how Margin is calculated. Currently, all of our Label Anchors are set to "Begin," which means that Margins are relative horizontally to the parent's Left and vertically to the parent's Top (see Figure 9.9).

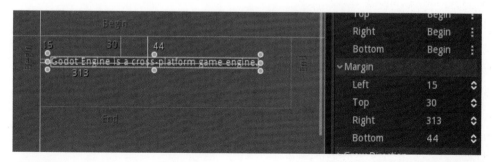

FIGURE 9.9
How Margins are calculated relative to Anchor. (Right Anchor set to "Begin.")

Let's try setting Right Anchor to "End." This will make our Right Margin relative to the parent's Right (see Figure 9.10).

FIGURE 9.10
How Margins are calculated relative to Anchor. (Right Anchor set to "End") Notice an unchanged boundary and difference in Margin value.

Anchor also dictates how the Control is resized if the parent is (see Figure 9.11) because Controls try to keep the Margin constant.

FIGURE 9.11
Resizing the parent. (Right Anchor set to "End") Notice an expanded boundary and constant Margin value.

Try experimenting with other sides too (Control's Left, Top, and Bottom). You can also use the "Anchor" menu to set Anchors and Margins automatically.

Rect

This also contains properties related to boundary and sizing. The transformation similar to that of Node2D's can be found here. Let's look at each one:

▶ **Position**: location of the Control relative to its parent.

▶ **Size**: size of the Control's boundary.

▶ **Min Size**: how small the Control can be resized. This has no effect if it's smaller than the intrinsic Control minimum size. You might want to set this property manually to keep an interface visible and readable.

▶ **Rotation**: Control's rotation around the pivot in degrees. Positive is clockwise.

▶ **Scale**: Control's scale, expanding or shrinking from the pivot.

▶ **Pivot Offset**: location of the pivot relative to the upper-left corner.

▶ **Clip Content**: whether e content outside the boundary is drawn.

Hint

This is the text that appears when players hover their mouse cursor on it for a while. It can be used to tell additional information related to the Control, e.g. contents that are too long to be displayed, the purpose of the Control, etc.

Focus

This lets you define nearby Controls manually. Note the engine can find another Control automatically when players press tab to focus on the next Control. This option lets you override it in case it chooses the wrong Control node.

Size Flags

This contains properties related to sizing inside Containers. Flags vary by Container types. In general:

- ▶ **Fill**: Fills the Container along that axis.
- ▶ **Expand**: The Control takes all available space but won't fill it with content. (as a spacer).
- ▶ **Fill and Expand**: Takes all available space and fills, it with content.
- ▶ **Shrink Center**: The Control keeps itself small and adjusts itself in the center.
- ▶ **Shrink End**: The Control keeps itself small in the right side or bottom.
- ▶ **Stretch Ratio**: The Control's size is relative to that of its siblings. Imagine two Controls being siblings, one with a Stretch Ratio of "2" and another with "1". The one with a Stretch Ratio "2" has the size doubled of another Control.

Theme

Theme is a resource that contains information related to panel drawing. It also contains predefined values for Controls, such as default margin, size, color, and font, etc. If a Control is not given its own Theme, it will inherit its Theme from its parent, resulting in an interface with a uniform look. Theme is discussed later this hour.

Custom Values

This lets you override values defined in Theme individually, in case the predefined ones don't look good in a specific setting. For our Label, you can set a new font, font size, shadow color, shadow offsets, and so on. Try giving our Label a shadow by selecting a check box in front of the "Font Color Shadow" property.

Signals of Control

Like most of the objects of Godot Engine, Control also has signals you can use to execute functions. The following is a nonexhaustive list of signals from the base Control class only. There are more signals available in each specific Control.

- **focus_entered()/focus_exited()**: called when Control has or loses focus
- **gui_input(InputEvent ev)**: called when input event happens inside Control area or while Control has focus for key input
- **mouse_entered()/mouse_exited()**: called when mouse cursor enters or exits the boundary
- **resized()**: called whenever the size is changed

Know Your Controls

There are many Controls bundled with the engine. In this topic, we will get to know some that are used often in game interfaces.

Label

Label is a Control that displays text. Usually, players cannot interact with this Control because it's used only as a display. Here are some of its important properties:

- **text**: a displayed String.
- **align and valign**: text alignment in horizontal and vertical axes.
- **autowrap**: allows resizing, wrap lines that are longer than the width, and adjusts height automatically.
- **clip_text**: allow resizing, but won't automatically adjust the height. As a result, displayed text will be truncated to the Control's height.

RichTextLabel

This is a more advanced label that supports styling via BBCode. Edit the **text** property to use. It's similar to normal Labels.

Text Inputs

Sometimes you want to get text from players. One example is letting players type their character's name using a keyboard. Following are the Controls that provide a text area in which players can type.

LineEdit

LineEdit is a single-line text area. Here are some of its interesting properties:

- **text**: text inside the LineEdit that can be edited by players.

- **editable**: whether players are able to type in the text area.

- **secret**: whether to display text as asterisks. (*) This is useful when making a password input box.

- **placeholder_text**: text that is displayed when the box is empty. It can be used as a hint of what players should enter, for example, "Player name," "Host IP," etc.

TextEdit

TextEdit is a multiple line text area. You may use `set_text(String text)` or `get_text()` to change and retrieve text inside.

Range

Sometimes you also want to get numeric data from players. In games where characters have hit points, you may want to display it using a gauge interface so that it's easier to understand, and it looks better than plain numbers. In games with a trading feature, you might want to know how many items they are going to buy or sell from merchants. This topic discusses Controls that help you get numbers from players while providing an easy-to-use interface. But before that, let's look at some properties these Controls have in common.

- **min_value/max_value**: minimum and maximum value.

- **value**: the current value held by the Control. It will not be below min_value and exceed max_value.

- **step**: a constant number that may be added or subtracted to value.

ProgressBar

Also known as a "loading bar," the ProgressBar is a horizontal control that shows progress as it's being filled with color. Usually, players cannot interact with this Control.

TextureProgress

A more customizable variation of ProgressBar. TextureProgress lets you replace the bar with images. A circular progress bar is also supported.

Slider

Slider is a Control with a dragable button that changes the value.

SpinBox

This is a Control similar to what you've used in the Inspector. It changes the value by clicking the up and down arrows or by clicking and dragging the arrow up or down.

BaseButton

Buttons are useful when you want to know how users want to proceed, whether the form is submitted or discarded, which menu is shown, and so on. Since BaseButton is an abstract class that all buttons are inherited from, it is important to know some of its properties and signals. Some of its interesting properties are listed below:

- ▶ **disabled**: decides whether users can interact with this button.
- ▶ **toggle_mode**: decides whether the button can stay pressed.
- ▶ **pressed**: the current state of the button. It's mostly useful with toggle_mode on.
- ▶ **shortcut**: an input event that triggers the button's action.
- ▶ **group**: only one of all buttons in the same group can be selected. This is mostly useful with toggle_mode on.

Useful signals of BaseButton are listed below:

- ▶ **button_up()/button_down()**: called when the button is released or pressed.
- ▶ **pressed()**: called when the button executes an action, which by default, is when it is unpressed. It can be configured to emit when being pressed by setting the action_mode property. However, the signal will be fired before the player has a chance to cancel the action.
- ▶ **toggled(bool pressed)**: called when the button executes an action while toggle_mode is on.

Button

A simple button has a custom caption and an optional icon.

TextureButton

This is a more customizable variation of Button that uses images. You'll need "normal," "pressed," "hovered," "disabled," and "focused" textures.

CheckBox and CheckButton

These buttons are set to toggle_mode on by default. CheckBox shows check marks inside a box when pressed. CheckButton looks like a switch and displays "ON" when pressed and "OFF" otherwise.

OptionButton

OptionButton is a dropdown menu that lets users select an item.

ColorPickerButton

ColorPickerButton is a button that shows a color picker when clicked. A chosen color is kept as a property. You can use this Control to easily create customization settings for player characters, for example. The **color_changed** signal is emitted when a new color is chosen.

Popup

Popup is a window that displays on top of other Controls. It usually tells users an action is required for another action to complete. Popups are hidden during runtime. To display a Popup, use any of the popup*() methods.

PopupPanel

PopupPanel is one of the simpler types of Popups as it only has a panel as a background and nothing else.

PopupMenu

PopupMenu displays selectable items. It will emit **id_pressed** and **index_pressed** signals upon selection.

WindowDialog

WindowDialog is a PopupDialog with a customizable title bar. It can be set to be resizable.

AcceptDialog

AcceptDialog is a WindowDialog with an accept button captioned "OK" by default. **Confirmed** signal is called upon a button press.

ConfirmationDialog

ConfirmationDialog is an AcceptDialog with a cancel button.

FileDialog

FileDialog is a complex dialog that is used to browse for files and folders. Interesting properties are listed below:

▶ **mode**: the dialog's access mode. The dialog configures its interface to match this setting.

▶ **access**: the file path to which the dialog has access. Note that the resource path usually isn't accessed for writing at runtime, only reading.

▶ **filters**: only files with one of these extensions is displayed.

▶ **show_hidden_files**: whether hidden files and folders are displayed.

The following lists all signals of FileDialog:

▶ **dir_selected(String dir)**: called when a folder has been selected

▶ **file_selected(String path)**: called when a file has been chosen

▶ **files_selected(PoolStringArray paths)**: called when files are selected while the dialog is set to "Open Many" mode

ItemList

ItemList displays items, which can be text or icon, in a nice-looking table. One example is the lower part of the editor's FileSystem dock. Items are interacted with and signals are emitted accordingly.

TextureRect

A TextureRect displays an image constrained by its boundary. Image can be set to tiling mode, scaling to fit or fill the area, or fixed in the center using the **stretch_mode** property.

ColorRect

This is a simple Control that displays nothing but color inside the boundary. Use the **color** property to set the color.

NinePatchRect

This is an image-displaying Control with unique scaling. The image used should have "corners," "sides," and "center." The Corners size is constant. Sides are expanded or tiled in one axis until they meet the other end. The center is expanded or tiled in both axes to fill the middle part. This is useful when making a panel using a custom texture.

Containers

The Anchor and Margin system can be a bit difficult to use and it takes time to achieve the desired outcome, especially when dealing with multiple Controls in the same level. Containers are designed for this situation. They are used as a parent for Controls that are in the same level, because they automatically adjust their child nodes. Note some Container types squeeze the children into their minimum size unless they are set with the appropriate size flags or given a custom minimum size.

BoxContainer

BoxContainer is useful when you want a child Control arranged in a row or column. For HBoxContainer, the first child Control will appear on the left and subsequent children will go to its right in order. It's the same thing with VBoxContainer, but working from top to bottom.

SplitContainer

SplitContainer contains two children separated by a drag-able bar that resizes both children.

MarginContainer

This is a simple Container that gives its child a custom margin. Note these margin values are located in the "Custom Constants," not "Margin."

ScrollContainer

This Container type automatically shows scroll bars when its child is larger than itself.

TabContainer

TabContainer, despite acting similar to other Containers, is not listed as a Container type. It puts its children in a tabbed interface, shows the one selected, and hides the others. Note its children can be of any CanvasItem type and are not limited to "Tabs" as most starters mistakenly assume from the name.

Making an Interface

Let's make an interactive interface using some of the Controls from previous topics. We will create an AcceptDialog that displays what we've typed in a LineEdit. Because there is a Popup in the interface, we will set the root node as a generic Control node to keep the Scene Tree structure in order. Let's begin by adding nodes to the Scene Tree as follows in Figure 9.12.

FIGURE 9.12
A simple interface.

The interface preview in the 2D editor looks a bit messy (Figure 9.13). Don't worry about it. It can be fixed easily as long as the tree is in order.

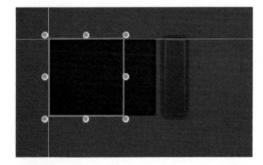

FIGURE 9.13
An unfinished interface.

As you've learned from previous topics, Control size is relative to the parent's boundary. To make use of all available space easily, we will set the root Control to fill the whole screen using "Full Rect and Fit Parent" in the Anchor menu (see Figure 9.14).

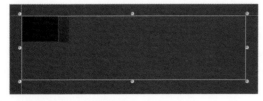

FIGURE 9.14
An unfinished interface.

The changes aren't visible because the child nodes with contents aren't affected. Select the HBoxContainer node and do the same (see Figure 9.15).

FIGURE 9.15
An unfinished interface.

The LineEdit and Button appear in a vertical shape because of the size flags. Select both Controls and change the vertical size flag to none. Then select the LineEdit node and set the horizontal size flag to fill and expand (see Figure 9.16).

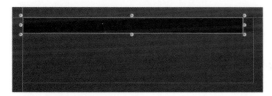

FIGURE 9.16
An unfinished interface.

The interface now looks a little more like what we want. Add a placeholder and a caption for both Controls (Figure 9.17).

FIGURE 9.17
A simple interface.

All that is left is coding the logic. You can attach a script to any node as long as the node paths are correct. This example in Listing 9.1 uses the root node as a script Container. Create and attach a new GDScript to the root node.

LISTING 9.1   Script for the Root Control Node

```
extends Control

func _ready():
    $HBoxContainer/Button.connect("pressed", self, "button_pressed")
    $HBoxContainer/LineEdit.connect("text_entered", self, "show_dialog")
```

```
func show_dialog(name):
    if name == "": name = "anonymous"
    $AcceptDialog.dialog_text = "You are %s." % name
    $AcceptDialog.popup()

func button_pressed():
    show_dialog($HBoxContainer/LineEdit.text)
```

We can't connect both signals to the same function, because they have a different number of parameters. Now save the scene and run it. Type some text, then press the button or enter key (see Figure 9.18).

FIGURE 9.18
AcceptDialog shows the text inside LineEdit.

The interface should now work as expected. Also, thanks to the HBoxContainer, the scene should be responsive to window resizing.

Theme

It is understandable to want to give your game a unique look and feel. The default user interface theme might not match your game aesthetic. Godot Engine provides an easy way to customize the look while keeping it consistent throughout the components. To create a new Theme, go to the Inspector and click the "Create new Resource" button. Find "Theme" resource in the list, choose it, and click "Create." The bottom panel will have a "Theme" option available (see Figure 9.19).

FIGURE 9.19
Theme configuration panel.

To add a new entry to the Theme, click the upper-left menu button that says "Theme," and choose "Add Item" as shown in Figure 9.20.

FIGURE 9.20
Theme configuration menu.

A dialog will appear. Click the ".." button to show the list of available items or manually type an option in the box (Figure 9.21).

FIGURE 9.21
Add Theme Item dialog.

You can find the names and the data type of a Control in the documentation of that Control in the GUI Theme Items section (see Figure 9.22).

FIGURE 9.22
GUI Theme Item section in Godot Engine documentation.

Click "Add" to add it to the Theme resource (see Figure 9.23).

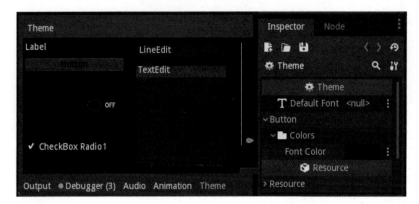

FIGURE 9.23
New Theme Item and preview.

The preview will show how it looks, as shown in Figure 9.24.

FIGURE 9.24
The preview.

StyleBox

StyleBox is also a resource and dictates how panels, boxes, and the like are drawn. There are three types of StyleBox:

▶ **StyleBoxEmpty**: draws nothing

▶ **StyleBoxFlat**: draws a single color

▶ **StyleBoxTexture**: draws an image similar to a NinePatchRect

We'll try adding a new StyleBox to a Normal button. Choose "Theme," then "Add Item." Pick "Type: Button," "Name: normal," "Data Type: Style," then click Add. Click on the new Item, "<null>" and choose "New StyleBoxTexture." Click on it again to configure it. Try adding a default Robot icon as Texture, set all margins to "4," and set modulate color to R:30, G:30, B:30, and A:255 to darken it (see Figure 9.25).

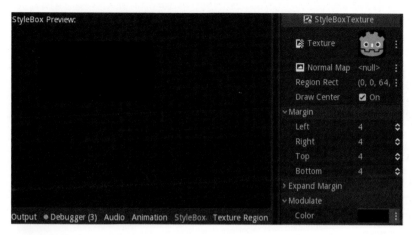

FIGURE 9.25
A configured StyleBoxTexture.

Go back to the Theme resource by clicking "<" icon in the Inspector. The buttons are replaced by the Robot icon. Note that this only affects the "normal" state of buttons (see Figure 9.26).

FIGURE 9.26
Button with custom StyleBoxTexture.

Save the Theme using the "Save Resource" button and then apply it with the root Control of the scene from the previous topic (Figure 9.27).

FIGURE 9.27
Button with custom StyleBoxTexture.

You may notice the button's appearance changed despite the Theme being put in the root Control and not the button node. This is because child Controls inherit their parent's Theme if they aren't given one.

Try using StyleBoxEmpty and StyleBoxFlat with other types of Control.

Custom Control

Controls bundled with the engine should fulfill most use cases. But what if you can't find what you want? In this final topic of this hour, we will learn how to make a control that doesn't come with the engine. We'll make a ColorRect that changes color according to the cursor position inside it.

The first thing to consider is, "Is there any similar Control to inherit from?" For our example, it is ColorRect. But if there's none, you can always inherit from a generic Control node. Now create a ColorRect node, set it to "Full Rect and Fit Parent," and attach the following GDScript shown in Listing 9.2.

LISTING 9.2   Script for a Custom Control Inheriting from ColorRect

```
extends ColorRect

func _gui_input(ev):
    if ev is InputEventMouse:
        var v = ev.position/rect_size
        color = Color(v.x, v.y, 1, 1)
```

The **_gui_input** works like **_input** but only when the input event happens inside the boundary or the Control is focused. We use this callback to change the **color** property of the Control.

Save the scene and give it a meaningful name. To use this custom Control, simply instance that scene. You can instance it multiple times in the same scene because the properties won't interfere with one another.

Summary

In this hour, you learned about important Controls, their properties, and signals. You learned about Containers and how they can help build an interface. You've tried making an interface using various Controls, such as LineEdit, Button, HBoxContainer, AcceptDialog, ColorRect, etc. You've made a custom Theme and applied it with a Control. And finally, you've created a custom Control that makes use of the **_gui_input** callback.

Q&A

Q. Can I use drag-and-drop with Controls?

A. Yes, there are methods for handling dropped data. Drag-and-drop is one of the more advanced implementations of Control. Godot Engine Demo repository offers a demo on this feature.

Q. Can I create custom Containers using GDScript?

A. Yes, by inheriting Container and handling the sort_children signal.

Q. **Can I use Controls in 3D?**

A. Controls are 2D-node types. To use them in 3D, you may put them in a Viewport and display as ViewportTexture. To make them responsive to input events, you can raycast from the root Viewport, and then pass an input event to the UI Viewport using **input**().

Workshop

Answer the following questions to make sure you understand the content of this hour.

Quiz

1. True or False: Controls can be rotated.

2. If you want a Control to stick with the parent's bottom-right corner, what are the Anchor settings.

3. True or False: Margin values cannot be negative.

4. True or False: You are limited with predefined names for Theme Items.

5. True or False: Controls can be created by GDScript.

Answers

1. True. Controls can be rotated using rotation property or inheriting the parent's transform.

2. All Anchors are set to "End."

3. False. Negative Margin value moves the Control in the opposite direction.

4. False. You can use any name. A custom-named Theme Item will be ignored by the engine, but you can refer to it using GDScript.

5. True. Almost every one of Godot Engine's objects can be created with GDScript. Because Controls are nodes, they need to be added to the SceneTree using **add_child** to be operational.

Exercises

Try to execute the following exercises to get more acquainted with the user interface in Godot Engine:

1. Make a simple Music Player using AudioStreamPlayer node with "Open," "Play/Pause," and "Rewind" buttons.

2. Choose any application on your machine and try to replicate its interface inside Godot Engine. You don't have to include all of its functionality, but make sure the interface can handle window resizing.

3. Customize parts of the engine using Theme. The Editor Theme can be set in **Editor menu > Editor Settings > Interface > Theme > Custom Theme.**

HOUR 10
Animation

What You'll Learn in This Hour:

▶ Becoming familiar with the animation editor
▶ Creating and saving a new animation
▶ What keyframes are, how they work, and how to create them
▶ Calling animations from GDScript
▶ Calling GDScript from within an animation
▶ Blending two animations together
▶ Smooth transitioning between subsequent animations

Animation is a key aspect in most games. It's used to simulate running, jumping, grabbing, shooting, and many more actions that happen over time. Even when a character is standing still, it's often given an idle animation, in which it moves up and down to give the impression that the player is breathing.

In this hour, you'll learn how to use the animation editor, how to create animations, how to assign them to sprites, and how to control them with code.

Animation Editor

The animation editor, as the name suggests, is where you create and edit your animations. Every animation starts here.

Opening the Editor

To open the animation editor, click on the word **Animation** at the bottom of the window (Figure 10.1). It should open a new pane, which looks like Figure 10.1.

FIGURE 10.1
The animation editor window.

As you can see, the editor is blank and all the buttons are grayed out. You can't create an animation out of the blue or assign animations to random nodes. Instead, every animation needs to be assigned to a node called the **AnimationPlayer**.

The AnimationPlayer Node

There are two things you need to remember about this node:

▶ It can play any animation you give it.

▶ It can only play one animation at a time.

For example, you have many enemy monsters crawling around your game. They are all playing their own "crawling" animation simultaneously and therefore each of them needs their own **AnimationPlayer** node as a child.

On the other hand, you can create one global **AnimationPlayer** node that plays all singular animations, such as fade-to-black scene transitions or shaking the screen.

So, create a Sprite and attach an **AnimationPlayer** node to it. Once you select the **AnimationPlayer** node, the animation editor should light up and give you some options (Figure 10.2).

FIGURE 10.2
The (very simple) node setup used for animations.

Creating a New Animation

To create a new animation, click the ▉ **New Animation** button. It will open a dialog asking you for the animation name (Figure 10.3).

FIGURE 10.3
The New Animation dialog. Replace "New Anim" with
the name you want to give your animation.

After entering your desired name and clicking **OK**, you'll have even more options. Don't worry, we will explore most of them in the upcoming chapters when we will actually create an animation.

Saving and Loading Animations

Once you've created an animation, it's important to save it. The first reason is, obviously, that you don't want to lose your hard work. The second reason is saving the animation in a file allows you to use this same animation multiple times in other places.

For example, every monster in your game might use the same "crawling" animation. It would be tedious to recreate it for each and every one of them. Save it in a file and reload it in the other AnimationPlayers.

To save an animation, press the 🖫 **Save Animation** button. The first time you do so, it will ask you where you want to save it and under which name.

NOTE

Why Save It Under a Different Name?

There's an important distinction between the name of the animation and the name of the file that contains the animation.

The name of the animation is used to call the animation from code. So, say your running animation is called "Run," you would use that name to play it from code.

The name of the file is merely useful for you, the animator, to easily find animations in your FileSystem. For example, you might use a different naming convention for these files, such as "RunningMonster" or "Run-Version1." In an ideal situation, the programmer should never need to bother with the file names. It improves workflow to keep the programmer's tasks separate from those of other people in the team.

To load an animation (that you previously saved), press the ◻ **Open Animation** button. Locate the animation file and open it.

On the Concept of Animation

Generally, people distinguish between two types of animation: spritesheet and keyframe.

Spritesheet animation is the "old school" way of animating. You might remember those old flipbooks where you have hundreds of pages with drawings, each only slightly different from the previous one. If you look at the pictures one-by-one, they seem like a bunch of similar pictures. If you flip through them with your finger, though, your eyes see it as an animation and the drawings seem to come to life.

Spritesheet animation does this. You create multiple drawings of your character in (slightly) different positions, and put them in a single image, which is called a spritesheet. Then, you tell the game to "play frame 2, 3, 4, and 5 really fast," and it suddenly looks as if the character is moving (Figure 10.4).

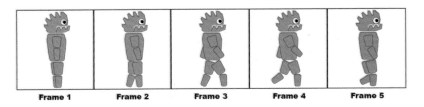

Frame 1   Frame 2   Frame 3   Frame 4   Frame 5

FIGURE 10.4
A spritesheet that shows the start of a running animation. (Or, if we're very mean to our player, a jumping off a building animation.)

Keyframe animation is what's most often used these days. Instead of drawing every single frame yourself, you only set the most important ("key") frames. The software then interpolates between those positions, automatically creating movement (see Figure 10.5).

Keyframe 1   ... arm automatically rotates over time ...   **Keyframe 2**

FIGURE 10.5
The same animation, but with keyframes. We only need to set two keyframes at the "extreme positions", and the animation player does the rest. Note in this case, we'd need separate keyframes for the other arm and both the legs. (Those weren't shown in the image for clarity purposes.)

In Godot, the keyframe system is used, because it can be used for both 2D and 3D, and it's more powerful. The next chapters explain the keyframe system.

NOTE
___

But What If I Really Want Spritesheet Animation?

There's a special node for that: the **AnimatedSprite** node. It won't be discussed further, as it's beyond the scope of this chapter.

Alternatively, you can achieve spritesheet animation with keyframes as well! (That's how useful they are.) All you need to do is make every single frame of the spritesheet a separate keyframe.

___

Timeline and Keyframes

A large part of the animation editor is dedicated to the so-called **Timeline**. That's a good thing, because it's by far the most important element. The timeline contains what happens at every step of the animation (Figure 10.6).

FIGURE 10.6
The timeline, with a few tracks on it. (Tracks are explained in a bit.)

Animation Duration

At the bottom of the animation editor (Figure 10.7), you'll find all the controls for animation length and view.

FIGURE 10.7
The toolbar for controlling animation length and how fine-grained your control is.

First, let's set the length of the animation. To do so, edit the **Length** property, which is in seconds. Then, it's important to set the **Step** property. You might think that you can just place keyframes anywhere in your animation, but that's not true. Think about it. If you could place a keyframe anywhere, you'd soon run into precision errors. One keyframe could be a few milliseconds off and you wouldn't notice.

Godot, therefore, automatically divides the whole animation into steps. The default setting is **0.1**, which means every tenth of a second you can place a keyframe. This ensures all keyframes within the same step line up perfectly. If you want more fine-grained control, you can lower this number.

The slider on the left is used for zooming in and out of the view. It doesn't actually change the length of the animation, but rather how much of it you can see. If you zoom in more, you can see the step lines.

Lastly, if the 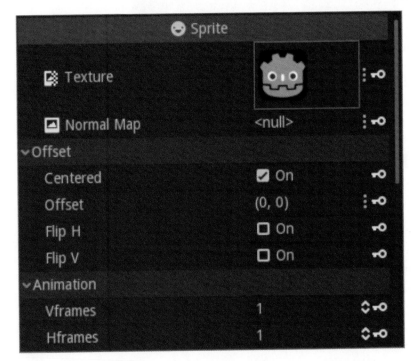 **Loop Button** is toggled on, the animation loops. This means that, when the animation reaches its end, it automatically jumps to the beginning and starts again.

NOTE

Nothing Is Fixed

You can always edit all properties of the animation later. If it turns out you need a longer animation, just update the length. In the next paragraphs, when you learn about keyframes, you'll also see you can move them around and change everything on the fly.

Creating Tracks and Keyframes

Now comes the best part! In Godot, everything can be keyframed: all of the properties of all of the nodes in the scene tree, as well as their resources. So, if you select our Sprite, its properties suddenly look like Figure 10.8.

FIGURE 10.8
What the inspector looks like with the Animation window open. Notice the keyframe symbol behind every property.

To create a keyframe, simply click on the 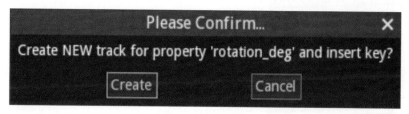 Keyframe symbol behind the property you want animated. If it's the first keyframe, Godot will ask you if you want to create a new track. This is merely a confirmation dialog—you always need a track for every animated property. In this case, we'll keyframe the rotation property (see Figure 10.9).

FIGURE 10.9
Track confirmation dialog.

Once a track is created, clicking on the 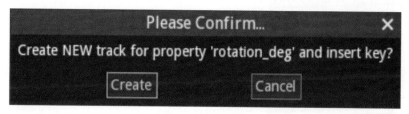 Keyframe symbol creates a keyframe on the existing track. Alternatively, you can press the **Insert** key to create a keyframe.

Modifying Keyframes

Keyframes are always placed at the position of the cursor in the timeline. The cursor is the vertical blue line. So, before you create a keyframe, always check if the cursor is at the right time. If not, you might accidentally override previous keyframes. To move the cursor, click on the top part of the timeline (see Figure 10.10).

FIGURE 10.10
Click somewhere on this box and the timeline cursor jumps to the position you clicked.

To move a keyframe around (after you've created it), click and drag it horizontally within the same track.

To have closer control, select a keyframe (by clicking on it) and click the 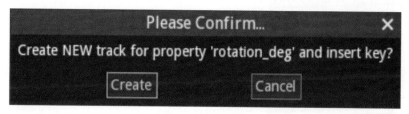 Edit Keyframe button (at the bottom right). This opens a small pane where you can precisely set the **Time** and the **Value** (Figure 10.11).

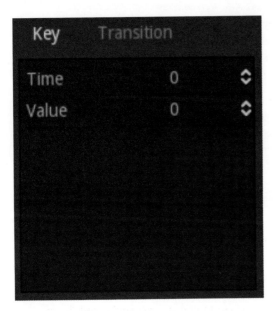

FIGURE 10.11
Pane for precise keyframe editing. This keyframe is
located at 0 seconds within the animation and sets
the rotation of the Sprite to 0 degrees.

Of course, animations are only interesting if there are multiple keyframes. So, we go ahead and
create another keyframe for the Sprite. We move the timeline cursor to **0.5s**, rotate the Sprite
180 degrees, and click the keyframe symbol again. Our track now looks like Figure 10.12.

FIGURE 10.12
A simple animation that smoothly rotates our Sprite upside down.

Testing the Animation

Now that we have the animation, we obviously want to run it and see how marvelous it looks. For
this, we use the symbols in the top left corner (see Figure 10.13).

FIGURE 10.13
Controls for animation playback.

You're probably already familiar with these symbols. To play the animation from the start, use the
Rewind & Play Button. To play the animation from where the cursor currently is, use the
Play Button. To pause playback, use the **Stop Button**.

The counter on the right shows the current step of the animation. You can use the up/down arrows to jump from step to step and see the animation in great detail.

Transform Animation

Even though everything can be keyframed, there's one thing that's almost always animated: one of the three transform properties (location, rotation, and scale). Luckily, Godot has an even quicker method for animating these (see Figure 10.14). At the top of the scene view, you'll find three words and a **Keyframe symbol**.

FIGURE 10.14
Buttons for quick transform keyframing.

By clicking on them, you can turn the words "**loc**", "**rot**", and "**scl**" green. Once you click the **Keyframe symbol**, all the properties that are green automatically get keyframed. So, in figure 10.14, location and rotation receive a keyframe, but scale does not.

Try It Yourself

Now it's time for you to create your own amazing animation with everything you've learned.

TRY IT YOURSELF ▼

A Bouncing Character

In this Try It Yourself, we'll create a character that bounces up and down.

1. Create a **Sprite** node, pick any image you want, and attach an **AnimationPlayer**.

2. Open the **Animation** window and create a new animation. Call it whatever you want, such as bounce or jumping.

3. Save it within your project. The name for the animation file doesn't have to be the same as the animation name.

4. Make sure the **Animation** window is open and the timeline cursor is at **0 seconds**.

5. Select the **Sprite** and go to its **Transform** properties.

6. Click the **Keyframe symbol** to create the first keyframe. When asked to create a track, confirm.

7. Now move the timeline cursor to **0.5** seconds and move the Sprite upwards (to a lower y-coordinate).

8. Click the **Keyframe symbol** again and a second dot should appear on the animation track.

9. Now move the timeline cursor to **1.0** seconds and move the Sprite downward again to its original position.

10. Click the **KeyFrame symbol** one last time and a third dot should appear.

11. Play the animation and your character should move up and down.

12. Do not forget to save your animation after you've changed it.

13. BONUS: See if you can keyframe the scale property as well, so that the sprite "squishes" when it hits the ground and "elongates" when it's in the air (for that cartoony feel).

Easing Functions

With the last Try It Yourself, you may have noticed something. Your Sprite moves up and down, but it doesn't really feel like a bounce, because it moves in a linear fashion. When a real person jumps, he starts very fast, but gradually slows down as he gets higher and higher. (And, conversely, when that person falls down, he starts falling faster and faster until he hits the ground.)

How the animation interpolates between keyframes (Figure 10.15), is decided by an easing function. For example, a linear animation—which is the default—is the result of a linear easing function, which is a straight diagonal line.

In case you've been wondering that's what the buttons at the right side of every track represent.

FIGURE 10.15
Buttons controlling interpolation of keyframes.

The ➕ **Add Keyframe button** provides a quick way to add another keyframe to this specific track.

The second button toggles between **continuous easing** (in which it uses the easing function) and **discrete easing** (in which it completely abandons the easing function, and simply jumps from keyframe to keyframe).

The third button is the overall **easing function**. Within the editor, you can only choose **linear** and **cubic** (which is curved and the one you need to get a realistic bounce). With GDScript, you can set more easing functions.

The last button toggles **easing on loop**. When set to wrap loop interpolation, it interpolates between the last and the first keyframe as well (which is what you often want, if your animation loops).

Try It Yourself

In Hour 7, "Handling Input," you learned how to handle input. We'll use that knowledge now to play an animation whenever the user presses a certain key.

TRY IT YOURSELF ▼

A Bouncing Character—Again

In this Try It Yourself, we'll use the bouncing animation we made earlier. When the user presses the up arrow key, our Sprite should jump and bounce.

1. Add a script to the **Sprite** node.

2. Check if your **AnimationPlayer** still has the previously created *bounce* animation. If not, you can test your skills now by recreating it.

3. Within the script, check for input with the `func _input(event):` function

4. Write an if statement to check whether a key was pressed, which is done with `if event is InputEventKey`

5. Write an if statement that checks whether the up arrow is pressed, which is done with `if event.scancode == KEY_UP:`

6. OPTIONAL: Now, the event will fire as long as the up arrow is pressed down. If you only want to play the animation when the user releases the up-arrow, add an additional check with `&& event.pressed == false`

7. Within the if block, tell the animation to play with `$AnimationPlayer.play("bounce")`

8. Save it and test it.

Scripting Animations

So, let's say you've made an animation called "run" and it's loaded into the **AnimationPlayer**. Eager to try out your new animation, you start your game—and nothing happens. That's because we haven't told Godot which animation we want to play and when.

If you have a very simple setup, **Autoplay** can help you out. By clicking the **Autoplay button** on a certain animation, it automatically plays when the **AnimationPlayer** node is added to the game (which is, in this case, when the game starts). Because the **AnimationPlayer** can only play a single animation at a time, you can only have one animation set to **Autoplay**.

Most games, however, need something way more complex. They need to dynamically call animations from a script (Listing 10.1). The following is a script that should be placed on the Sprite and plays the animation called "run."

LISTING 10.1   Simple Animation Call

```
extends Sprite

func _ready():
    $AnimationPlayer.play("run")
```

The next thing you want to be able to do is stop and pause the current animation (Listing 10.2).

LISTING 10.2   Stopping and Pausing

```
$AnimationPlayer.stop() # this stops the animation, and resets it to the beginning
$AnimationPlayer.stop(false) # this merely pauses the animation
```

OK, so we have a run animation we can play and stop. It is tempting to write a function that checks whether a certain key is pressed (say, the left arrow key), and if true, it plays the animation. This will most likely result in horror and confusion. Why? Because, every time you call play(), it plays the animation again from the beginning. So, calling it every frame results in the animation getting stuck in the first few milliseconds.

To work around that, you could check whether the animation is already playing, like what is shown in Listing 10.3.

LISTING 10.3   Checking the Current Animation

```
if $AnimationPlayer.is_playing() && $AnimationPlayer.get_current_animation() == "run":
    # do nothing, it's already playing
else
    $AnimationPlayer.play("run")
```

Animation Signals

As with all nodes, the **AnimationPlayer** emits signals. These are extremely useful. Even though they can be replicated with some code, it's recommend to use signals. Why? For example, your character has a "wood chopping" animation. Every time that animation ends, you want the tree he's chopping to release one wood Sprite. Then you can use a signal (Listing 10.4).

LISTING 10.4   The AnimationPlayer Signals

```
animation_changed(old_name, new_name)
        # fires whenever the animation changes. The old animation is given by
old_name, the new one by new_name

animation_finished(anim_name)
        # fires whenever the current animation finishes (anim_name holds the name
of the current animation)

animation_started(anim_name)
        # fires whenever a new animation starts (anim_name holds the name of the
current animation)
```

If you want even better control, you can, in a sense, create your own signals. Thus far, we've added tracks that can keyframe certain properties. We've done that by clicking the ⬤ **Keyframe symbol** behind the desired property.

There is one extra type of track, though, we haven't seen yet, which must be created in a different way. It's the **Call Func** track. To create it, press the ➕ **Add Track button** (lower right of the animation editor), and choose **Call Func**.

A new window opens, asking you which node you want to attach it to. Choose the **Sprite**.

As the name suggests, this type of track calls a function. For example, we want to call the function wood_chop() halfway through an animation. These are the steps we should take:

1. First place the timeline cursor at **0.5s**.

2. Then, press the ➕ **Add Keyframe button** on the **Call Func** track.

3. Select the new keyframe you created and press the ✏ **Edit Keyframe** button.

4. Type wood_chop in the **Name** field.

5. Add the function wood_chop() to the script on the **Sprite**, like what is shown in Listing 10.5.

LISTING 10.5   Receiving the Call from the Call Func Track

```
func wood_chop():
    print("It works! Choppie choppie.")
```

Blending and Transitioning Animations

With keyframes and the **AnimationPlayer** node, we can already make many powerful animations. There are, however, two "problems" left: we can only play a single animation at a time and the transition from one animation to the next is very harsh—it just suddenly jumps from one animation to the start of the next.

The first problem can be solved with **blending**. The second problem can be solved with adding a **transition**. Both of these can be accomplished with the special **AnimationTreePlayer** node.

The Setup

First, do the same thing as always: add the **Sprite** (or whatever node you want animated) and attach an **AnimationPlayer** node. Next, attach an additional **AnimationTreePlayer** node (Figure 10.16).

FIGURE 10.16
How to setup your Sprite to use an AnimationTreePlayer.

Go to the properties of this new node and set the Master Player to the **AnimationPlayer** node also attached to the Sprite. This means the animation tree we're about to create will use animations from that specific player.

Animation Tree Editor

With the **AnimationTreePlayer** node selected, an additional pane has appeared next to the animation editor. This animation tree editor should look like Figure 10.17.

FIGURE 10.17
An empty animation tree.

You might notice that it looks familiar to the visual scripting language Godot has and that's because it is. Using the ➕ **Add Node** button, you can add any type of node to the tree. Once added, you can connect nodes by clicking and dragging from the output of one node to the input of another.

As you can see, now the animation tree is invalid. Eventually, all nodes should lead to this "Output" node, and when that happens (correctly), it tells you the animation tree is valid.

With the 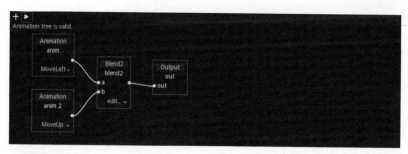 **Play Tree button,** you can activate the animation tree. You can also activate/deactivate them within GDScript, using the `set_active()` function.

Animation Trees "Replace" Animation Players

When an animation tree is not active, it has no influence at all on the game. When the animation tree is active, it overrides anything the **AnimationPlayer** node is trying to do. Therefore, if you decide to use an animation tree for your character, you'll most likely need to include all your animations in the tree (idle, run, jump, fall, walk, and so on).

Blending Animations

Let's say we have an animation "MoveLeft" (in which our Sprite moves to the left), and an animation "MoveUp" (in which our Sprite moves up). Now we want to blend these two together, so that the character moves diagonally upwards instead.

To do so, add both the animations to the animation tree (using the **Animation** node) and add a **Blend2** node. The final tree should look like Figure 10.18.

FIGURE 10.18
An animation tree that blends two animations.

As you might expect, the **Blend3** and **Blend4** nodes blend 3 and 4 animations, respectively.

On the **Blend2** node, you can press **edit** to get a slider. This slider determines how much of each animation is used. So, in our case, we want to set it to the halfway point, to use 50 percent of the first animation, and 50 percent of the other.

That's all you need to do! Activate the tree and the Sprite should move diagonally. Play around with the blending slider if you want to see the effect.

Creating Transitions

Say our Sprite is moving to the left, but halfway through the animation, we want it to go upwards instead. If we switch the animation with code, it would look horrible. Why? Because it would immediately switch to the "MoveUp" animation, instead of gradually easing into it. We can fix that by adding a **Transition** node to the animation tree.

Once added, you'll see the **Transition** node has only one input. To add another input, right-click on the node, and choose **Add Input**.

Now, remove the **Blend2** node. We can't blend two animations together and perform a transition, because both animations are already playing. Connect the animation nodes to the transition node and it should look like Figure 10.19.

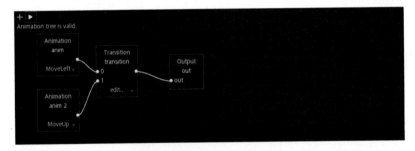

FIGURE 10.19
An animation tree that transitions between two animations.

Again, by clicking on **edit** on the **Transition** node, you can set some properties. The most important is the **X-fade time**. This determines how much time it takes to transition from one animation to the next. If you set it to 0.1s, then both animations will blend for a tenth of a second and afterward the new animation is the only one playing.

As mentioned before, the **AnimationTreePlayer** node replaces the **AnimationPlayer** node. Therefore, if you want to transition from the 0 animation to the 1 animation, you need to do so with the following lines of code in Listing 10.6.

LISTING 10.6   Changing the Animation Tree

```
$AnimationTreePlayer.transition_node_set_current("transition", 1)
# the first parameter is the <name> of the node, which you need to supply
because you can have multiple transition nodes with different names
```

Summary

In this hour, you've learned where to find the animation editor and how to use it. You've learned how to create animations, save them, and open them in an **AnimationPlayer**. You've learned how to animate anything by creating keyframes. You've learned how to manipulate animations from code and how to call code from within the animation. Finally, you've learned how to create seamless transitions between animations playing right after one another.

Q&A

Q. Is there a limit to the amount of AnimationPlayers, animations, tracks, or keyframes?

A. No, though it's always recommended to keep them to a minimum. Animations are often the culprit when it comes to lagging games or weak performance. If unsure, press the **Animation Tools** button and choose **Clean-Up Animation**.

Q. Animating every single body part of the character is tedious. Is there no better way for such complex animations?

A. Why yes, there is. It's called Inverse Kinematics, and can be found under Edit > Skeleton. You create a skeleton made of bones that run through the character and, by moving a certain body part, the rest naturally follows along. It's way too complicated to explain here, but be sure to give it a try if you're into complex and realistic character animations.

Q. Can I delete tracks?

A. Yes, simply select the track and press the **Delete Track** button (in the lower right corner). In fact, there's also a **Delete** button at the top, which deletes the whole current animation.

Q. Can I rename animations?

A. Yes. Press the **Rename** button (top toolbar) and enter the new name in the dialog.

Workshop

Now that you have finished the hour, take a few moments to review and see if you can answer the following questions.

Quiz

1. True or False: you do not always need an **AnimationPlayer** node to play animations.

2. True or False: a single **AnimationPlayer** node can play as many animations as you want.

3. Pressing the ___ key adds a new keyframe for the currently selected node.

4. True or False: you can place keyframes anywhere on the timeline.

5. True or False: you can switch the current animation with GDScript.

6. True or False: you cannot perform code within an animation.

7. To blend two animations, one needs a ___ node, with the master player property set to a ___ node.

Answers

1. False, you always need one.

2. False, it can only play one at a time.

3. Insert

4. True; the step in the editor acts as a helper, but you can use any float value for your keyframe's time.

5. True, use the `play("anim_name")` function.

6. False, a **Call Func** track can call any function within a script.

7. AnimationTreePlayer, AnimationPlayer

Exercises

Exercise: We've learned a lot this hour, so this exercise touches on many different key points. We will create a monster/security guard/whatever that patrols an area, and makes a backflip when he changes direction.

1. Create a **Sprite** and add a script.

2. Create two animations: **MoveLeft** (which moves 200 pixels to the left), and **MoveRight** (which moves 200 pixels to the right).

3. Within the **MoveLeft** animation, the **Sprite** should rotate 90 degrees to the left. Within the **MoveRight** animation, the **Sprite** should rotate 90 degrees to the right. (Or try something else, you want to visually see the Sprite facing either left or right. There should be a distinction.)

4. At the end of the **MoveLeft** animation, call the function `finished_move_left()`. At the end of the **MoveRight** animation, call the function `finished_move_right()`.

5. Create an animation tree. Connect the two animations to a transition node and set a certain x-fade time (though not too long). Activate the animation tree.

6. Within the script, use the two functions you've created to transition to the other animation. (So, when the **MoveLeft** animation is finished, start **MoveRight**, and vice versa.)

7. Create an input handler (in the same script), which checks if the user presses the up arrow key. If so, change the x-fade time to a random value, using `transition_node_set_xfade_time("name", newtime)`

Bonus Exercise: I've mentioned the differences between spritesheet animation and keyframe animation. Now that you know all about animations, try to create a spritesheet animation using keyframes.

1. Find any spritesheet you like.

2. Create a **Sprite**, and set the spritesheet as the image of the **Sprite**.

3. Within the **Sprite** properties window, you should find two properties called **Vframes** (vertical frames) and **Hframes** (horizontal frames). These "cut" the spritesheet into frames for you. For example, if a spritesheet has 6 frames arranged in 2 rows and 3 columns, you should set **Vframes** to 2 and **Hframes** to 3.

4. Find the frame property of the **Sprite**, and keyframe it.

5. Move the timeline cursor a bit, change the frame to the next number and keyframe it again.

6. Repeat the last step until you've used up all the frames.

7. Play the animation and enjoy life.

HOUR 11
Game Flow

What You'll Learn in This Hour:

- ▶ Pausing the scene and stopping node processing
- ▶ Changing to another scene
- ▶ Loading resources while providing visual feedback
- ▶ Controlling game behavior when the quit button is pressed

One can think of a video game as a show on stage, but interactive. It is "live," i.e., things you see on the screen are being dynamically rendered at the time you are playing. There are several scenes, and you are going through them one at a time. There is also a "backstage," where tasks are managed behind the scenes, such as setting up the scene, retrieving objects and resources, etc. However, most of the time, the player is in control and may choose which scene to play or to take a break.

In this hour, our focus is on the "stage," or the Scene Tree. You'll learn how to use it to control game flow, selectively pause the game, and switch scenes. You'll also learn about Resource Loader, a "backstage," and use it to load large resources without the game freezing while it waits for them. Finally, you'll learn how to handle "quit" requests from players and respond properly.

After Launching the Game

Have you ever wondered what actually happens when you launch the game executable?

A game cannot start if there is no operating system. Thus, it begins with the module that speaks directly with the system—the OS singleton.

OS

OS is a singleton that abstracts interactions with the system and tries to make it consistent, regardless of the platform. It is also one of the first modules that are loaded, before other singletons and the scene system. A Main Loop must be given to keep the engine running. Without a Main Loop, the engine will quit, because there is nothing else to process, kind of like renting a theater with no plays to show. This is useful for stand-alone scripts, for example, which will have to inherit the Main Loop class.

Main Loop

Main Loop is a class capable of keeping the engine running after initialization. It will receive callbacks on each tick ("iteration") throughout the duration since the last tick ("delta"). When launching a game, a subclass of Main Loop called Scene Tree is automatically created by the engine, and provides the interface to manage the current scene. Main Loop or Scene Tree can be accessed via `Engine.get_main_loop()`.

Scene Tree

Scene Tree is a class derived from Main Loop. As mentioned previously, besides preventing the engine from quitting, Scene Tree manages the current scene. It has a viewport called "root" that acts as the root of the tree. Here are some of the functions regarding scene management:

- **change_scene(String path)**: Loads the scene file pointed to by the provided path and change the current scene to it. An example of this path parameter is `res://main.tscn`.

- **change_scene_to(PackedScene packed_scene)**: Changes the current scene to a loaded scene. PackedScene of a scene file can be acquired by `load()` or `preload()`. For example, `var scene = preload("res://main.tscn")` will load "main.tscn" as PackedScene "scene." Then you can call `change_scene_to(scene)`.

- **get_current_scene()**: Retrieves the root node of the current scene.

- **is_paused()**: Notifies whether the current Scene Tree state is paused.

- **set_pause(bool paused)**: Sets the Scene Tree pause state.

- **quit()**: Closes the game.

- **reload_current_scene()**: Loads the current scene file from the disk.

- **set_auto_accept_quit(bool enabled)**: If set to "true," the game will exit immediately when the player presses the exit button or the quit key combination (Alt+F4).

In addition to being the nodes manager, Scene Tree is also capable of calling multiple nodes of the same group, high-level networking, and more, but those are out of the scope of this hour.

Scene Tree is always accessible via the mentioned `Engine.get_main_loop()` method. It is optional to check whether the returned Main Loop is a Scene Tree, as most of the time, that is what it will be. Another way is to call `get_tree()` from any nodes in the tree. If successful, `get_tree()` will return a Scene Tree. It is important to know that `get_tree()` will not work if called from nodes that are not in the tree.

Once Scene Tree is created and loads your main scene, calling `tree_entered` signal and `_ready` method, your game will finally be running.

Pausing the Game

You can call `get_tree().set_paused(true)` from any nodes inside the tree to pause the game. However, your game will become unresponsive from that point on, because all nodes inside the tree stop processing. You'll need to whitelist some nodes that you want processed regardless of the pause state. Nodes can be set to stop, continue to process, or inherit a parent's setting via the pause_mode property. If set to inherit, scene root will stop processing when paused.

Let's see pausing in action. Create a new node, add a child accept dialog named `PauseMenu`, and attach the following GDScript to the node, as shown in Listing 11.1.

LISTING 11.1   Simple Counter with Pause Functionality

```
extends Node

var label = Label.new()
var counter = 0

func _ready():
    label.text = str(0)
    $PauseMenu.dialog_text = "Paused"
    $PauseMenu.connect("popup_hide", self, "unpause")
    $PauseMenu.popup_exclusive = true
    add_child(label)

func _process(delta):
    counter += delta
    label.text = "%.1f" % counter

func _input(event):
    if event is InputEventKey:
        if event.scancode == KEY_ESCAPE:
            $PauseMenu.popup()
            get_tree().set_pause(true)

func unpause():
    get_tree().set_pause(false)
```

The script above creates a label that tells time once the game is launched. When the escape key is pressed, it pops up an accept dialog that says "paused," and pauses the game. When the accept dialog is closed, the game resumes. Try running the scene and press "escape." You'll notice that the timer stops when the Scene Tree is paused. This is the expected response (see Figure 11.1).

FIGURE 11.1
Simple game pause dialog.

However, when you try to unpause the game by clicking the "OK" button, it doesn't let you, because the dialog is also paused.

Now try setting the pause mode of the pause menu to "process" and restart. Alternatively, you can add the following line in `_ready,` as shown in Listing 11.2.

LISTING 11.2   Setting the Pause Mode to Process

```
$PauseMenu.pause_mode = PAUSE_MODE_PROCESS
```

The "OK" button should respond to input now, and the timer continues when you press it.

Switching Scenes

It is possible to never switch a scene by using one scene that loads and unloads its children. For simple games, this is overkill. It is advisable to use Scene Tree to switch scenes.

Scene Tree is responsible for scene switching. You can call `get_tree().change_scene (String path)` to load a scene and set it as the current scene. If you want to load the scene beforehand, you can use `preload()` or `load()` and save the scene in a variable. Then, call `get_tree().change_scene_to(PackedScene)` with that variable as a function parameter.

Let's try switching scenes. Create two scenes. One has a Sprite with a default robot icon as texture for visualization. Save the Sprite scene as res://sprite.tscn. Another has a node as the root node with the following GDScript attached, as shown in Listing 11.3.

LISTING 11.3   Scene Switching

```
extends Node

var label = Label.new()

func _ready():
```

```
        label.text = "Press Start"
        add_child(label)

func _input(event):
    if event is InputEventKey:
        get_tree().change_scene("res://sprite.tscn")
```

Try running the node scene. The text saying "Press Start" should appear (see Figure 11.2).

FIGURE 11.2
Scene switching

Pressing any key should bring you to the Sprite scene (see Figure 11.3).

FIGURE 11.3
Sprite scene

To go back to the node scene, you can add another GDScript to the Sprite node that changes the scene back.

Background Loading

Sometimes, the resource is too large to be loaded in a couple of frames. The game will be unresponsive until the loading is complete. It is generally undesirable to not provide visual feedback of long operations.

Resource Interactive Loader

Resource Interactive Loader is a class capable of loading Resource in steps. It can be created by the Resource Loader singleton by calling `ResourceLoader.load_interactive(String path)`.

- ▶ **preload()** loads resources at compile time. You may not use variables as the function's argument, and the file must exist.

- ▶ **load()** loads resources at run time. The file does not have to exist at the time of loading, making it useful when loading user data.

Example

The following example will require a scene with many references. You can find it in the official demo projects. Download a project, and copy both scenes and resources into your project root. Rename the scene file name to "scene.tscn." Create a new scene and node, then attach the GDScript shown in Listing 11.4.

LISTING 11.4   Background Loading

```
extends Node

var label
var loader
var clock = 0

func _ready():
    label = Label.new()
    add_child(label)
    loader = ResourceLoader.load_interactive("res://scene.tscn")

func _process(delta):
    clock += delta
    var err = loader.poll()
    if err == ERR_FILE_EOF:
        print(loader.get_resource())
        get_tree().quit()
    label.text = "%d / %d loaded (%.1f s)" % [loader.get_stage(),
loader.get_stage_count(), clock]
```

The script above will load the scene interactively in stages and display the progress. Note that it's greatly slowed down so you can easily see the progress. Each call to `ResourceInteractiveLoader.poll()` increases the progress. You might notice that the timer is continuously counting up. This means the game doesn't freeze while the resource is being loaded (Figure 11.4).

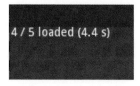

FIGURE 11.4
Interactively loading a scene.

If the loading is finished, it will return `ERR_FILE_EOF`. You can get the resource using `ResourceInteractiveLoader.get_resource()`. If you want the resource instantly, calling `ResourceInteractiveLoader.wait()` will halt the game until the resource is loaded.

Handling a Quit Request

When a game receives an exit signal, there is a chance the player did not mean to quit, and it can be infuriating if he has not saved for a while. Loss of game data can adversely affect the reputation of your game. It is a good idea to have a dialog that pops up asking if the player wants to save first or auto-save when quitting. Any quit requests should be properly handled.

Let's see how this is made possible with the notification system. Create a new node and attach the GDScript shown in Listing 11.5.

LISTING 11.5   Manually Handling a Quit Request

```
extends Node

var dialog = ConfirmationDialog.new()

func _ready():
    dialog.dialog_text = "Are you sure?"
    dialog.get_ok().text = "Yes"
    dialog.get_cancel().text = "No"
    dialog.connect("confirmed", self, "end")
    add_child(dialog)
    get_tree().set_auto_accept_quit(false)

func _notification(what):
    if what == MainLoop.NOTIFICATION_WM_QUIT_REQUEST:
        dialog.popup()

func end():
get_tree().quit()
```

The script above will intercept NOTIFICATION_WM_QUIT_REQUEST of Main Loop and respond by popping up the dialog that says, "Are you sure?" The game will quit when you press the button that says, "Yes" (see Figure 11.5). Otherwise, the game will continue to run.

FIGURE 11.5
Manually handling a "quit" request.

This gives you a chance to save the game before quitting.

Summary

In this hour, you've learned about Main Loop and its importance of keeping the engine running. You've also learned about a type of Main Loop called Scene Tree that also manages the scene that is currently playing. You should be able to query Scene Tree to pause the game and switch the scene. When there's a large resource that takes time to load, you've learned that the Resource Interactive Loader can help load it in stages. Finally, you know how to intercept a quit request and do things that are necessary before closing.

Q&A

Q. How do you switch between scenes with a transition effect such as fading?

A. The simplest way is to make both scenes children of another scene that applies effect. If that is not applicable, there are several ways to achieve this. One way is to apply a fade effect to both scenes. Fade out the old scene before switching, and fade in the new scene when it's ready. Another way is to add a fade effect on top of both scenes by adding it as a root viewport's child and making it render on top. If the effect requires images from the old scene, such as a crossfading effect, you can capture the viewport before switching.

Q. Can you skip the interactive loading and get resources immediately?

A. Yes, by calling ResourceInteractiveLoader.wait().

Q. Can you handle quit requests from killing the process?

A. No. The game will exit immediately.

Workshop

Answer the following questions to make sure you understand the content of this hour.

Quiz

1. What is the class that manages the current scene and its nodes?

2. What property of a node should be modified if you want to pause the Scene Tree without the game becoming unresponsive?

3. What is the difference between `SceneTree.change_scene()` and `SceneTree.change_scene_to()`?

4. What is returned by `ResourceInteractiveLoader.poll()` when the resource is done loading?

5. To what class does `NOTIFICATION_WM_QUIT_REQUEST` belong?

Answers

1. Scene Tree.

2. pause_mode.

3. change_scene() must be given a scene file path; `change_scene_to()` must be given a PackedScene.

4. ERR_FILE_EOF.

5. Main Loop.

Exercises

Try to execute the following exercises to get more acquainted with Scene Tree:

1. Add a pause dialog to your game or a demo project.

2. Display the pause dialog when a player makes a quit request.

3. Choose two demo projects, merge them into one, and make a main menu with options to choose which to run.

HOUR 12
File System

What You'll Learn in This Hour:

- ▶ Special Godot paths
- ▶ Creating and saving configuration files
- ▶ Saving general files, such as save games
- ▶ Using encrypted files
- ▶ Managing files and directories with scripting

Godot has capabilities to deal with the file system of the player's device, which is important when creating and managing configuration and save files. This hour will focus on the scripting API that helps you handle this in a portable, multi-platform way.

Special Paths

Apart from the standard file system paths available from the user's operating system, Godot provides two special portable file paths: The **Resources** directory and the **User** directory.

Resource Path

The root folder of your project is the **Resource Root**. From there, all the resources are loaded to the game. It is identified with the `res://` prefix, which acts as a protocol in standard paths (such as `file://` or `http://`), and can be used like a regular path in the functions.

The Resource path is where your project lives. It is great for reading project resources in a portable way, since it's the same for every platform. However, you should not try to write on it. You can write on the Resource path inside the editor, because it's just your project folder, but it will likely be a read-only path when the game is exported. This is especially true for mobile, as the file system access is restricted. Even on desktop platforms, the game is exported in a single read-only package (a Godot-specific file, as we'll see in the hour about exporting).

TIP

Case Sensitiveness

The file system on Windows is not case-sensitive; therefore, it does not matter if you change a capital letter to a lowercase correspondent. This is not true for other operating systems, however, so it's important to keep the case of the file names in your code as they are in the system.

A general rule of thumb is to name all files in lowercase.

User Path

In a similar manner, there's a special path that can be accessed by the `user://` prefix. This path is meant to store user-specific information, such as configurations and game saves. The actual location of this directory varies from one operating system to another, but it uses the common user-data location. It is a reliable place to write files in-game so they don't get lost.

NOTE

User Path Location

The user path has different locations for each platform to follow the standards of the user's operating system. If you want to find the files, here's a list of locations per OS:

- **Windows:** `%APPDATA%/.godot/app_userdata/project_name`

- **Linux and MacOS:** `~/.godot/app_userdata/project_name`

- **HTML5:** The file system is mocked using the LocalStorage API.

- **Android, iOS, and UWP:** These platforms have restricted access to the application data.

Note that you can remove the `.godot/app_userdata` from the path and just use `project_name` (which is a path-safe conversion of your project's name). To do that, enable **Use Shared User Dir** on Project Settings under the **Application/Config** section.

Game Configuration

One very common thing in games is the options menu. The user can select the difficulty, video and audio settings, control configuration, etc. The player also expects the game to remember these options between sessions. To deal with that, you need to save a file in the player's machine with the selected options so that the game can save and load the next time.

Godot provides a special class called **ConfigFile**. This class has methods to add, edit, and retrieve options in a INI-like formatted file. It can deal with sections in the file to better organize the content, and is responsible for loading and saving the file in the disk. An example usage of the `ConfigFile` class is shown in Listing 12.1.

LISTING 12.1   Saving Configurations

```
extends Node

func _ready():
    save_config()

func save_config():
    var path = "user://config.ini" # The path to save the file
    var config = ConfigFile.new() # Create a new ConfigFile object
    config.set_value("options", "difficulty", "hard") # Save the game difficulty
    config.set_value("audio", "music_volume", 42) # Save the music volume

    var err = config.save(path) # Save the configuration file to the disk
    if err != OK: # If there's an error
        print("Some error occurred")
```

In this sample, we add two values to the `ConfigFile`: the game difficulty and the music volume. The `set_value()` function receives three arguments: the section, the property name, and the property value. After setting the values, we need to call `save()` with the path to actually write the file to the disk. This function returns an **Error** value that can be checked against any of the `ERR_` prefixed constants from the `@Global Scope`.

Loading Configuration Files

After you save the file to disk, only half the work is done. When the game starts again, you need to load the file from the disk and change the options to match the file. `ConfigFile` will also help you with that (see Listing 12.2).

LISTING 12.2   Loading Configurations

```
extends Node

func _ready():
    print(load_config()) # Should do something meaningful, but let's print for test
purposes

func load_config():
    var path = "user://config.ini" # The path to load the file
    var config = ConfigFile.new() # Create a new ConfigFile object

    var default_options = {    # Create a dictionary of default options
        "difficulty": "easy",
        "music_volume": 80
    }
```

```
    var err = config.load(path) # Load the file from the disk
    if err != OK: # If there's an error return the default options
        return default_options

    var options = {} # Create a dictionary to store the loaded options

    # Get the values from the file or the predefined defaults if missing
    options.difficulty = config.get_value("options", "difficulty", default_options.
difficulty)
    options.music_volume = config.get_value("audio", "music_volume", default
_options.music_volume)

    return options # Return the loaded options
```

The `load_config()` function starts by creating a dictionary of default options. Then it tries to load the file from the disk. If it fails (which may be the case in the first run of the game), it returns the default options. This ensures the output is always in a valid state. After that, it creates a new dictionary to store the loaded options.

There are two calls to the `get_value()` function from the `ConfigFile` class. This function receives three arguments: the section, the name of the property, and the default value (the default is an option argument, and will be `null` if not provided). In the code, try to load the settings defined earlier. If for some reason they are not defined (maybe the player deleted them manually), load from the default options.

After building the options dictionary, return it for the calling function so it can do the appropriate task such as changing the music volume or, in this case, printing the options to the output.

TIP

Avoiding Redundancies

The `ConfigFile` class has methods for retrieving the sections and the properties in a section. You can use them to make a loop that fills the options dictionary based on the file instead of listing the properties manually once again, which might be troublesome if you forget to add or remove one option, or if you change the section of another.

If you centralize the places where options are stored and retrieved, you can save work in the future and avoid the nasty hard-to-find bugs caused by the redundancy.

Dealing with Files

While the `ConfigFile` class is great for storing configuration, it is very limited in what it can do. It is not recommended to deal with more complex save games. Godot provides a general class to read and write to files in a general way. The `File` class can create files with any kind of content, including binary formats. It has options to store and retrieve any type of data, and is able to compress and encrypt files.

Creating and Writing to Files

The first thing you need to do to write to a file is create a new `File` object. Then you need to open a file from the disk. The class has functions to write Variant type to files, which may help you deal with the content. Listing 12.3 gives an example of how to write player data to a file.

LISTING 12.3   Writing Data to File

```
extends Node

# Some variables to store
var player_name = "Link"
var player_score = 550

func _ready():
    create_file()

func create_file():
    var path = "user://save.dat"
    # Create a new File object
    var file = File.new()

    # Open the file for writing
    var err = file.open(path, File.WRITE)
    # Simple error checking
    if err != OK:
        print("An error occurred")
        return

    # Store the player data
    file.store_var(player_name)
    file.store_var(player_score)

    # Release the file handle
    file.close()
```

The code opens a file for writing. Note that if the file doesn't exist, it will be created; otherwise, it will be truncated (cleared). The `store_var()` function stores a Variant type with metadata (such as type and size) so that it can be retrieved later.

TIP

Open Modes

The second argument of the `File.open()` method is the mode to open the files. There are four modes available, all of which are constants in the File class:

▶ **READ**: Open for reading. Will return an error if the file exists.

▶ **WRITE**: Open for writing. Create the file if it doesn't exist and truncate if it exists.

▶ **READ_WRITE:** Open for reading and writing. Return an error if it doesn't exist; don't truncate if it exists.

▶ **WRITE_READ:** Open for reading and writing. Create the file if it doesn't exist and truncate if it exists.

These may be a bit confusing to remember, but you can always check the built-in help if needed.

Reading from Files

Writing to a file can only be useful if you can read the data later. The `File` class has similar methods for reading as for writing (e.g., if you use `store_double()`, you can later retrieve with `get_double()`). Let's try to get back the player data from the file (see Listing 12.4).

LISTING 12.4   Retrieving Data from the File

```
extends Node

func _ready():
    read_file()

func read_file():
    var path = "user://save.dat"
    # Create a new File object
    var file = File.new()

    # Open the file for reading
    var err = file.open(path, File.READ)
    # Simple error checking
    if err != OK:
        print("An error occurred")
        return

    var read = {}
    read.player_name = file.get_var()
    read.player_score = file.get_var()

    file.close()

    return read
```

This code is like that in Listing 12.3: it creates a `File` object and opens the file for reading. Note that an error will be returned if the file doesn't exist. After it's open, retrieve the variables and put them into a dictionary so the values can be returned.

Data Order Matters

If you are writing binary data to a file, be sure to use the same order when reading. If the order is changed during the development process, the old files may be wrongly read or simply unreadable. This may also be needed to update the game (add data or change a data type). Be sure to have a consistent format and versioning in your binary files to avoid losing data, especially when dealing with player data. No one likes to lose their game progress after an update.

Text Formats

Instead of simply storing variables directly, you can save the data as text. Godot has support for the popular JSON format (JavaScript Object Notation), which can be used easily by other applications. It may not be suitable for save games if you don't want the player to tamper with them, but it can be useful for configuration storage.

You can use the `to_json()` and `from_json()` functions to convert from a dictionary to text and vice-versa. Then simply use `File.store_string()` and `File.get_as_text()` methods to store and retrieve the JSON from the file.

Compressing and Encrypting Files

The `File` class has special variations of the `open()` method to use compression or encryption in your files. When you use them, the file will be automatically dealt with following the way it was opened. Note that encryption and compression needs a **flush** (the process that stores data to the disk). You need to call `close()` on the file object to flush the data; otherwise, you may lose it.

The `open_encrypted()` and `open_encrypted_with_pass()` functions both open files with encrypted data. They can be used to open files for writing and reading the same way as the regular `open()` method. The difference between `open_encrypted()` and `open_encrypted_with_pass()` is that the first receives a binary key (as a `PoolByteArray`), and the other receives a string password that will be used to decrypt the file when opened in read mode.

The same applies to the `open_compressed()` method. This method receives an optional argument to determine the compression mode. You can use the `COMPRESSION_` prefixed constants from the file class. The default method is FastLZ, which has a nice compromise between compression ratio and speed.

Compressing and Encrypting the Same File

Godot does not offer a direct API to compress and encrypt a file at the same time, but it is possible to work around that. If your data is in an array or in a string, you can convert it to a `PoolByteArray`.

This kind of array has compression functions, so you can compress it and store the result as a buffer in the encrypted file, then follow the reverse steps to get back the data.

This may be a bit convoluted, but if you really need to do it, it's possible to abstract it away with a few functions.

NOTE

Encryption and Security

It's important to note that even if you encrypt save games, the key to decrypt must be somewhere in your application, and dedicated hackers could get their hands on it. Also, if the application uses the same key for all users to store save games, it won't stop players from exchanging save files.

The rule of thumb is to never trust the client. If your game relies on an online multiplayer experience that could be ruined by cheaters, be sure to enforce the rules on the server, where you have control.

Dealing with Directories

Besides the File class, Godot also contains a `Directory` class. This one is responsible for managing folders in the file system. It can list, delete, rename, and move files.

Listing the Files in a Folder

A simple way to start is to list all the files in a certain directory. Godot has a few functions to make this behavior possible. This is a bit different from how it's usually handled, so let's look at an example, shown in Listing 12.5.

LISTING 12.5   Retrieving Data from the File

```
extends Node

func _ready():
    # Create a new directory object
    var dir = Directory.new()

    var err = dir.open("res://")
    if err != OK:
        print("An error occurred")
        return

    # Start listing the directories
    dir.list_dir_begin()
    # Retrieve the first file or dir
    var name = dir.get_next()
    # Start a loop
```

```
while name != "":
    # Test if it's a dir and print as appropriate
    if dir.current_is_dir():
        print("dir : ", name)
    else:
        print("file: ", name)

    name = dir.get_next()

# End the listing
dir.list_dir_end()
```

The first step, as always, is to create a new `Directory` object. Try to open the resources directory, and if there's an error, stop the function. Then call a method to start the listing of files and directories. Start a loop, and at each iteration, call `get_next()` to advance in the list. There's a test for the current entry: if it's a directory, prefix the print with "dir"; otherwise, use "file." When the loop ends, call a function to stop the listing and close the stream.

NOTE

Special Directory Entries

If you ran the code above, you may note that the first two entries are a dot (.) and a couple of dots (..). These are standard notations in file system paths. The single dot means the current directory, and the double dot means the directory above the current one. You can use them for relative navigation.

If you don't need them or want to skip them when listing the files, you can pass true as the first argument of the `list_dir_begin()` call.

Managing Files and Directories

There are a handful of methods in the `Directory` class that can act as full-fledged file explorers. In fact, these functions are in use by the engine internals in the file dialogs. Let's walk through some possibilities with this powerful class.

Creating Directories

Two functions can create folders: `make_dir()` and `make_dir_recursive()`. The difference between the two is that the latter creates all the intermediate directories if they do not exist, while the former just returns an error if that happens.

Deleting Files and Directories

The `remove()` method of the `Directory` class acts as a delete function for both files and directories. Note that to remove folders, they must be empty. There's no function to delete a directory recursively, but you can implement your own in GDScript.

Moving, Renaming, and Copying Files

The `rename()` method can be used for renaming and moving files. If the destination path is different from the source, the file will be moved there. This behavior is akin to the "move" command of Unix-like platforms.

To copy files, you can use the `copy()` method. Its arguments are the same as the `rename()` function: the first is the source, and the second is the target. Both methods overwrite the destination if it already exists.

Checking for Existence

The `Directory` class has two methods for checking existence in the file system: `dir_exists()` and `file_exists()`. Both work with relative and absolute paths. Note that if you call `dir_exists()` with the path to a file, the function will return false, and vice-versa.

TIP

FileDialog

If you need a graphical way for the user to select files and directories, you should use the `FileDialog` control. It has all the appropriate functions and interface to navigate within the file system and let the user select a file. This control is very similar to the file dialogs encountered in the Godot engine editor.

Summary

This hour covered the aspects of the file system and how Godot deals with it. You saw the special portable paths of the engine that can be used in any platform. You learned how to create configuration files and store them to the disk, followed by general files and how to deal with them. In the end, you saw how the `Directory` class can navigate and interact with the files in the user's operating system.

Q&A

Q. Can Godot access any path in the file system?

A. Yes. However, it follows the operating system's permissions, so the game cannot change files to which the player doesn't have access or permission to edit.

Q. Do the file system functions apply to any OS?

A. Yes. Godot functions are truly portable. Some functions are OS-specific when there is a need (like access to the Windows drives) but in general, you can rely on the access to work in any operating system.

Q. Does Godot deal with binary files from other applications?

A. Godot can manage any kind of file. However, if you are trying to use files from other programs, you need to implement your own parser to analyze the file format.

Workshop

Here are a few questions to help you review the contents of this hour.

Quiz

1. Where's the user path located?

2. True or False: `ConfigFile` automatically detects your game configuration and saves it.

3. Is it possible to load a file with `File` class if it was saved with `ConfigFile`?

4. True or False: Godot games can create, modify, and delete files and directories.

Answers

1. The user path resides in the common application data for the user's operating system.

2. False. `ConfigFile` can be used to save the configuration, but you need to provide the information via code.

3. Yes. The `File` class can open any file, including those created with `ConfigFile`.

4. True. Games have full access to the user's file system (if the user has permissions). These functions should be used wisely.

Exercises

Take some time to solve the following exercises. They may require some coding experience, but solving them will improve your understanding of the file system functions.

1. Modify the directory listing to show the subdirectories. This requires a recursive function. Be careful to not fall into an infinite loop by going into the special relative paths ("." and "..").

2. Abstract the configuration saving and loading to functions that receive and return a dictionary. Pass the file path as an argument.

3. Try to implement a configuration saver and loader using JSON.

4. Make a system of save slots. Each slot can be a file, and the player may be able to delete them.

5. **Advanced**: Implement the abstraction so that you can compress and encrypt the save game at the same time.

HOUR 13
3D Graphics

What You'll Learn in This Hour:

▶ Adding 3D nodes to your game

▶ Importing meshes and models

▶ Working in the 3D editor view

▶ Manipulating 3D objects

▶ Placing, enabling, and scripting cameras

So far, everything in this book has been in 2D. It's simple, straightforward, and cozy, and it's easy to understand. But sometimes, you want more—an extra dimension or a different lens through which to view your game. Sometimes, you want three sides of the coin. That's why we'll explore 3D graphics in this hour.

In this hour, you'll learn how to add 3D objects to your game and manipulate them in the editor and through code, and how to set up cameras to view your game properly.

Spatial Node

Godot was built from the ground up to fully support 2D and 3D. Because of that, everything in 3D works and looks very similar to the process in 2D. Just as 2D nodes have a base node called ⊙ **Node2D** and GUI nodes have a base node called ⊙ **Control**, the base node of all 3D nodes is the ⊙ **Spatial** node.

Just like the ⊙ **Spatial** node, all 3D nodes have a red color. And if you know how to use a certain 2D node, there's a good chance you'll find the same node for 3D simply by removing the letters "2D" from the node name.

Let's add a ⊙ **Spatial** node to a scene.

The New Transform

In the inspector, take a look at the transform properties for this node (Figure 13.1). You'll notice that it looks similar to the 2D transform, yet slightly different. The reason for this, of course, is that we now have a third axis.

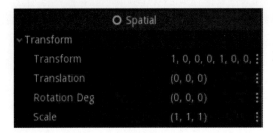

○ Spatial	
˅ Transform	
Transform	1, 0, 0, 0, 1, 0, 0, ⦂
Translation	(0, 0, 0) ⦂
Rotation Deg	(0, 0, 0) ⦂
Scale	(1, 1, 1) ⦂

FIGURE 13.1
The new transform properties, which are present in every 3D node.

Just as every 2D node has a position, a rotation degree, and a scale, every 3D node has a translation, a rotation, and a scale.

▶ **Translation:** the offset of this node from the origin of the scene.

▶ **Rotation:** the rotation of this node, in degrees, around each axis.

▶ **Scale:** the scale of this node along each axis.

If you look in the 3D editor, the "origin of the scene" is depicted by the point where the three axes (red, green, and blue) meet (Figure 13.2).

With 3D nodes, an additional property is present: transform. This is a matrix of 12 numbers, and you can use it to set translation, rotation, and scale at the same time. This requires complex math, so it won't be discussed further here.

The Three Axes

In 2D, everyone knows there's an **x-axis** that runs horizontally, and a **y-axis** that runs vertically. But how does this translate to 3D? Well, there are two schools of thought:

▶ Y is up: The x-axis is left/right, the y-axis is up/down, and the z-axis is forward/backward.

▶ Z is up: The x-axis is left/right, the y-axis is forward/backward, and the z-axis is up/down.

These differences stem from the background of people using 3D. For example, the "z is up" version is usually attributed to architects. They first draw a floor plan on paper in 2D (using x and y axes), leaving the z-axis for when they start building toward the sky.

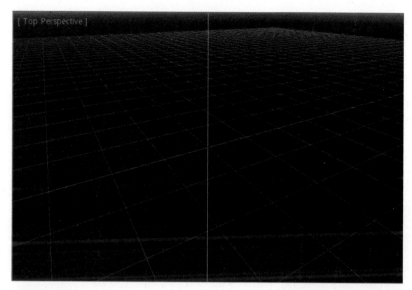

FIGURE 13.2
The origin of the scene, shown in the editor. In code, it's simply the point (0,0,0).

In Godot, the "y is up" variation is used. However, it is possible that other software uses the "z is up" strategy, in which case you will run into problems when importing your models. More on that later.

NOTE

Axes Are Color Coded

Throughout all of Godot and most other 3D software, the three axes are color coded exactly the same way: the x-axis is red, the y-axis is green, and the z-axis is blue.

The Metric System

In 2D, everything was measured in pixels. In 3D, we can't do the same thing. When we place the camera differently, the size of objects and the distance from the camera changes. In fact, we might even use a split screen in which each camera only uses half the screen width. This means using a fixed pixel unit doesn't work in 3D.

Instead, the metric system is used. When you set a node's translation to, say, (50, 50, 0), it moves 50 meters to the right and 50 meters up within the scene.

All professional 3D-modeling software uses this convention, so if you ensure that objects are the right size in your software, they should look perfect once imported to Godot.

Models, Meshes, and Primitives

If you look in your 3D editor, you don't see anything, because the 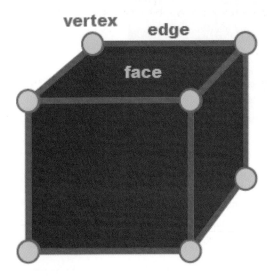 **Spatial** node has no geometry attached to it. It's an empty node, just as **Node2D**. In fact, all 3D nodes have no visual presence, except for meshes.

A mesh is nothing more than a collection of vertices (or dots), connected to each other to make edges (or lines), which are connected to get faces (or surfaces). In the image below, you can see that a cube has eight vertices, 12 edges, and six faces (Figure 13.3).

vertex **edge**

face

FIGURE 13.3
How meshes are built. (Obviously, there's also a backside to this cube, but it doesn't show in a 2D image.)

A **model** is a collection of meshes that belong together. For example, a character might consist of multiple meshes—one for his head, and two for both his arms.

A **primitive** is a "standard mesh," such as a cube, sphere, pyramid, or cylinder.

In the next chapter, we'll look at how to import 3D models into Godot.

NOTE

Dynamic Meshes

Sometimes, you'll need to change meshes during the game or create new meshes on the fly. Godot offers the possibility to generate and manipulate meshes using GDScript with the **ImmediateGeometry** node, but it's beyond the scope of this lesson.

Note that this is different from animating an object. Everything you've learned in Hour 10 about animation also applies to 3D, and you can animate any object any way you want by keyframing the translation, rotation, or scale.

Importing Meshes and Models

In this chapter, I'll assume you have 3D-modeling software installed on your computer, and that you know how to use it (at least a little). If not, Blender is a professional, free modeling software that you can install and use. All you need to do—for now—is add a cube to your scene and export it as an .obj file.

When it comes to importing, there are two options:

▶ Importing a single mesh: This gives you more control, as you import each and every mesh yourself, but you lose textures and animation (and other properties) associated with the mesh.

▶ Importing a complete model/scene: This gives you less control, but it imports a complete scene with all its properties.

Importing a Mesh

As soon as you add an .obj file to the Godot project directory, it will be automatically imported. A scene in which your mesh resides will be created. In the case of the simple cube, it looks like the one in Figure 13.4.

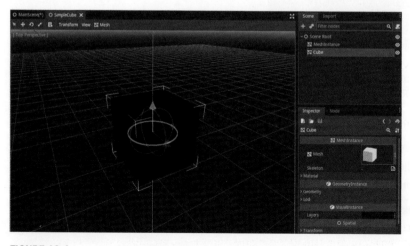

FIGURE 13.4
A scene containing the cube node. The cube is black because there is no light source, only a mesh.

If you're not happy with the way your mesh was imported, you can select it in the FileSystem window and open the Import tab (next to Scene). There, you can change settings and click "reimport" (Figure 13.5).

FIGURE 13.5
The reimport window. It also works if you select multiple files of the same type.

One disadvantage is that the automatically created scene cannot be edited. You have two options to fix this:

▶ If you double-click the scene to open it, it will warn you and give you the option to create a new inherited one.

▶ Right-click an existing node (in a different scene), and choose ⊠ **Merge from Scene.** Locate the .obj scene, click the cube node, and click "OK."

As you might have noticed, the mesh of our 3D model is displayed by a ▨ **MeshInstance** node. This is always the case—every single mesh needs a single ▨ **MeshInstance** node.

NOTE

MultiMeshes

The 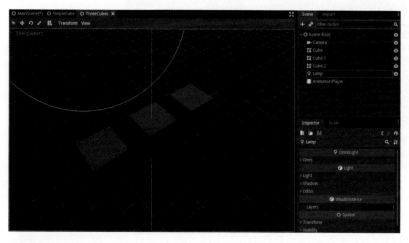 MeshInstance is quick and powerful, but if you're using hundreds or thousands of instances of the same mesh, it will severely affect performance. For this, look at the MultiMesh node as the solution.

Importing a Model/Scene

Importing a scene uses the same process, just a different file format. The file format to use is .DAE. Unfortunately, some software has a really broken export system for this, which you must first fix:

▶ Maya/3DS Max: uses "OpenCollada" plugins.

▶ Blender: On the Godot website, under downloads, you'll find a "Better Collada Exporter."

Once you have your scene exported, add it to the folder of your Godot project, and it will automatically import. Below is a scene with three cubes. Notice in Figure 13.6 how Godot also imported the light, the camera, and an animation player.

Note: A new standard asset exchange format called glTF has been released. It has significant advantages and will replace Collada in the near future.

FIGURE 13.6
A complete scene, imported automatically.

3D Editor

Now that we have something in our scene, let's see how we can move around our 3D world and change the view.

First, it's important to be in the 3D editor view. You can get to the 3D view by clicking the word "3D" at the top, pressing the F2 key, or selecting any 3D node in the Scene view.

Moving the Camera

It's very important to be able to move the camera around easily. It saves you a lot of time, and it allows you to quickly move around the scene and look at objects from all angles. The default controls are as follows:

▶ Zoom in/out: scroll wheel

▶ Orbit around selection: middle mouse button + drag

▶ Pan left/right/up/down: shift + middle mouse button + drag

If you don't like these controls, you can change them to a different popular configuration in the editor settings (Figure 13.7).

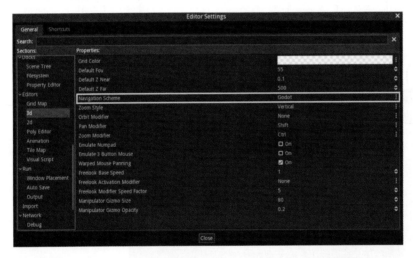

FIGURE 13.7
The 3D editor settings. There are many properties you can change are not covered in this lesson.

Changing Camera View

By default, the editor camera is in perspective view (as can be seen in the top-right corner of the view). Sometimes, however, it's more useful to look at the world in 2D to see if things line up perfectly.

To do so, click on the "Perspective" text, which opens a window.

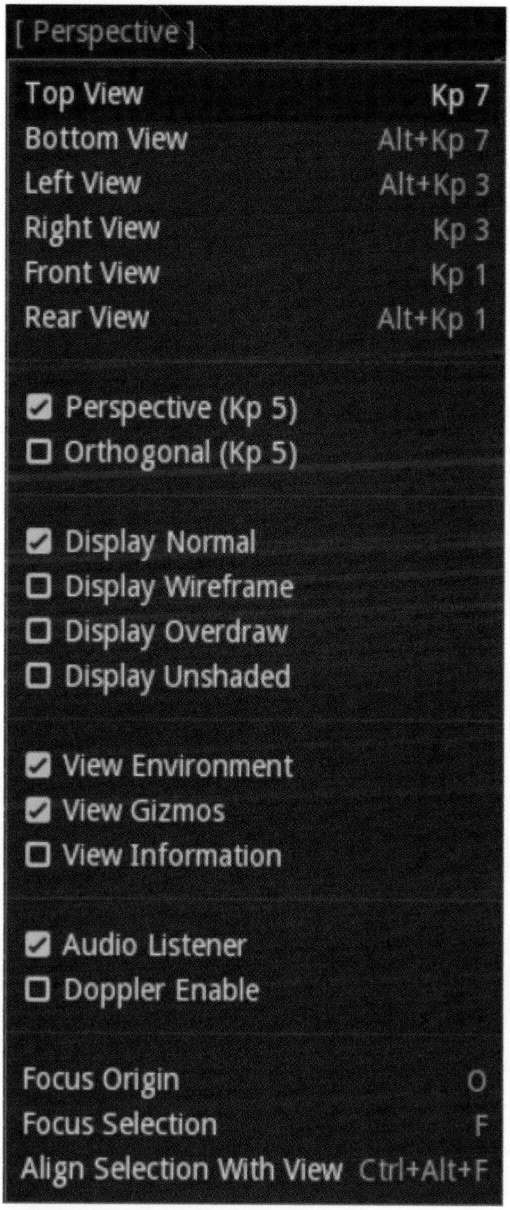

[Perspective]

Top View	Kp 7
Bottom View	Alt+Kp 7
Left View	Alt+Kp 3
Right View	Kp 3
Front View	Kp 1
Rear View	Alt+Kp 1

☑ Perspective (Kp 5)
☐ Orthogonal (Kp 5)

☑ Display Normal
☐ Display Wireframe
☐ Display Overdraw
☐ Display Unshaded

☑ View Environment
☑ View Gizmos
☐ View Information

☑ Audio Listener
☐ Doppler Enable

Focus Origin	O
Focus Selection	F
Align Selection With View	Ctrl+Alt+F

FIGURE 13.8
The camera view list. Every view is quite self-explanatory; the top view, for example, views the world as if the camera were watching it from above. In this list, one can also turn on/off certain visuals within the editor.

Additionally, we can also split the screen into multiple views. To do so, click the "View" button to get the following dropdown list:

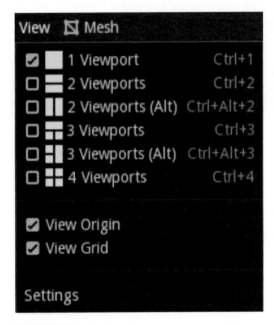

FIGURE 13.9
You can split the screen into up to four viewports. It's common to set the top-right viewport to perspective and the others to top, left and front. This ensures that you can see the scene from all sides. You can also turn on/off the origin lines and the grid.

Transforming Nodes

You probably already noticed that, in 3D view, there are circles and arrows drawn around an object. These are called gizmos, and they can help you translate, rotate, and scale the node quickly. They do not show up in the final game.

To use a particular gizmo, hover over it with your mouse until it turns white, then click and drag it.

Gizmos are nice, but sometimes they can be in the way, especially if you want to transform only one element (such as scale). To switch to a singular transformation mode, use the buttons on the upper left.

Of course, if you know exactly how many units you want to translate/rotate/scale a node, you can simply edit the number in the properties of the node in Inspector.

Cameras

We've thus far learned everything about placing objects in our scene and working within the 3D editor. However, if you only have 3D models in your scene, you would see nothing when you

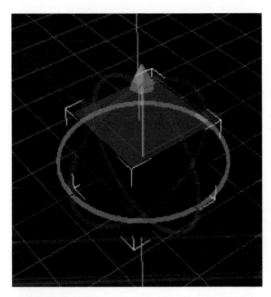

FIGURE 13.10
Gizmos displayed around a cube.

FIGURE 13.11
From left to right: default
setting, only translation,
only rotation, only scaling.

started the game! Without a camera in the 3D world, there's no way to show the world, because the engine doesn't know from which angle and distance to view the world.

Creating a Camera

To put a camera into the world, we use, not surprisingly, the ▣ **Camera** node. Make sure you don't accidentally choose the Camera2D node.

The new camera will be instantiated at the origin, and you can move it around and rotate it using gizmos. To preview what the camera sees, press the ▣ **Preview** button at the top right of the editor view.

Camera Settings

Like every node, the camera has important properties that can be edited in Inspector.

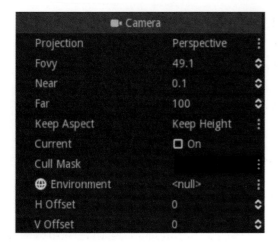

FIGURE 13.12
The main camera settings.

The **projection** property has two options: perspective and orthogonal. The perspective type is the default type, with objects getting smaller as they are further away. With orthogonal projection, sizes stay the same, and you basically convert a 3D world to a 2D one on the screen.

The **fovy** property stands for "field of view," and determines how much the camera is zoomed in. What's the difference with moving the camera closer? By increasing the field of view, objects get "warped" around the edges of the screen, as if you're applying a fisheye effect. On the other hand, decreasing the field of view gradually turns a perspective camera into an orthogonal one.

The **near** and **far** properties determine how close and how far the camera can see. For example, if you have a camera following a player, you might want to cut away all objects closer to the camera (than the player) to have an unobstructed view.

Lastly, we have the very important **current** property. To understand what it does, we must first learn about viewports.

About Viewports

Every camera must answer to a viewport. Look at it this way: The camera registers part of the world, then hands this picture over to the viewport, which is responsible for actually displaying it on the screen.

The root node of every scene is automatically a viewport. Godot does this for you, so our current camera, a child of the root node, has a viewport. Because it's the only camera, everything works as expected.

If we added another camera as a child of the root node, we'd run into problems. A single viewport can only display the picture from a single camera, so we have to choose. This is where the current property comes into play. By setting the current property on a █▌ **Camera** node to "on," it becomes the active camera for its viewport.

Below is an example script that switches to a different camera when the game starts.

LISTING 13.1   Camera Switching

```
func _ready():
    $Camera.set_current(false)
    $CameraTwo.set_current(true)
```

Working with Multiple Cameras

There are cases, however, where you want to use multiple cameras at the same time; for example, in a split-screen game or when you want to display a minimap. If that's the case, you'll need to add your own viewports for each camera.

This is discussed in great detail in Hour 21 ("Viewports and Canvas").

Manipulating the Camera

Most likely, you won't have a static camera. The camera will follow your main player, or, as often seen in strategy games, the player can freely move the camera around the map.

The easiest way to make the camera follow the player is to make the █▌ **Camera** node a child of your ▨ MeshInstance node. However, this is also very restrictive and results in jagged movement, as the camera follows exactly what your player is doing.

A better way is to control the camera with code. Here's an example of how to make the camera follow a node called Cube from a safe distance. (This script should be placed on the parent node of the camera and cube.)

LISTING 13.2   (Very) Simple Camera Follow

```
extends Spatial
func _process(delta):
    $Camera.set_translation($Cube.get_translation() + Vector3(0, 25, 25)) # offset
the camera from the cube
    $Camera.set_rotation(Vector3(-45,0,0)) # rotate it so it faces the cube
```

As you can see, in 3D, we work with `Vector3(X,Y,Z)` instead of `Vector2(X,Y)`. Also as expected, `get_position()` becomes `get_translation()`, and all 3D functions accept Vector3 arguments only.

If you test this code, it will work, but it will still feel choppy. Luckily, Godot offers an alternative to the █▌ **Camera** node, which is the ▨▨ **InterpolatedCamera** node.

Interpolated Camera

The  InterpolatedCamera node is the same as a regular camera, but with a useful addition, which you can see in Inspector.

FIGURE 13.13
The extra properties for the interpolated camera.

You can set a target node, and it will smoothly follow the node wherever it goes. So if the node abruptly moves, the camera will interpolate positions and slowly move with it (instead of jumping around).

There's one important pitfall: the InterpolatedCamera node moves to exactly the location of the target node, instead of following from a distance. So it's best to set a Position3D node as the child of the cube, offset it by a certain distance and make it face the cube, then use that Position3D node as the target:

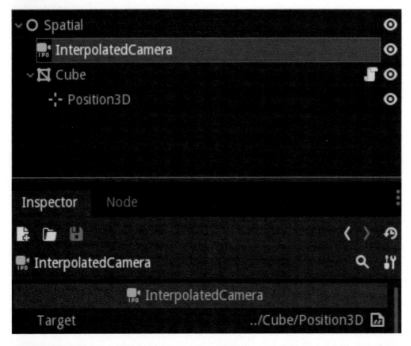

FIGURE 13.14
A working configuration for a smooth camera follow.

In the end, it depends on what kind of camera behavior you want. The ![icon] **InterpolatedCamera** node provides a quick and easy way to get a smooth camera follow, but it's highly likely that you'll need something more advanced or unique. In that case, you can just use a ![icon] **Camera** node and script the desired behavior yourself.

Summary

In this hour, you've learned about the spatial node, and how to recognize and use 3D nodes. You've learned how to import 3D models and meshes into Godot and use them in a scene. You've learned how to navigate around the 3D world, and how to make the most of the 3D editor. Finally, you've learned how to create and set up cameras, what to do with multiple cameras, and how to script camera behavior.

Q&A

Q. Can I use 2D nodes in a 3D game?

A. Yes, 2D nodes can be used, and they will be fixed to the camera screen. Obviously, you can use all ![icon] **Control** nodes, which are 2D by nature, for the GUI of your game. Other 2D nodes, such as the ![icon] **TouchScreenButton**, work exactly the same in 2D and 3D, and should be used in both. But besides that, most 2D nodes should be replaced by a 3D counterpart or a GUI node. And some nodes simply don't do anything in 3D, such as the ![icon] **Camera2D** node.

Q. How do I detect what's under my mouse in 3D?

A. In 2D, if you want to check if a Sprite was clicked, you can just use an Area2D and signals that check whether the area was entered or exited.

As you might have guessed, it's not so simple in 3D. Usually, raycasts are used, which are invisible lines shot from the camera toward the 3D world. These raycasts check whether the line is obstructed by any object. They are too complex to discuss here, but remember them, as they are very useful.

Q. Help—my object doesn't rotate the way I want it to! What do I do?

A. 3D rotation is a tough subject. If you rotate multiple axes at the same time in the wrong way, you could get something called "gimbal lock." It's a transform configuration in which you suddenly lose a degree of freedom and can only rotate around two axes. Usually, people resort to other rotation measures, such as quaternions or using the transform matrix that was covered earlier.

Workshop

Now that you have finished the hour, take a few moments to review and see if you can answer the following questions.

Quiz

1. Which three fundamental actions can you perform on any 3D node?

2. One can switch to the 3D editor by pressing the _____ key.

3. Which axis points upward in Godot?

4. True or False: Importing in Godot happens automatically when you place a file in the project folder.

5. True or False: A .obj mesh can also contain other elements, such as lights and cameras.

6. True or False: You can only have a single camera per viewport in a 3D scene.

7. True or False: The **Camera** node automatically smoothens movement.

8. Which data type should be used to contain 3D (X, Y, and Z) data?

Answers

1. Translate, rotate, and scale.

2. F2.

3. The y-axis.

4. True. You can, however, choose different settings and reimport if you want.

5. False. A mesh contains only a single 3D object, while a .dae scene contains everything.

6. False. You can have multiple cameras per viewpoint, though you need to choose which one you want to use by setting the current property.

7. False. You need to script that yourself or use an **InterpolatedCamera** node.

8. The `Vector3 (X, Y, Z)` data type.

Exercises

In this exercise, we will be creating a 3D "city" and writing a script that allows the camera to navigate it, just like in a city-building game.

1. Go to your favorite 3D-modeling software and create something that vaguely resembles a (small) city. Use cylinders, cubes, and pyramids to create simple buildings.

2. Import your creation into Godot. Make sure you allow the individual buildings to be edited one way or another.

3. If not already in the scene, add a light so that you can see the city well.

4. Add a camera and point it toward the city. Attach a script to the camera so that it moves left/right/forward/backward when you press the arrow keys on the keyboard. (Bonus points if you can make that movement smooth.)

5. Allow the camera to zoom in/out when the user scrolls his mouse scroll wheel.

6. BONUS: Create an animation for a building that makes it jump up and down. Start this animation when the camera gets within a certain distance of this building.

7. BONUS (hard): Write a script so that every building within the vicinity of the camera starts jumping up and down. (I don't recommend an animation for this, but rather using code to make buildings jump.)

Bonus Exercise: We'll be creating a very simple racing game.

1. Create a simple 3D mesh (such as a cube), and import it in to Godot. This will be a car.

2. Duplicate this mesh a few times and number each logically.

3. Attach a camera to each car and make sure each camera follows its own car.

4. Write a script that keeps track of which car you're currently controlling. When you press a certain button (say, "K"), it should switch to the next car.

5. In the same script, add an input handler. Write code so that the car you're currently controlling (and *only* that car) responds to the arrow keys for movement. For the best visual results, rotate the car in the right direction. (In such a simple environment with few reference points, it can otherwise be hard to tell where your mesh is actually going.)

6. Now you should be able to control one car at a time and jump from car to car by pressing the "K" button.

HOUR 14
Project Management

What You'll Learn in This Hour:

▶ Importing resources into a Godot Engine project
▶ Organizing the project directories
▶ Using Version Control Software (Git) with the project

In this hour, we will look at some of the tasks related to the project directory. We'll learn about types of resources and how to import resource files to use in the project. Then, we'll look at the preferred way of organizing project files that work well with the engine. Finally, we will learn about how to use Version Control Software, such as Git, with a Godot Engine project in a way that minimizes unnecessary conflicts.

Importing Resources

Before a file can be used as a game resource, it needs to be imported so that the engine knows what to do with it. Some files need to be processed prior to usage.

Supported Extensions

Godot Engine supports many resource extensions. It is advised that you check if the format is supported by the engine before creating resources, as converting them afterward might adversely affect their quality (Table 14.1).

If the file is not supported by the engine, it will not show up in the FileSystem dock at all.

TABLE 14.1   **Recognized Extensions and Their Corresponding Resource Type**

Resource Type	Extensions
AudioStreamOGGVorbis	.ogg
AudioStreamOpus	.opus
AudioStreamSample	.wav
Texture	.dds, .pkm, .pvr
StreamTexture	.exr, .hdr, .jpg, .jpeg, .png, .svg, .svgz, .tga, .webp
GDScript	.gd, .gdc, .gde
VisualScript	.vs
NativeScript	.gdns
Theme	.theme
Translation	.csv, .po
DynamicFontData	.ttf, .otf
BitMap	.pbm
Mesh	.obj
PackedScene	.tscn, .gltf, .glb, .obj, .dae
Resource	.tres (plain text), .res (binary)

Drag and Drop

The simplest way to import resources is to drop it inside the project directory where the project. godot file is located. Once you switch back to the engine, it will start the import process automatically with the default preset. The import process may take a while and cannot be interrupted. Once it's done, it will show up in the FileSystem dock with a resource type icon at its upper-left corner.

Import Dock

If the default preset is not desired, you can select them in the FileSystem dock, go to the Import dock (Figure 14.1), change import the settings, and then click the "Reimport" button. If you want the subsequent files to be imported with the same parameters, click "Preset" and choose "Set as Default."

FIGURE 14.1
Import Dock.

Using the Import Dock to Import Pixel Art

By default, Godot will import Textures with the filter enabled so that they are interpolated when scaled. This works well for most images, but pixel art might look blurry, because their pixels are not meant to be interpolated.

1. Get a pixel art image or create one.

2. Drag and drop it inside the project root.

3. Switch back to the Editor, apply it to a Sprite2D node and scale it. Notice that it looks blurry.

4. Select the file in the FileSystem dock, go to the Import dock and remove the check mark at the 'Filter' option. You can also click 'Preset' and select '2D Pixel.'

5. Click 'Reimport' and look for differences in the scaled Sprite2D node.

Post Import

When the editor finishes importing, it will create a `*.import` file for each imported asset. These files contain import parameters of the asset file with the same name. Imported data will be inside the `res://.import` folder. If this folder is deleted, the editor will regenerate it using the resource files and its respective `*.import` file.

Organizing Project Directories

The heart of the Godot Engine is at its Node system. To maximize productivity, project organization must take the Node system into account. This extends to directory organization inside a project.

Small Projects

For small projects containing about ten scenes or less, you can put your files and folders in whatever way you find them most comfortable. You can also put everything at the project root as long as you can find what you want quickly (see Listing 14.1). The organization of directories in small projects is generally not much of a concern.

LISTING 14.1   Arrange All Project Files in the Project Root

```
/
/project.godot
/main.tscn
/level_1.tscn
/level_2.tscn
/player.tscn
/player.png
/enemy.tscn
/enemy.png
```

Larger Projects

When your scenes and resources grow, you might think about organizing them in some way. Many will try to put them in folders by type (Scenes, Audio, and Images) as many other engines require this specific folder structure and users of these engines are used to it (see Listing 14.2). This is not the case with Godot and is **not recommended** because the in-game contexts between files are lost.

LISTING 14.2   Arrange Project Files by Type (Not Recommended)

```
/
/project.godot
/scenes
/scenes/main.tscn
/scenes/level_1.tscn
/scenes/level_2.tscn
/scenes/player.tscn
/scenes/enemy.tscn
/images
/images/player.png
/images/enemy.png
```

Organize by Content

The recommended way to organize project directories is to put the scene files and resources of the same in-game object in one folder. Then arrange the folders by in-game context (see LIsting 14.3). This way, a scene and its resources are in the same place and can be easily looked up, edited, and refactored. Moreover, this structure works well with the Node system, as most nodes in a scene are arranged by their in-game relationship.

LISTING 14.3   Arrange Project Files by Content

```
/
/project.godot
/main.tscn
/levels
/levels/level_1.tscn
/levels/level_2.tscn
/entities
/entities/player
/entities/player/player.tscn
/entities/player/player.png
/entities/enemy
/entities/enemy/enemy.tscn
/entities/enemy/enemy.png
```

Version Control Software

Version control software (VCS) is a program that can be used to track changes between versions, synchronize and merge files from various contributors, find a specific version that introduces an issue, and so on. They're mostly used in programming, but can be adapted for use in other works. Godot is created with open-source and VCS in mind, thus, project files can be saved in a text format that is compatible with most VCS. In this topic, we'll learn about how to use Git, a widely used VCS, with a Godot project. This topic assumes that Git is already downloaded and installed.

Text Format

VCS works well with files that are in plain text, such as source code, but does not work as well with binary files, such as samples or images. Scenes and resources can be saved in a VCS-friendly text format (see Listing 14.4). You can do this by choosing the .tscn extension for scenes, .tres for resources, and .gd for GDScript when saving. Saving project files in plain text format has a lot of benefit and is recommended even if no VCS is used. The data are human readable and can be changed with a text editor in case they are corrupted and cannot be opened in the Godot Engine editor.

Godot Engine text format is inspired by TOML (Tom's Obvious, Minimal Language). It has been modified to adhere to Godot's own specifications.

LISTING 14.4   Example of Text Format Resource File (default_env.tres)

```
[gd_resource type="Environment" load_steps=2 format=2]

[sub_resource type="ProceduralSky" id=1]

radiance_size = 4
sky_top_color = Color( 0.0470588, 0.454902, 0.976471, 1 )
sky_horizon_color = Color( 0.556863, 0.823529, 0.909804, 1 )
sky_curve = 0.25
sky_energy = 1.0
ground_bottom_color = Color( 0.101961, 0.145098, 0.188235, 1 )
ground_horizon_color = Color( 0.482353, 0.788235, 0.952941, 1 )
ground_curve = 0.01
ground_energy = 1.0
sun_color = Color( 1, 1, 1, 1 )

[resource]

background_mode = 2
background_sky = SubResource( 1 )
background_sky_custom_fov = 0.0
```

Content of the file is divided into sections inside square brackets. A member variable name is to the left side of an equal sign and its value is to the right. One line defines one variable only. This is because VCS operates at line level for text files. Source code files from various developers can be merged automatically assuming they didn't change the same portion of the code.

Repository Structure

There are at least three ways to create a repository for a Godot project. It is advised that you choose the folder structure carefully before making a repository, because moving folders around often will make it more difficult to view older changes.

Project Root as Repository

The simpler way is to create the repository so that the project root and repository root are in the same directory. The repository root, where the `.git` folder is, should contain the `project.godot` file. This is very straightforward, as shown in Listing 14.5.

LISTING 14.5   Project Root as a Repository Root

```
/
/.git
/project.godot
/main.tscn
/player.tscn
/player.png
/enemy.tscn
/enemy.png
```

Project as a Sub-Directory

There might be some files related to the project that are not part of the game, such as concept art, storyline, and level design. You might want these files managed by VCS too. This can be done by having the project root at least one subfolder deep in the repository (see Listing 14.6). You can put these files you want to be managed by VCS inside the repository but outside of the project.

LISTING 14.6   Project Root as a Repository Root

```
/
/.git
/game
/game/project.godot
/game/main.tscn
/game/player.tscn
/game/player.png
/game/enemy.tscn
/game/enemy.png
/concept
/concept/player_draft.png
/docs
/docs/storyline.txt
```

Multiple Projects in a Repository

This method might be suitable for situations where there is a large number of small projects, such as a demo or showcase. You may create a repository once and create multiple projects inside it as subfolders (see Listing 14.7). The Godot Engine demo projects repository uses this method.

LISTING 14.7   Project Root as a Repository Root

```
/
/.git
/hello_world
/hello_world/project.godot
/hello_world/main.tscn
/test_physics
/test_physics/project.godot
/test_physics/main.tscn
/multiplayer_demo
/multiplayer_demo/project.godot
/multiplayer_demo/main.tscn
```

Create a Repository

This can be done using the operating system's command prompt or terminal. Navigate to the directory you want to be the repository root and type `git init`. This will create a hidden folder named `.git` inside. Then, launch the editor and create a new project inside the repository as planned in the previous step. You can also move the existing project inside too. Finally, stage and commit changes to the repository using `git add` and `git commit`.

Clone a Repository

If you work in a team and want to make changes to the project without overwriting others' changes, you may clone the repository using `git clone`, make changes to your local copy, commit and push it back to the original repository using `git push`.

Making a Branch

Branching is useful when you want to test new features, but don't want to risk breaking the existing code. New branch can be created using `git branch` command.

Cloning a Godot Demo Projects Repository

The following list shows you how to download demo projects using Git.

1. Git clone https://github.com/godotengine/godot-demo-projects.git

2. cd godot-demo-projects

Fork, Clone, and Push

The following list shows you how to push changes back to the original repository (assuming the branch and remote name are not changed).

`'upstream'` is godotengine/godot-demo-projects on GitHub.

`'origin'` is /godot-demo-projects on GitHub.

1. Use Fork function on the repository page on GitHub

2. Git clone https://github.com/godotengine/godot-demo-projects

3. cd godot-demo-projects

4. Make some local changes and commit.

5. Git push origin master

6. To make a Pull Request to upstream (godotengine), please look at `CONTRIBUTING.md` in the upstream's main repository first (godotengine/godot).

TIP

GITIGNORE

You can create a file named `.gitignore` that contains the name of the files or folders that you don't want to be included to the repository. You can also use the asterisk (*) as a wildcard, i.e. adding `*.exe` to it will tell Git to ignore changes done to any Windows executable files inside the repository folder.

Summary

In this hour, we've learned about importing the workflow of the Godot Engine. Importing can be done by moving asset files inside the project folder with the editor will taking care of the process automatically. If you want to customize how assets should be imported, use the Import Dock to set the import parameters and reimport. We've also learned about organizing files and folders inside the project. Generally, you want to arrange them by in-game context. Finally, we've tried using VCS with a Godot project.

Q&A

Q. Why is TTF and OTF fonts imported as DynamicFontData, and not DynamicFont?

A. This is because of the fact that DynamicFont can contain more than one DynamicFontData as fallback. DynamicFont must be manually created in the Inspector. After that, you can add one or more DynamicFontData to it.

Q. How do you import and use a CSV file for translation?

A. If imported successfully, importer will generate `.po` files from the CSV file. You may put them in `'Translation'` inside the Project Settings dialog (`Project > Project Settings > Localization > Translations`).

Workshop

Let's recall the contents of this hour by answering these questions.

Quiz

1. Which one of the following extensions is supported by Godot Engine: `mp3`, `ogg`, `mid`, `mp4`, or `m4a`?

2. Which one of the following extensions is **not** supported by Godot Engine: `png`, `jpg`, `svg`, `gif`, or `tga`?

3. Where do you adjust parameters for imported textures?

4. Where are the imported data stored?

Answers

1. `ogg` (OGG Vorbis)

2. `gif` (Graphics Interchange Format)

3. Import Dock

4. `res://.import` folder

Exercises

Try to execute these exercises to get acquainted with this topic.

1. Create a new project and import at least one file for each of the following extensions: `ogg`, `svg`, `csv`, `ttf`, `gltf`.

2. Use VCS with projects from previous chapters.

HOUR 15
Materials and Shaders

What You'll Learn in This Hour:

- ▶ Making 2D materials in Godot
- ▶ Making 3D materials
- ▶ Applying multiple material passes
- ▶ Writing simple shaders

In this hour, you'll learn about materials in Godot. First, you'll see the simple 2D materials, then you'll learn about the complex but powerful 3D materials. You'll also learn how to write shaders and add nice effects to your scenes.

Canvas Item Materials

Materials are special resources that change the appearance of the objects, which are especially useful for 3D models. The 2D materials are extremely simple. There's nothing much you can do in this matter, because the 2D engine is based in pixels and textures drawn directly into the screen and without the need to process vertex positions and lighting, which is needed in 3D.

To add a material to a node, it must be derived from ⦿ Node2D or ⦿ Control. Then, using Inspector, you can set the material property to a new ▭ CanvasItemMaterial resource. If you click to edit it, you'll notice there's only two properties.

Blend mode sets up how the node will be inserted into the canvas. It's like what you can see in graphical editing software. The options are not as extensive, but they are enough for most of the games. Table 15.1 shows the different blending modes, and the effects are shown in Figure 15.1.

TABLE 15.1   **Blend Modes**

Property	Description
Mix	Mixes the image in the regular way, i.e., renders it on top of the background, replacing the pixels.
Add	Sets the color as the addition between the background and the texture, summing the RGB values.
Sub	Subtracts the color values of the texture from the background. It can generate an effect of a negative if the background is transparent.
Mul	Multiplies the values of the background and the texture colors.
Premult Alpha	Pre-multiplies the alpha values of the texture. Usually, the RGB values are independent from the alpha, but with this mode, the final output is the color values multiplied by the alpha value. This is used to achieve a more correct blending between objects, but it has to be set in the texture at import time as well as in the material.

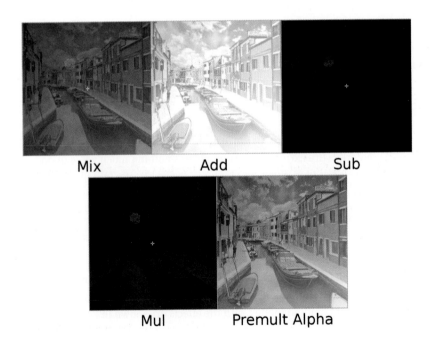

FIGURE 15.1
Effects of different blending modes.

The other option for this type of material is the Light mode. It indicates how lights interact with an object, and is useful for creating a masking effect, as will be seen in the next hour.

Render Priority and Next Pass

These two options are common in every type of material, including the shader and particle types. The Render Priority is used for objects with no depth test to decide which will be shown in front (higher priority objects are shown first).

The Next Pass property allows you to set up a chain of materials that are used in order. This allows you to make more complex effects and, for instance, add a shader code to regular material.

Other Canvas Item Properties

Despite not being part of materials, there are a few properties in the ✎ CanvasItem node that have functions to change the appearance of objects.

The Visible property name speaks for itself. This is the property with which you interact when clicking the eye icon in the Scene dock. Another simple property is the Show Behind Parent. Usually, the nodes lower in the tree are shown on top, so this property allows you to reverse the behavior for certain items.

The Modulate and Self Modulate settings apply a tint to an object, and the alpha value can be used to make it transparent. The difference between the two is that Self Modulate applies only to the object, while Modulate also applies to the object's children.

Spatial Materials

Spatial materials are applied to 3D models, so the project can become quite complex and full of options. Still, most of the options are quite common for 3D artists and can be found on modeler software. Godot 3 uses a physically based rendering (PBR) workflow, the current modern standard for 3D shading, as opposed to the classic Phong shading.

⬢ SpatialMaterial can be either imported from an external model such as a GL Transfer Format (GLTF) file exported from a 3D modeler software or developed directly in Godot itself using Inspector. You can create a new ⬢ SpatialMaterial resource by setting the Material property of an object that accepts it (such as the **MeshInstance** node or the **Mesh** resource).

Flags

The first section of the material properties is called Flags (see Table 15.2). It sets a few options that change how the material behaves in general. These options may take a hit on performance, so you'll need to consider what you really need when changing them (see Figure 15.2).

TABLE 15.2   SpatialMaterial Flags

Property	Description
Transparent	If enabled, the material will be treated as transparent. This is not enabled by default, because transparent objects are rendered with a different, more expensive technique. Some effects need opaque materials to work (such as SSAO), and won't be available for transparent items.
Unshaded	Disables the effect of light onto the object and shows its own default color.
Vertex Lighting	Godot uses a per-pixel lighting by default, which usually gives better results. But this can be too costly in some cases, especially on low-end devices, so you can enable per-vertex lighting, which needs less computational power. Note that only directional lights produce shadows if this is enabled.
No Depth Test	Usually, objects appear in front of the ones in the back. You can change this behavior by enabling this option so that objects are drawn in front of everything else, independent of position. With this, you can make use of the Render Priority property presented in the last note.
Use Point Size	If the imported geometry is made of points (instead of triangles, as is more usual), you can use point size to render. Check the Parameters section to specify the point size.
World Triplanar	If you're using triplanar mapping, this makes the material use coordinates in world-space instead of the default local-space.
Fixed Size	When this is enabled, the object is always drawn in the same size, irrespective to its distance to the camera.

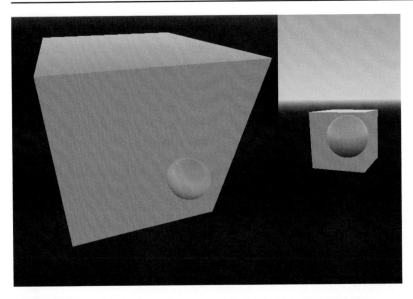

FIGURE 15.2
The sphere has a fixed size and no depth test, so it's always in front and doesn't get smaller with distance unlike the cube. This can be used for visual indicators.

Vertex Color

Usually, Godot ignores the vertex colors of the geometry. If you want to use them, you'll need to enable the Use as Albedo property. Many 3D modeling software uses the SGRB color space when exporting, so if the vertex colors are in this format, you'll need to tell the engine to correct the colors.

Parameters

The following section in the material configuration has several parameters to set up rendering details. You can use this to tweak the material or achieve special effects.

Diffuse Mode

In this mode, you can select a different algorithm for diffuse. This changes how the light is scattered when it hits an object. Table 15.3 lists the available modes, and Figure 15.3 shows the modes.

TABLE 15.3   SpatialMaterial Diffuse Modes

Mode	Description
Lambert	The default mode. It reflects the light equally from all viewing angles, and isn't affected by roughness.
Lambert Wrap	Extends the previous algorithm to cover a larger area when roughness increases.
Oren Nayar	Creates a virtual roughness to the material and treats the surface as imperfect, which changes the reflection of light depending on the angle (from the viewer's position). This is an interesting effect to apply on clothing and clay.
Burley	Uses the original physically based shading (PBS) material developed by Brent Burley at Walt Disney Animation Studios.
Toon	In this mode, the light is cut hard (like a cartoon). The smoothness can be tweaked with the roughness property.

FIGURE 15.3
Different diffuse modes (in the order presented in Table 15.3).

Specular Mode

This affects the specular highlight point on the object. This is an important detail in determining the shape and position of objects by the human eye, and also represents the shape of the light source.

The Schlick-GGX mode is the most common in modern PBR engines, and is a sane default for most applications. Blinn and Phong modes are used by old renderers and are available for compatibility purposes, but they aren't very useful unless you're going for a retro feel. Toon mode creates a cartoon-like specular blob, and its size varies with the roughness property.

TIP

Disabling the Specular Highlight

While the Specular highlight is a cool effect that gives a somewhat realistic feel to your scene, sometimes it gets in the way. You can disable it completely by selecting this option in the Specular mode property.

Blend Mode

Determines how the material will be mixed into the scene. This is the same as the one available in **CanvasItemMaterial**, so you can refer to Table 15.1 to see what each mode does.

Other Parameters

You can change the Culling mode of the objects too. The default is Back mode, which hides the back faces of the object. If set to Front mode, only the back faces will be visible. Disabled mode makes the object double-sided.

You can also specify depth rendering using the Depth Draw mode property. This especially affects how partially transparent objects, such as foliage or hair, will look and cast shadows. You can set to draw depth for opaque only, which is the sane default. It's possible to set it to Always or Never, too. The remaining option is the Opaque Pre-Pass mode, which will make a pass for opaque parts and a second pass on top for transparent parts.

Line Width and Point Size adjust the size of the lines and points, respectively. Line Width is usually not available on modern hardware, and Point Size only makes sense for point-based geometry.

Billboard mode specifies how an object faces the camera. Enabled mode will make the negative Z-axis of an object always face the camera. The Y-Billboard option will align the X-axis instead. There's also a mode specific for particles, which enables animation options.

The Grow option makes the vertices of the objects move away, following their normal vectors. This can be useful in a second-pass material for some effects. The Alpha Scissor option cuts the alpha of the material based on a threshold, so it's rendered always as 0 or 1, never in between. This can also be useful, as the material can be treated as opaque and receive the mid- and post-processing effects that rely on this (such as SSAO and SSR).

Albedo

This is where the main colors of the object are defined. This was done in the Diffuse channel in previous rendering engine generations, but the Albedo does more than diffuse light. This is the only thing visible if the Unshaded option is enabled.

There's both a color and a texture, which can be used together since their values are multiplied to get the final color. If the color is white, the albedo texture will be shown as is. The resulting alpha value will be used from a transparent if either the Transparent flag or the Alpha Scissor option is active.

Metallic and Roughness

These are the main parameters of the PBR workflow used by Godot 3. They are important settings in the PBR workflow, and most materials can be reproduced by fine-tuning them.

The Metallic property determines the reflectivity of a material. A higher value makes it reflect more light. Note that it's impossible to make a material totally unreflective. Even if you set this property to 0, Godot will use the minimum reflectivity of four percent.

Roughness indicates how the reflection happens. A material without roughness acts as a perfect mirror (see Figure 15.4). As you add to this value, it starts blurring the reflection, mimicking the effects of a micro-surface as in real life.

FIGURE 15.4
Different values for Metallic and Roughness properties. The first row shows 0
Metallic with both 0 and 1 Roughness. The second row shows the same values for
Roughness but with Metallic set to 1.

NOTE

Specular/Glossiness versus Metallic/Roughness

You may have heard this discussion if you searched the web for PBR. Godot 3 supports only the Metallic/Roughness approach, which is more closely related to how materials work in the real world. Other game engines use the Specular/Glossiness workflow, while some support both. This is something to keep in mind when designing your assets, since the conversion between the two systems isn't straightforward.

Other Properties

There's a lot of detail in the 🔷 SpatialMaterial properties. Table 15.4 shows properties not mentioned so far. You can get more information by looking at Godot's documentation.

TABLE 15.4   Remaining SpatialMaterial Properties

Property	Description
Emission	Makes the object emit light. It will not illuminate its surroundings unless used within a GIProbe.
Normal Map	Changes the angle of the reflecting light, allowing for greater detail without making the geometry more complex.
Rim	Makes a micro rim around the object, like the fur around some types of fabric. Note that this depends on incident light.
Clear Coat	Simulates the effect of coating or waxing the object.
Anisotropy	Changes the Specular highlight to make it follow the surface. It works better when combined with a flow map (which can be set in the same section).
Ambient Occlusion	Lets you set a texture with the baked occlusion from ambient light. This can make the scene look better than with a generated occlusion (such as SSAO).
Depth	Allows you to add a depth map, which can increase the effectiveness of a normal map by giving the illusion of depth without complex geometry.
Subsurface Scattering	Simulates how light penetrates a surface and is reflected back to the exterior after being scattered. This is very useful in creating realistic-looking skin.
Transmission	Sets up the transmission of light from the lit side to the dark side. It's useful for thin objects.
Refraction	Changes the alpha blend mode to show the content behind the object in a distorted way, similar to how refracted light would behave in the real world.
Detail	Uses a secondary albedo and normal map to achieve detailed textures, allowing you to combine them in interesting ways.
UV1 and UV2	Lets you change the scale, offset, and triplanar properties of the two UV channels supported by Godot.
Proximity and Distance Fade	Adds effects that change the transparency of objects based on their proximity to other objects or the distance from the viewer. Can be used for interesting effects, but should be used with care because of the added transparency.

Shader Basics

Shaders are programs that run directly in the GPU. They change the appearance of items on the screen and dictate how they should be drawn. Internally, every material in Godot is a shader, but this is abstracted away from you for the sake of simplicity and flexibility. Still, Godot gives you the ability to create custom shaders that complement or replace the regular material.

NOTE

Shader Language

If you're familiar with the graphics pipeline or with other engines, you might be used to writing shader code in GLSL or HLSL (the shader languages for OpenGL and DirectX, respectively). Godot does not allow you to write the code directly for the GPU.

Instead, it provides its own shading language very similar to GLSL by letting you write simple shaders without having to worry about the entire pipeline. This has the added benefit of letting you see the shader changes in real-time in the editor and detect errors as you type.

Shader Material

The first step to take when you want to write shaders is to create a new ![icon] **ShaderMaterial** resource and apply it to the Material property of the node. This can be done for 3D and 2D objects alike. Then you'll need to set the Shader property to a new ![icon] **Shader** resource, which will show the editor for your code.

Shader Language

Since the language is like GLSL, it follows the same conventions, which are akin to C++ too. The code is case-sensitive, and each statement needs to end with a semicolon (;). Variables are declared by stating the type followed by the variable name (see LIsting 15.1). Similarly, functions are declared using the return type followed by the function name, then all the need arguments are placed between parentheses. The function body is delimited by curly braces ({ }).

The first line of your shader code must specify the shader type. Three possible values are available: `spatial` (for 3D objects), `canvas_item` (for 2D and Control items), and `particles` (for the particle system). After that, you can optionally specify the render modes.

There are three phases of the shading process, which can be accessed by using specially named functions. The Vertex processor alters each vertex in the object. The Fragment function runs for every pixel before the output. Finally, the Light function affects how the light is applied to the object. For particle shaders, only the Vertex function is used.

LISTING 15.1   Shader Structure

```
shader_type spatial;
render_mode cull_disabled, diffuse_toon;

void vertex() {
    // Vertex Processing
    VERTEX.x += sin(TIME);
    VERTEX.y += cos(TIME);
}

void fragment() {
    // Fragment processing
    ALBEDO.r = 1.0;
}

void light() {
    // Light processing
    DIFFUSE_LIGHT = ALBEDO * ATTENUATION;
}
```

TIP

Uniforms

Uniforms are used to pass values from the outside world into the shader code. These are variables declared on the top level of the code, and their values are available in all the shader processing functions.

Once a Uniform is declared, its value can be edited in Inspector on the ⬛ **ShaderMaterial** resource properties. It can also be set via code using the `set_shader_param()` method.

Vertex Processing

The first step in the shader process is vertex shading, which handles both the position and the vertex in the geometry. For instance, you can create waves in an ocean by changing the position of vertices over time.

TRY IT YOURSELF ▼

Simple Vertex Shader

In this simple exercise, we will make a very basic vertex shader to manipulate the geometry of a primitive mesh.

1. Create a new scene in the editor.

2. Add a ⬤ **Spatial** node as the root.

3. Add a ▦ **MeshInstance** node. Set the Mesh property to a new ⊕ **SphereMesh**.

4. In Inspector, set the Material property of the **MeshInstance** to a new **ShaderMaterial**.

5. Create a new **Shader** for the material's shader property.

6. The shader editor will show up. Paste the following code there:

```
shader_type spatial;
render_mode cull_disabled;

void vertex() {
    VERTEX.z *= sin(TIME);
}
```

7. Observe the mesh change in the editor over time. This shader simply multiplies the Z-position of each vertex by the sine of the `TIME` variable, which is generated by Godot. Since the sine will always return a value between −1 and 1, it will collapse the sphere into a flat surface then revert its direction, repeating over time. Hence, the `cull_disabled` mode is enabled, because otherwise the sphere will look different when the faces are in the opposite direction (you can try to remove the render mode definition to see how it looks).

Vertex shaders are useful in altering the geometry of objects. You can use it to create motion effects and deformation. Note that if an object is intended to interact with other objects via the physics engine, changing its geometry will do nothing to its physical shape. Shaders are only useful for visual effects.

NOTE

Geometry Shaders

Godot 3 supports only the OpenGL ES 3.0 specification, which does not include modern geometry shaders. While the modern geometry shader is more appropriate for changing the geometry of meshes, it's not supported by low-end hardware, especially on mobile devices. Godot values better flexibility for all types of hardware over focusing on more powerful machines.

Fragment Shader

The next step of the shader process is Fragment processing. This is called by every pixel in the render, and can be used to alter how the pixels are shown.

This type of shader is used to set the final color of the object, which can be a calculated color result or part of a texture to be applied over the geometry. This can also be used to move the texture over time, making the detail of an object change (Figure 15.5).

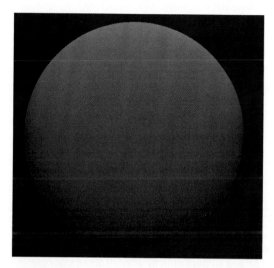

FIGURE 15.5
A simple fragment shader that replaces the Albedo
with the Normal vector. This can also be used to
debug geometry or other material properties.

Light Shader

The final step in this chain is the Light processor. Like Fragment processing, this is called for every pixel but is also called per light in the scene. If there are no lights, it will never be called. This processing is completely optional, and does not directly affect performance if set, so there's no extra cost for using Light shaders.

This can be used to change how light interacts with the material. You can change how the final lighting looks by writing to the diffuse_light variable. It's possible to completely ignore the light and act as an unshaded material. It's also possible to change the specular reflection by writing to the specular_light variable.

TIP

Converting SpatialMaterial to ShaderMaterial

Godot offers an interesting option to convert regular ⬡ SpatialMaterial into shader code. This way, you can see basically how the material behaves and tweak usage of the parameters.

To do this, click on the little down arrow beside the Material property in the inspector (or right-click it) and select the ⬛ **Convert to ShaderMaterial** option. You cannot convert it back, so be careful with this option.

Summary

In this hour, you learned about materials in Godot. You saw how to make the simple materials for 2D objects, then you learned about the different options for 3D materials. Finally, you saw the basic concepts for writing your own custom shaders.

Q&A

Q. **Can I set multiple materials to a mesh?**

A. If the imported geometry has multiple material slots, you can set each one individually in Inspector.

Q. **Why does Godot not use GLSL directly?**

A. Godot uses its own shading language for usability and portability purposes. It's much easier to write a shader in Godot, because you don't need to deal directly with attributes or color buffers (among other things), as the engine already deals with it. This also allows the editor to have code completion, error checking, and real-time visualization. It is also possible to use the same shader in different rendering backends, such as DirectX and Vulkan, if they are eventually supported.

Workshop

Try to answer the following questions to better grasp the contents of this hour.

Quiz

1. How can you add custom material to an object?

2. Where can you set the main texture of a 3D object?

3. True or False: You can't pass values from the script to a shader.

4. True or False: You can convert a 🔷 SpatialMaterial to a ⬛ ShaderMaterial.

Answers

1. By setting its Material property in Inspector.

2. In the Albedo property of the material.

3. False. You can add a Uniform variable in the shader and set it via script with the `set_shader_param()` method.

4. True. Godot has a built-in function to convert a 🔷 SpatialMaterial to a ⬛ ShaderMaterial.

Exercises

Follow this exercise to gain some insight into materials and shaders.

1. Create a new scene and add a **Spatial** node as the root. Save the scene.

2. Add a **MeshInstance** node.

3. Set the **Mesh** property to a new **SphereMesh**.

4. Add a **DirectionalLight** to the scene. Rotate it to change the default angle, making the light come from above and move down.

5. Set the **Material** property of the node to a new **SpatialMaterial**.

6. Change the **Albedo** color to something other than the default white.

7. Set both the **Metallic** and **Roughness** properties to 0.5.

8. Change the **Diffuse** and **Specular** modes to watch the difference between them.

9. Experiment with other parameters and properties.

10. Convert the material to a **ShaderMaterial**.

11. Look at the code.

12. Try changing some of the operations, and see how they affect the object.

13. Try to use the `TIME` parameter to change some properties over time.

HOUR 16
Lights and Shadows

What You'll Learn in This Hour:

▶ How to add and position lights in Godot
▶ Different types of light
▶ How to configure shadows
▶ Types of shadow filters

During this hour, you'll see how to set up lights in Godot, and how to add them to the scene and position them using the editor. You'll see how to set up the properties of lighting. You'll learn how to enable shadow and configure its properties, and how filtering works for shadows. You'll also learn about techniques such as ambient occlusion and shadow mapping.

Light Sources

An important part of a 3D scene is the lighting. It can make the mood of the scene and improve the focus of the action. You can have an outside setting where the sun is the main light source and everything is visible. You can have a claustrophobic room in a horror game with only the beam of a flashlight as a light source. These details can enrich the atmosphere of your scenes.

There are many ways to light a scene in Godot. You can use the lighting nodes, use ambient lighting from the environment, or make use of emissive materials. The combination of these techniques makes a scene shine in your game.

Directional Light

This type of light is very common in games. It represents a big source of light that is very far away, like the sun. You can have it in your scene by adding a ⬡ **DirectionalLight** node. The position of the light does not matter, so you can move it around to place the editor gizmo where it doesn't disturb you. The only important setting is the direction, which is defined by the node's rotation (Figure 16.1).

FIGURE 16.1
Directional lighting applied to a simple scene.

Since this is a very simple light, it does not have any specific properties. It's also very light on performance, because the light rays all travel in the same direction (though it doesn't have the easiest shadow mapping, as we'll see later). Still, there are a few properties inherent to every light node (see Table 16.1).

TABLE 16.1   Light Properties

Property	Description
Color	The color of the light. Setting it for something other than white will tint the environment. Setting it to black will be the same as having no light.
Energy	Sets the amount of light emitted by the node. Zero means that no light will be emitted, and values over 1 will overexpose the scene.
Negative	If enabled, the light source will emit a "shadow" (i.e., remove light from other sources).
Specular	Specifies how much of a specular highlight the materials will receive from the light source. If the value is 0, the specular property of the materials won't have any effect.
Cull Mask	Sets up the masking for reflection, and is used with a ⬇ **ReflectionProbe** node. The probe will only reflect if the masks match.
Editor Only	If enabled, the light will only be visible in the editor, not in the game. This is useful when adding extra illumination to your scene while designing a dark level.

Directional Lighting

Follow this simple exercise to see the effect of light in a scene:

1. Create a new scene and add a ⊙ **Spatial** node as the root.

2. Add a ▣ **MeshInstance** node. Set its Mesh property as a new ⬤ **CapsuleMesh**.

3. Create a ⊕ **WorldEnvironment** node and add an empty ⊕ **Environment** to it.

4. Add a ✦ **DirectionalLight** to the scene.

5. Change the rotation of the light. See how it changes the illumination of the mesh.

6. Change the position of the light. Notice that this type of light isn't affected by its position.

Omni Light

The ⦿ **OmniLight** node disperses a light in all directions from a single point (Figure 16.2). This is the equivalent of a light bulb without a lampshade, and also means that the light is attenuated for objects farther away from the source (see Table 16.2).

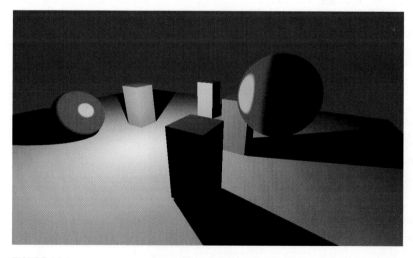

FIGURE 16.2
A simple scene with an Omni Light in the middle.

TABLE 16.2   OmniLight Properties

Property	Description
Range	Sets how far the lighting goes. It can also be edited by moving the gizmo in the visual editor.
Attenuation	Configures the attenuation curve of the emission. Higher values will make it attenuate faster (i.e., show a weaker light on distant objects).
Shadow Mode	Selects the shadow mapping technique. Dual Paraboloid is a faster method, so it has better performance (at the cost of accuracy). The Cube mode produces more accurate shadows.
Shadow Detail	Specifies the focus of the shadow detail. If you're casting the shadow onto a wall, select Vertical; if it's being cast onto a floor, select the Horizontal detail.

In the real world, lights attenuate by an inverse square law, but since that can be tricky to work with in an artistic setting, Godot provides an option to adjust the attenuation curve. This allows you to use less intense light that reaches farther away than a real lamp would. You can also do the opposite: create a bright light that doesn't reach very far.

Spot Light

The last type of 3D light node is the ▲ **SpotLight**. This is not very different than an OmniLight, except it focuses as a cone instead of spreading the light in every direction. It is very useful for flashlights, street lamps, or any source that can be pointed.

The properties of the ▲ **SpotLight** (Figure 16.3) aren't very different from the ◉ **OmniLight's**. The range is not a radius but the distance from the source. There's also an Angle property, which lets you configure the aperture of the light to make it narrower or wider. This type of light also attenuates over distance.

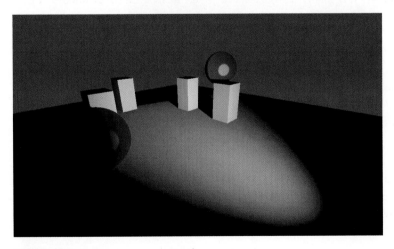

FIGURE 16.3
A SpotLight applied to a simple scene.

TIP

Choosing the Right Type of Light

Each type of light can be used in a specific situation. Note that you can put many light sources in a scene, so you are not limited to a specific one. You should mix and match different types to achieve the desired effect.

Directional lights are used to emulate the sun, and is great for outside scenes. Sometimes, you can get away with it as your single light source. Omni lights are used for sources that go in all directions, such as a lamp bulb. The spot lights can be used for flood lights and even for tractor beams.

Essentially, you should think of how the light will flow from the source. You can try different types to see what looks best for your scene. Also note that not every illumination needs to come from a light node; you can use ambient light and emissive materials too.

Other Light Sources

Besides the lighting nodes, you can use some other sources for illumination. Most come from the environment, which will be covered in greater detail in Hour 18. For the sake of completeness, let's go through the other ways to add light to a scene.

Ambient and Sky Light

The ⊕ **Environment** resource can provide illumination by itself. It can use the light from the sky or from a custom color. Note that such lighting does not have a specific source: it lights every pixel with the same intensity, so it won't produce a shadow.

Emissive Materials

The materials of the objects can emit light too. They need a 🔳 **GIProbe** node (a special node to make Global Illumination, which will be shown in Hour 18) to properly illuminate the environment around them, but this can be easily achieved. While this should not be abused and works best for static items, it provides an interesting effect, and works great for glowing objects.

Indirect Lighting

The 🔳 GIProbe node also provides indirect lighting for the scene by calculating the light that bounces off objects to illuminate others. This isn't a light source per se because it depends on other sources, but it can provide an atmospheric effect for objects that aren't lit by direct light.

Shadows

The polar opposite of a light is a shadow. To create a realistic effect, you'll need to keep light from reaching areas where the object blocks it. Objects that do not cast shadows don't seem to belong in the game world, so shadows are quite useful for creating a nice ambience.

Shadows are a property of lights, so you can configure each individually via **Light** nodes. You can even disable the shadows for a specific light (in fact, they are disabled by default). Table 16.3 shows the properties of shadows available in the Light nodes.

TABLE 16.3 Properties of Shadows

Property	Description
Enabled	Enables the propagation of shadows from the light source.
Color	Sets the color of the shadow. Realistic shadows are usually black, but you can change this for an effect or to debug lighting issues.
Bias	Adjusts where the shadow should begin. This is a useful setting for self-shadowing meshes.
Contact	If the shadows aren't touching the bottom of an object, you can adjust this value to increase the contact point.
Reverse Cull Face	If enabled, this uses the reverse face to cast the shadow (i.e., the internal faces of the mesh).

NOTE

Self-Shadowing Meshes

Sometimes, a mesh can cast a shadow upon itself. This depends on the light type and position as well as the mesh shape. It makes it hard to predict where the shadows should hit; this is why the Bias property is available.

If you're having issues with self-shadowing, even on meshes that should not do it, try adjusting the Bias and see how it affects the scene. Often, the look can be improved by changing the properties of the nodes.

Directional Light Shadows

One thing to consider when placing a DirectionalLight is that it illuminates large areas. This may become an issue, since the resolution of the shadow texture is limited. You can improve the look of the shadows by choosing a different mapping mode.

Orthogonal mode uses the same number of pixels for the entire scene, so it will use the same detail even for places far away from the camera. To mitigate that, you can use the Parallel Split Shadow Mapping (PSSM) mode, which divides the scene in two or four sections and uses less detail for farther objects, since they're visually smaller anyway. This option comes with a performance hit, as more splits consume more power.

Shadow Mapping

The term "shadow mapping" is a general concept that represents the process of computing the shadows of dynamic objects in computer graphics. The engine generates a texture that indicates where the shadow will be applied (the "map") and uses it to draw the scene.

While the algorithm is provided by Godot, it is up to the artist to configure its properties to make the scene look better.

Omni Light Shadows

For Omni Lights, generating the shadow map is also a bit troublesome, because it's hard to use a single texture that maps 360 degrees of light rays. Essentially, Godot offers two solutions for this: dual-paraboloid mapping and cube mapping.

Dual-Paraboloid Shadow Mapping (DPSM) is a fast technique that relies on a paraboloid-shaped shadow map (Figure 16.4). It facilitates the calculation of the map, but it's not very accurate. It may have poor results on weaker systems, such as mobile phones. It also may have problems if the objects aren't well tessellated (i.e., it might require more vertices in the meshes to look good). Still, if the scene looks good with this, it's likely the best option.

Cube mapping relies on a cube around the map, so it needs six textures (one for each face), and comes at the cost of GPU memory. It also needs more passes to render the shadow, making it more expensive. This mode produces more accurate shadows, though, so it might be necessary for some scenes.

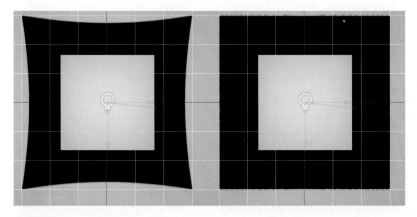

FIGURE 16.4
Dual Paraboloid Shadow Mapping (left) compared to a cube map (right). The first method is faster, but leads to imperfections.

TIP

Shadow Filter

To make the shadows look softer and less blocky, Godot uses a technique called Percentage Closer Filtering (PCF). It consists of taking more samples to decide which fragments fall under the shadow. The more samples it takes, the softer the shadow looks (at the cost of GPU resources).

The default is a safe bet, but you can change it in Project Settings (under Rendering > Quality) if you intend to have higher hardware requirements for your game.

Ambient Occlusion

Another technique to increase the shadowing of the scene is **Ambient Occlusion**. This consists of darkening the parts of the object that wouldn't be reached by direct ambient light. This type of shadow isn't generated by the lights: instead, it takes light from the material of the mesh or the environment properties.

There are essentially two possibilities for adding ambient occlusion in Godot: Screen Space Ambient Occlusion (SSAO) and the occlusion texture in the material. SSAO has the advantage of being generated by the engine, but it isn't as good-looking as a properly crafted occlusion texture.

Lights in 2D

Godot also offers the possibility of lighting in 2D games, though in a much simpler fashion given the limited dimensions for light to flow. Still, it can add a nice effect to some games.

The ⬤ Light2D node is responsible for adding light into a 2D world (Table 16.4). For it to work, you'll need to add a texture to give it shape and color. This texture will be cast onto the other objects on the screen to give them light. Notice that it doesn't affect the viewport background.

TABLE 16.4   Properties of Light2D

Property	Description
Enabled	Enable or disable the light effect.
Editor Only	Has the same function as for 3D lights. If enabled, it will only affect the editor and not the running game.
Texture	Sets the texture that makes the color and shape of the light. Gradients with alpha works very well for this property.

Property	Description
Offset	Changes the position of the light in respect to its transform. Can be used to effectively change the pivot point of rotation, and to make shake effects without affecting the transform. Also affects the point from where the light is propagated, which makes a difference when using shadows.
Texture Scale	Modifies the size of the light texture. You can use this to make the light bigger or smaller, independently of the scale of the node.
Color	Tints the light color. This is useful for making different light colors with the same texture. (Note that if you set the alpha to 0, the light won't have any effect.)
Energy	Affects how powerful the light is. A value of 0 has the same effect as disabling the light. You can set it to a value greater than 1 to have it overexposed.
Mode	Changes the alpha blending mode of the light.

NOTE

Light Range and Normal Mapping

The 🔆 **Light2D** node has a Range property section with which you can set up how the light will interact with different layers of objects. You can set a limit to the Z-range, which will affect only items that have their Z-property in that (inclusive) range. The same applies to the layer, which applies to objects that are children to a 🟦 **CanvasLayer** node.

You can also set the height of the light, though this only has a meaningful effect for Sprite nodes with a Normal Map applied. This can give the player a sense of depth without going into a 3D game.

Shadows in 2D

To stop the light from propagating, you'll need a 🔆 **LightOccluder2D** node. This prevents the light from reaching a certain area and creating shadows. Note that it only makes a difference if the 🔆 **Light2D** node has its shadows enabled.

Once you add the node, you can create a new polygon for it using the 🔹 **Create Polygon** tool in the editor. You'll need to close the polygon for it to work as intended, even if you don't need it to be closed (you can right-click in the editor to close it). While the polygon is shown with a darker tint in the editor, it won't be seen like this in the running game. Instead, it just stops the light from crossing its border (see Figure 16.5).

FIGURE 16.5
Lights and shadows in 2D.

NOTE

Light Cull Mask

Another property of the 🔆 **Light2D** node is the Light Cull Mask. This affects how the occluders are selected. A light will only affect occluders that have the same light mask, allowing you to be selective about how lights and shadows will be formed.

For instance, you can have the player character emit a light from its center but not be affected by it, while still casting shadows from other light sources.

The 🔲 **OccluderPolygon2D** resource has a couple of properties. Cull mode can change how the light is blocked, so it's possible to make an object that is fully lit but casts a shadow in the opposite direction of the light. You can also set the polygon as open so that the last side won't occlude the light.

TIP

Soft Shadows

It is possible to achieve soft shadows in 2D by changing the Gradient and Filter properties of the Shadow section in the 🔆 **Light2D** node. Check out the 2D Lighting demo available with Godot to see an example of this.

Summary

This hour covered the basic ideas of lights and shadows in Godot. First, you learned about the three direct light sources for 3D. Then you saw other options available for indirect lighting, and learned how to enable and configure shadows.

Q&A

Q. My shadows don't look right. What can I do?

A. Shadows are quite tricky to create. Essentially, you'll need to tweak the shadow settings to get a better look. Sometimes, you'll need to move things or change the geometry of your objects to help the generation of shadows.

Q. Can I have any number of lights?

A. You might hit some hard limits imposed by Godot if you add too much, but you'll likely hit hardware limits before that happens. Usually, having well-placed lights looks better than having a large amount of them.

Workshop

Answer the following questions to recapitulate this hour's content.

Quiz

1. What are the three light nodes for 3D scenes?
2. True or False: Only light nodes can provide illumination to a scene.
3. True or False: It does not matter if you change the position of **DirectionalLight**.
4. True or False: You can't have soft shadows in 2D games.

Answers

1. **DirectionalLight**, **OmniLight**, and **SpotLight**.
2. False. You can also have ambient light and emissive materials.
3. True. Directional lights simulate rays that come from a very far place, so its transform position isn't relevant.
4. False. Godot 3 provides configurable shadows in 2D that can cast soft shadows.

Exercises

Try this exercise to get a better feel of lights and shadows in Godot.

1. Create a new scene and add a ⬤ **Spatial** node as the root. Save the scene.

2. Add a ⊕ **WorldEnvironment** node. Create a new empty ⊕ **Environment** for it.

3. Create a ▧ **MeshInstance** node. Add a ◣ **PlaneMesh** primitive and set its size to (50, 50). This will be the ground.

4. Add another ▧ **MeshInstance** with a ⬡ **CapsuleMesh** attached to it. Increase its Y-axis position so it's above the ground.

5. Add a ✦ **DirectionalLight** to the scene. Enable shadow casting.

6. Change the rotation of the light. Note how it affects the illumination of the floor and the capsule.

7. Disable the visibility of the light so that it has no effect.

8. Add an ⬤ **OmniLight** node. Remember to enable the shadows on it.

9. Change its position and range. See the effects of the properties in the scene.

10. Disable the visibility on this light too.

11. Now add a ▣ **SpotLight** to the scene and activate its shadows.

12. Again, change its properties to light the object and see how it affects the objects in the scene.

Game 2: Bloxorz Clone

What You'll Learn in This Hour:

▶ Using 3D objects in a game project
▶ Making custom transformations on physics objects
▶ Detecting an out-of-bounds player for a losing condition
▶ Using the GridMap node
▶ Loading different levels dynamically

In this hour, you will make a 3D rolling block puzzle game. You'll see the main concept of the game and how it is structured. Then you'll see how to create the scenes and develop each level. From there, you'll add the scripts to handle the movements and detect winning/losing conditions. Finally, you'll play the game yourself and have fun!

Concept and Design

This game is a relatively simple, but challenging puzzle game. The player controls a rectangular prism, which has a square base and a height two times taller than the base. The player needs to roll it around to fit the square hole in the middle of the floor. Once he does so, he will advance to the next level. If he falls to the sides, he will lose and get respawned at the beginning. The floor consists of square tiles that form a different path each level. The player needs to be creative in each level to roll the block around and finish in the right position to fall through the ending level. Ideally, he should use the least possible number of moves.

Design Ideas

Let's take some time to decide how to structure our game scenes. First, the moving block should be a simple mesh, so we can use a ▨ **MeshInstance** node to hold it. The block itself can be a ⚙ **RigidBody** to make use of gravity when falling.

The floor is a square grid, which makes it easy to use a ▦ **GridMap** node to lay it out. This node acts as a TileMap (as shown in Hour 3), but for the 3D space, laying pre-made blocks in a grid. For this, you will need to also make a ▥ **MeshLibrary** even though it consists of a single tile type.

The ending will be checked with an ▣ **Area**, and another will be used to set the inbounds of the level. Once the player leaves this area, he won't be able to control the block until it respawns. Each level should have its own spawn point, which can be set with a ✚ **Position3D** node.

For the code part, you will make use of a few simple state machines to determine the transitions and winning/losing conditions based on the current orientation and rest position of the block (whether it's standing or lying). A few ▨ **Timer** nodes will set the wait times for respawning and avoid player movement before the block is ready. Signals will be used to communicate between different scenes. A singleton will be used to find the levels and to keep track of the current one.

Game Scenes

Break everything down in scenes to help structure the game with the employment of reusable components. Table 17.1 shows the description of each scene.

TABLE 17.1   Bloxorz Game Scenes

Scene	Description
Game	The main scene. This is where the game starts and everything is connected. Put here the ◉ **WorldEnvironment**, the ▓ **DirectionalLight**, and the ▣ **Camera**. It will also load the block and levels.
Block	The controllable block. This scene will be based on a ◉ **Spatial**. It will contain the ◉ **RigidBody** and ▨ **MeshInstance** to represent the block itself. There will be a couple of ▣ **Area** nodes to control the out-of-bounds checking. You'll also use a couple of ▨ **Timer** nodes for some controls.
Levels	Each level will be its own scene. You will make a base scene with all the components: ▣ **GridMap** for layout, ▣ **Area** nodes for ending and inbounds check, and ✚ **Position3D** for the spawning point. The specific levels will inherit this scene and change the parameters.
Meshlib	There'll be also a scene to convert into a ▨ **MeshLibrary** for use with the ▣ **GridMap**.

Making the Scenes

There's not much to change in the Project Settings. Since this is a 3D project, the window size is quite flexible, and resizing just changes the amount of area seen by the camera. Yet, there's a bit of configuration that can make life a bit easier.

First, let's change the default gravity. The block should fall quite quickly, so increase it to about 50. You can set that under **Physic > 3d > Default Gravity** in the Project Settings. You should also give names to the physics layers to make it easier to set on the objects without getting lost (Table 17.2). This can be done under **Layer Names > 3d Physics**.

TABLE 17.2   Layer Names

Layer	Name
Layer 1	**Floor**. This is the one applied to the ![icon] **GridMap**.
Layer 2	**Block**. This will be applied to your controllable character.
Layer 3	**Bound**. It represents the ending and inbounds areas.

TIP

Orthogonal versus Perspective

Since this is a grid-based game, it makes sense to use the orthogonal view so that all of the squares are equal in size. You can toggle the view between perspective and orthogonal in the Viewport menu (which is on the top left of each viewport) or by pressing the 5 key on the numeric keypad.

Mesh Library Scene

A good place to start is the Mesh Library source scene. This is the base for the ![icon] GridMap, and can be changed later to tweak the floor if needed.

Start by creating an empty scene. Add a ![icon] Spatial node as the root so it will be considered a 3D scene. In the ![icon] MeshLibrary, there are a collection of ![icon] MeshInstance nodes. Add one, and call it "Floor." For its **Mesh** property, add a new ![icon] CubeMesh. Set the size of the mesh to (0.95, 0.1, 0.95). This will make it a short square tile. It will be a little smaller than the unit square to make the grid more visible.

Add a ![icon] SpatialMaterial to the resource. Note to add it to the ![icon] CubeMesh resource and not to the ![icon] MeshInstance node. This will ensure that the material is properly applied to the final object in the ![icon] GridMap. A trick to add a simple outline is to add material to the **Next Pass** property. In this new material, set it to Unshaded, add a Grow of 0.01, change the Cull mode to front, and set its color to black. This outline is not perfect, but it should be enough for this simple game.

You'll want the player body to fall in the starting block and avoid falling through it when the game is lost. For this, you'll need a collision body. To acquire that in a Mesh Library, add a ![icon] StaticBody node as a child of the ![icon] MeshInstance. This will be kept when converted. You can then add a ![icon] CollisionShape node to it and set the Shape property to a new ![icon] BoxShape. Set its Extends to (0.45, 0.05, 0.45). This is half the tile size, because the shape uses this property as a radius and not as length. It's also a bit smaller than the actual size to make the ending hole wide enough for the block to fall through.

TIP

Better Graphics

This example game is very simple, and by that standard, it uses only simple materials without any texture. You can improve on this by making custom textures and tweaking the materials to make the visuals more vibrant.

With the mesh and its collision, the scene is complete. Save it as "meshlib.tscn" to be a reference if something needs to be changed. Then click on **Scene > Convert To > MeshLibrary** to create the resource. Save this as "meshlib.meshlib." The name is a bit redundant, but it's not an issue for this simple game. You can be more creative during larger projects.

Block Scene

The next scene to prepare is the Block. This is our controllable character that we can roll around when playing the game. The root of the scene is a ⬤ **Spatial** node, so we can have the 3D transform and work with it. The structure of this scene can be seen in Figure 17.1.

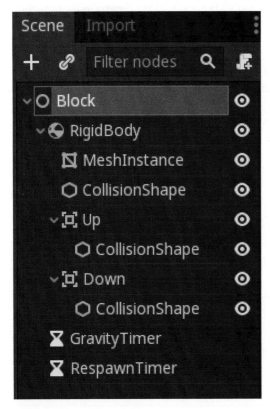

FIGURE 17.1
Structure of the block scene.

NOTE

Spatial as Scene Root

You may remember the tip in Hour 8 to make the physics body the root of the scene and everything else children to make them follow the transform. This tip still stands, and you can see in this structure that most of the nodes are under the 🔴 **RigidBody**.

The idea here is that because you need to rotate the body across an edge, you'll use the root 🔘 **Spatial** as a pivot point to facilitate the rotations. It makes the movements a little more complicated, because there's a need to adjust the body getting away from the parent (as you'll see in the scripting section), but in the end, it will be easier to make the rotations.

The 🔲 **MeshInstance** here will be set with a 🔷 **CubeMesh**. Create a 🔷 **SpatialMaterial** for the mesh and adjust it to your liking. You can look at the company project to see the exact parameters for our example. This mesh must have its size set to (1, 2, 1). This will make a prism with a square base and double the height, as proposed in our design. The 🔘 **CollisionShape** for the body is a 🟦 **BoxShape**, with half of that used for its Extents property.

The **Up** and **Down** 🔳 **Area** nodes are for checking the out of bounds parameters. When any of those areas leave the bounds, it's game over. They should have a 🔘 **CollisionShape** equal to the floor tiles and be placed slightly above the block. You can position each area in the center of each square base, and it will be enough.

Both 🟨 **Timer** nodes have their functions explicit in their names. **GravityTimer** will set the gravity of the body to zero when it finishes. This will allow the block to fall naturally at the beginning, but then it's controlled manually by the controls. Its wait time will be set to 0.5 seconds, but you can play around with this value. The **RespawnTimer** represents the amount of time the game will wait after the fall before respawning the block. One second should be enough. Both nodes should be set to One Shot, since we don't want them to keep being triggered.

Levels

The sample game has three levels, and they all inherit from the same base scene. Again, this scene is rooted with a 🔘 **Spatial** to make use of 3D transforms. The structure can be seen in Figure 17.2.

FIGURE 17.2
Base level scene structure.

The  **GridMap** will make the floor for the level. This is the main node to design the actual layout of the level. You'll first need to set the Theme property to the **MeshLibrary** we created earlier. When you select this node, the editor will change to show the list of available tiles, which will be only one in this case. You can select the tile and use your mouse to place it on the grid. Right-clicking will delete the tile. You can also use Ctrl + mouse wheel to change the elevation of the grid and the A, S, and D keys to rotate the tile before placing it.

Since the player block spawns in a different location each level, the **Start** node is need. It's simply a **Position3D** to hold the transform. The height of it is constant for every level, and in this sample, you'll use a value of 4.

The **Ending Area** node will be placed on the hole that ends the level. Its **CollisionShape** is a **BoxShape** with Extents set to (0.45, 2, 0.45). The base is smaller than the grid tile to avoid any edge contact due to numerical imprecision. Areas report the entering signal as soon as any part of the body touches them, so this size is wide enough to properly detect the winning condition.

When the player reaches the end successfully, the gravity should be turned back on, but only after the block completes its rotation, so it can fall naturally if it's outside of the game boundaries. That's what the **GravityTimer** is for. You can set it to One Shot, but the time itself will be set via code to match the block movement duration, so you don't need to change it.

The 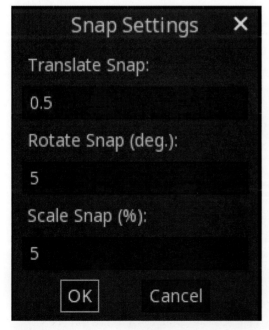 Inbounds Area defines the boundaries of the level. When the detection areas of the player block get outside the boundaries, the game is over. The ◼ CollisionPolygon makes it easy to draw a line that defines the level border. You'll need to rotate this negative 90 degrees in the X-axis so the polygon line matches the level position. You'll also need to set the depth property to a high value, like 15 or so, because the block spawns on a high position, and it should be inside the boundaries.

Note this is only the base scene, and you don't need to change the default position of the nodes. You'll need to create inherited scenes based on this one where you'll fill the GridMap, move the start and ending points, and create the inbounds polygon. Create a few levels and add them all to a directory called "levels." This will ensure they can be easily listed and fetched by scripts.

TIP

Grid Snapping

Since the game features a perfect grid, you can use the Godot Editor features to snap the objects into it. You can enable this by clicking on the **Transform > Use Snap** menu on the toolbar. Use the **Transform > Configure Snap** dialog to change the Translate option to 0.5. While the grid square has side 1, you may need to snap things in the center of squares. This is quite helpful when setting the start and end positions of the levels (Figure 17.3).

FIGURE 17.3
Grid snap configuration The Translate Snap makes things move perfectly into the grid.

NOTE

Pixel-perfect Inbounds Polygon

While you don't need to make the polygon fit the boundaries perfectly, it is nice to do so, since the game fits into a grid. The easiest way to do this is to simply make the polygon manually by clicking on the corners and using Inspector to change the array of points to the closest integer. This way, the polygon will snap into the grid nicely.

▼ TRY IT YOURSELF

Create a Level

Let's see how to create the first level of the game (see Figure 17.4):

1. Create a new scene inherited from the original level scene.

2. Click on the 🎮 **GridMap** node.

3. Use the floor tile to design the level. You can be creative or just follow the existing example.

4. Select the ➕ **Start** node.

5. Use the ✥ **Move** tool to set it over the level's spawn point. Use the snapping option to make it easier.

6. Move the ▣ **Ending** node and put it over the hole at the end of the level. Its bounding box should match the square hole.

7. Select the ◀ **CollisionPolygon** under the ▣ **Inbounds** node. Use the 🖉 **Create Polygon** tool to make it go around the level's tiles and enclose them. You can manually adjust the values of the points to make it fit exactly onto the grid.

8. Save the scene in the "levels" folder. This will make the script load it.

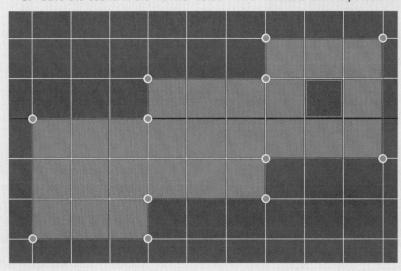

FIGURE 17.4
The layout of the first level.

Main Game Scene

The last step is to make the main game scene. This will put everything together and handle the environment settings. It will also be responsible for making the level's transitions and setting up the block spawn point. Figure 17.5 shows the main scene structure.

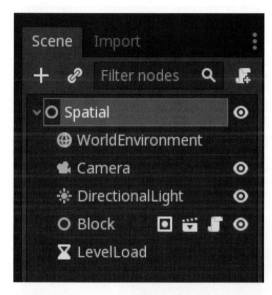

FIGURE 17.5
Main scene structure

First, you have the ⊕ **WorldEnvironment**. This allows you to set up the environment without relying on the default one. Use it to set up the clear color of the world, since the generated sky does not look good with an orthogonal perspective. There's also a 📷 **Camera,** which should be set to orthogonal with a Size Y of 10 to capture the entire level.

The 🔆 **DirectionalLight** is used to give illumination to the game. It's also responsible for giving a nice shadow to the block. For that, you'll need to enable its Shadow property. You may need to adjust the Color, Bias, and Contact properties to make the shadow look nicer.

There is a ⏳ **Timer** node here to make the game wait a little after the level is won before loading the next one. In our project, we set it to 2 seconds. It should also be set to One Shot.

Last, we have an instance of the ◉ **Block** scene. For testing purposes, you may also want to instance one of the levels before the level loading is set up. After that, you can save this scene and set it as the Main Scene in Project Settings.

Scripts and Input

Before adding the scripts, set up the input mapping. This way, you can change the keys used to control the block or add joystick support without changing the code.

The Input Map can be set in the Project Settings. In this game, you only need four: `left`, `right`, `up`, and `down`. These will be responsible to move the block. You can expand on this to add other functionality such as respawn, pausing, and level skip.

TIP

Input Configuration

The Input Map can be altered in runtime with scripting. You can set up and delete actions as well as change the keys and buttons associated with it. This means it's possible to make a menu screen the player can use to set up the keys that move the block.

You can refer to Hour 7 and check the official Godot documentation about the **InputMap** singleton if you intend to make something like this (Figure 17.6).

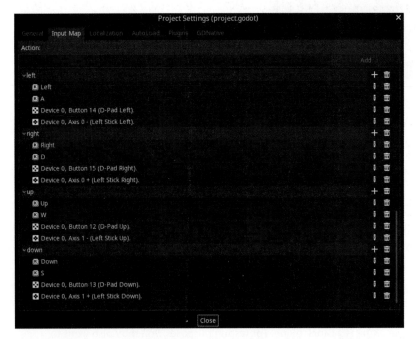

FIGURE 17.6
The Input Map configuration for the game Notice you can have multiple keys or gamepad buttons triggering the same action.

Controlling the Block

The most important and complex script is meant to move the block. It relies on state-keeping variables and a few magic numbers to move the block in the correct way. This section will follow each function and explain the most complex portions of the code (Listing 17.1).

LISTING 17.1   Block Input Code (block.gd)

```
extends Spatial

...

enum Direction { UP, DOWN, RIGHT, LEFT }
enum Orientation { PARALLEL, ORTHOGONAL }
enum RestPosition { STANDING, LYING }

var orientation = PARALLEL
var rest_position = STANDING

var is_turning = false
var interpolation = 0
var rotation_direction = null
var won = false
var lost = false
var respawning = false

var right_shift = Vector3(0.5, -1, 0)
var down_shift = Vector3(0, -1, 0.5)

func _input(event):
    if event.is_action_pressed("right"):
        start_turning(RIGHT)
    elif event.is_action_pressed("down"):
        start_turning(DOWN)
    elif event.is_action_pressed("left"):
        start_turning(LEFT)
    elif event.is_action_pressed("up"):
        start_turning(UP)

func start_turning(direction):
    if respawning or won or lost or interp != 0 or not $GravityTimer.is_stopped():
return
    is_turning = true
    match direction:
        RIGHT:
            rotation_direction = RIGHT
            adjust_transform(right_shift)
```

```
            DOWN:
                    rotation_direction = DOWN
                    adjust_transform(down_shift)
            LEFT:
                    rotation_direction = LEFT
                    adjust_transform(right_shift * Vector3(-1, 1, 0))
            UP:
                    rotation_direction = UP
                    adjust_transform(down_shift * Vector3(0, 1, -1))
        adjust_orientation()

...

func adjust_transform(shift):
    translation += $RigidBody.translation + shift
    $RigidBody.translation = -shift

func adjust_orientation():
    if rest_position == LYING:
        match rotation_direction:
            RIGHT, LEFT:
                    if orientation == PARALLEL:
                            rest_position = STANDING
            UP, DOWN:
                    if orientation == ORTHOGONAL:
                            rest_position = STANDING
    elif rest_position == STANDING:
        rest_position = LYING
        match rotation_direction:
            RIGHT, LEFT:
                orientation = PARALLEL
            UP, DOWN:
                orientation = ORTHOGONAL

func update_shifts():
    if rest_position == STANDING:
        right_shift = Vector3(0.5, -1, 0)
        down_shift = Vector3(0, -1, 0.5)
    else: match orientation:
        PARALLEL:
                right_shift = Vector3(1, -0.5, 0)
                down_shift = Vector3(0, -0.5, 0.5)
        ORTHOGONAL:
                right_shift = Vector3(0.5, -0.5, 0)
                down_shift = Vector3(0, -0.5, 1)

...
```

Listing 17.1 shows part of the block script. This part of the code is responsible for handling the input and preparing the block for movement while adjusting the state to match the direction of the movement.

The first lines define three `enum` structures to be used in the state code. Using these kind of constants ensures they are integers internally instead of strings, which requires less processor usage to compare them when needed. The structures we define here are used throughout the code to check and update the block state. It's useful to know which direction the block is oriented and whether it's standing or not, because its asymmetrical nature makes it harder to calculate the rotations without this information.

Following that, you will set a few variables to keep the state. Most of them aren't in use currently, but will be very soon. The names are quite descriptive, except maybe for `interpolation`, which keeps the position of the movement animation on a scale of 0 to 1. The `right_shift` and `down_shift` variables are basically "magic" numbers that help us move the pivot point of the rotation. Think of it like this: from the origin (center of the block), how much in each direction do you need to move the pivot point to the edge, where it rotates? To move it to the right, you need half a unit in the X-axis and 1 unit in the Y-axis downward (hence the negative). Those values change depending on the block orientation, so the `update_shifts()` function updates the values after each movement.

The `_input()` function essentially checks if an action was pressed and passes it around to another function so that you can reuse the code. This function is called automatically by Godot when there's a user input. The `start_turning()` function sets the state of the object to be rotated. This state will then be used on the process function (which we will check later). First, it checks if in a state where it cannot turn, such as if it's respawning or already turning. If so, it bails out of the function early. Then it checks the direction of the turn and calls a function to adjust the transform accordingly. After that's done, it calls another function to update the orientation of the block (it will only reach such orientation after the rotation is completed, but you set it early on).

To adjust the transform, you'll need to zero out the ⬤ **RigidBody** translation and shift it according to the direction of movement. For this, you'll move the root node the same amount as the body and add the shift, then set the translation of the body to zero minus the shift you need.

The orientation is adjusted by checking the current state and direction of movement. With a bit of logic, you can figure out what the next orientation will be. Updating the shift vectors is almost the same thing, but you'll need to reset the magic numbers once again.

Rotating the Block

The actual rotation is made in the `_physics_process()` function (Listing 17.2). It uses the current state of the block to apply the transform. The most important detail of this function is the axis of rotation. Godot uses the right-hand rule. This means that if you take your right hand, stick your thumb up, and imagine it as the axis of rotation, the closing fingers indicate the direction of rotation (Figure 17.7).

FIGURE 17.7
The right-hand rule for rotation Pointing your thumb in
the axis direction, the other fingers show the rotation
movement.

LISTING 17.2   Block Rotation (block.gd)

```
const movement_duration = 0.2;

...

func _physics_process(delta):
    update_labels()
    if is_turning:
        var step = (delta / movement_duration)
        var angle = (PI / 2.0) * step
        var body = $RigidBody
        match rotation_direction:
            RIGHT:
                body.transform = body.transform.rotated(Vector3(0, 0, -1), angle)
            DOWN:
                body.transform = body.transform.rotated(Vector3(1, 0, 0), angle)
            LEFT:
                body.transform = body.transform.rotated(Vector3(0, 0, 1), angle)
            UP:
                body.transform = body.transform.rotated(Vector3(-1, 0, 0), angle)

        interpolation += step
```

```
        if interpolation > 1:
            is_turning = false
            interpolation = 0
            update_shifts()
...
```

The function first calculates the `step`, which is how much movement will be made this frame, in a ratio value. From this, you can calculate the angle considering that by the end, the block will be rotated 90 degrees (which in radians is half of Pi). Then it rotates the transform of the block along one of the axes, depending on the direction of movement. At the end, it updates the state to stop the animation once it gets to the end.

Winning and Losing Conditions

The rest of the block code deals with win/lose conditions and properly resetting the properties to start a new level (or restart the same one).

The functions `respawn()` and `reset_properties()` are responsible for most of that burden. They update the state to the original values and zero the transforms. The ⧗ **GravityTimer** is used after respawning to disable the gravity once the block is on the floor.

There are two functions that will be triggered by the level areas, namely `win()` and `lose()`. They are responsible for setting up the routines for winning and losing conditions. The `won` signal is connected to the game code, which will trigger the loading of the next level.

Out of Bounds Checking

When any of the block Area nodes get out of the level boundaries, an `area_exited` signal is triggered. You'll use that to call the `lose()` function of the block, which will make it respawn (Listing 17.3).

LISTING 17.3   Out of Bounds Check (outbounds.gd)

```
extends Area

func _on_Inbounds_area_exited( area ):
    var body = area.get_parent()
    var parent = body.get_parent()
    if parent.won or parent.respawning: return
    body.gravity_scale = 1
    parent.lose()
    body.angular_velocity *= 2
```

Note that it gets the grandparent of the detected Area, since that will be our block node. This also increases the angular velocity of the body to make it rotate a bit faster and create an interesting effect.

NOTE

Script Attachment and Signals

You should note the `outbounds.gd` script is attached to the Inbounds node. This also has implications in the signal connection, since it's dependent on the node path. When connecting the signal using the editor, you'll need to select the correct node where the function is.

Winning Condition

The winning condition has a similar logic to out of bounds checking. The difference is the block doesn't fall if it's over the ending hole unless it is in a standing position. There's also a timer to reenable the gravity once the movement is completed to make the block fall. When the timer runs out, it will call the `win()` function on the block, which will handle the condition (Listing 17.4).

LISTING 17.4   Winning Check (ending.gd)

```
extends Area

const BlockClass = preload("res://block.gd")

func _on_Ending_body_entered( body ):
    var block = body.get_parent()
    if block.rest_position == BlockClass.STANDING:
        block.won = true
        $GravityTimer.connect("timeout", self, "_on_GravityTimer_timeout", [
block, body ])
        $GravityTimer.wait_time = block.movement_duration
        $GravityTimer.one_shot = true
        $GravityTimer.start()

func _on_GravityTimer_timeout(block, body):
    block.win()
    body.gravity_scale = 1
    $GravityTimer.disconnect("timeout", self, "_on_GravityTimer_timeout")
```

Accessing Constants from Scripts

You may have noticed the ending script preloads the "block.gd" file. This makes it possible to access the constants of that script. In this example, you'll only use the `STANDING` constant, so it's not much of a problem, but in a larger game, this pattern avoids repetition of code. If you simply tried to define the constant here, it would work, but it would need maintenance if you needed to change the value. And if you forget that it is defined in multiple places, it would lead to hard-to-find bugs.

Loading Levels

The logic of the level listing is done by a singleton keeping the state. The game code uses this to load the next available level. This is a regular ◉ Node, because while it needs to be a singleton in the tree, you don't need any special functions from any of the provided nodes. You can set this up in the **AutoLoad** tab of Project Settings. You'll need to set the path to script and the name of the node that it will have when in the scene. This name can then be used for reference. If you enable the Singleton field, it will be available directly by its name without the need to use the `get_node()` functionality (Listing 17.5).

LISTING 17.5   Level Keeping Singleton (levels.gd)

```
extends Node

signal levels_ended()

const levels_path = "res://levels"

var level_list = []
var current_level

func _enter_tree():
    var dir = Directory.new()

    dir.open(levels_path)
    dir.list_dir_begin()
    var file = dir.get_next()
    while file != "":
        if file == "." or file == "..":
            file = dir.get_next()
            continue
        level_list.push_back(levels_path.plus_file(file))
        file = dir.get_next()

    level_list.sort()
    current_level = -1
```

```
func get_next_level():
    current_level += 1
    if current_level == level_list.size():
        emit_signal("levels_ended")
        return ""
    return level_list[current_level]
```

The main logic is on the _enter_tree() function, which will be called when the script is loaded. This will get all the files in the "levels" directory (as provided in the levels_path constant) and put their full paths in a list. Then it will sort the list to make sure that "level1" is the first level (Listing 17.6). Note this makes the name of the level files important. Finally, this sets the current_level variable to –1, since it will be incremented by the game to 0, which is the first index on the list.

The other function is the get_next_level(), which will increment the level counter and return the file name as stored. If the game is over, it will return an empty string, and the caller function will have to handle the result.

LISTING 17.6   Changing Levels (game.gd)

```
extends Spatial

var current_level = null

func _ready():
    next_level()

func _on_Block_won():
    $LevelLoad.start()

func next_level():
    var next_level = Levels.get_next_level()
    if next_level == "":
        return

    if current_level != null:
        current_level.queue_free()

    current_level = load(next_level).instance()
    add_child(current_level)

    $Block.start_point = str($Block.get_path_to(current_level)) + "/Start"
    $Block.respawn()
```

The main game script is the last piece in the puzzle. This will be responsible for loading and instancing the levels into the scene.

First, note the `current_level` variable here is different from the one in the singleton. This one holds the actual level instance so that it can be easily referenced later. Also note the `timeout` signal of the 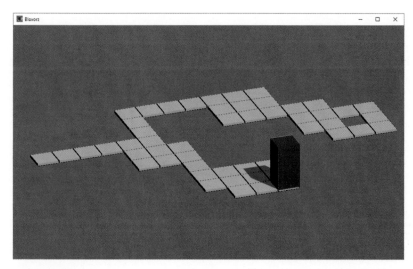 LevelLoad timer is connected to the `next_level()` function, and that the `won` signal of the block is connected to the `_on_Block_won()` function.

The `next_level()` function gets the next level path from the singleton. If it's an empty string, it does nothing, since this means the game is out of levels. Otherwise, it frees the current level (if there is one) and loads the next in the same variable. Then it adds the level to the game scene and sets the start point of the block. Finally, it tells the block to respawn, which makes it appear in the correct position.

Playing the Game

With all that done, the game is finally done and ready to be played! Run the main scene, and you should be able to move the block around with the arrow keys on the keyboard. You can roll the block around to see it falling out of the grid or getting into the winning hole (Figure 17.8).

FIGURE 17.8
The final game running Move around the block and test your puzzle-solving skills.

Summary

In this hour, we created a simple 3D puzzle game. You learned how to set up the camera, lighting, and environment. You also learned how to create your Mesh Library for use with the GridMap node. You saw how the instanced scenes come together to form a larger game, and how scene inheritance can help with that. You learned how to make scripts, and how they can call functions in other scripts and singletons. Finally, you saw how to put everything together and form a complete game.

Q&A

Q. Why use a GridMap instead of placing instanced scenes?

A. The ![icon] GridMap node has a great advantage in the editor, making it much easier to edit. It also uses batch instancing for the same tiles, resulting in a better overall performance.

Q. Do you need an interpolation in the processing function? Can't it be done with animation?

A. Theoretically, it's possible to make it via animation, but you'd need multiple animations for each variation, which isn't very practical. It's also possible to use the ![icon] Tween node to interpolate properties automatically.

Q. Why connect and disconnect the Timer signal in the ending script?

A. The connection function binds the block and body objects to be referenced when the time-out ends. Since these binds happen only at the connection, it's needed to disconnect and reconnect later. This is not a real problem in this game, since only one block exists, but this would avoid issues in more complex games with multiple objects.

Workshop

Take a moment to go through these questions and make sure you have a grasp of the content.

Quiz

1. Where can you reconfigure the input keys and buttons?

2. Why do we use different physics layers?

3. True or False: You can only connect signals using script.

4. True or False: You should only attach scripts to the root of the scene.

Answers

1. In Project Settings, under the Input Map tab.

2. To categorize the objects and avoid contact between certain categories.

3. False. You can also connect using the editor interface.

4. False. You can have multiple specialized scripts for many nodes in the same scene.

Exercises

Let's change the game a bit to make it more interesting.

1. Add a Label node to the block scene. Update its content to show the number of rotations. Remember to use the built-in function `str()` to convert the number into a string.

2. Add a few more levels to the game.

3. Change the order of the levels by renaming their scenes in the "levels" folder.

4. Add a "game over" screen that shows when all the levels are finished. Use the `levels_ended` signal of the singleton.

5. **Advanced:** The original Bloxorz game has buttons that activate blocks, opening or closing paths. Try to implement this functionality. You can make other types of tiles for the buttons and use areas in the levels to detect the presence of the block.

Environments

***

What You'll Learn in This Hour:

▶ Creating and manipulating World Environment

▶ Enabling environmental effects such as fog and depth of field

▶ Using skies and ambient lighting

▶ Adding and managing Reflection probes

▶ Improving global illumination with GI probes

This hour is focused on the ambient side of 3D worlds. Godot provides tools to create and enhance the environment of your game scenes. These tools include the ability to create an ambient imagery, be it a solid, clear color or a panoramic sky, depth of field blurring, fog, and many other adjustments. There are also two probe nodes, ReflectionProbe and GIProbe, that help create more realistic environments with better reflection and materials that emit light.

World Environment

Godot provide a special node, ⊕ **WorldEnvironment**, to deal with the ambience of the stage. Usually, you only need one such node per scene. Once it is placed on the tree, it starts to have an effect, because Godot searches for it by default. If you have do not have World Environment in your scene, the engine will use a default one.

Environment Resource

While important, the World Environment node by itself will do nothing. It needs an ⊕ **Environment** resource to set up the ambience of the scene. You can create one by using Inspector and then editing its properties.

TIP

Default Environment

When you create a new project, Godot automatically makes a file called **default_env.tres**, which contains the default settings for an environment. This will be used if a World Environment node is not available. You can edit this file by double-clicking it in the file system dock. It will be shown in Inspector, where it can be changed and saved.

You can also change the resource file to use or even remove the default by changing the **Default Environment** property in Project Settings, under the **Rendering > Environment** section.

NOTE

Camera Environment

While you can set a World Environment node to see the effect of its environment resource in Editor, it's also possible to set an environment resource directly into the **Camera** node. The camera's environment will override the others when the camera is active. This won't be shown in Editor (unless you use the camera preview), and can be useful if you want different ambiences depending on the active camera, e.g., a desaturated view for a CCTV image.

Sky

The first section of the Environment properties controls the background. There are some simple options, such as using the default project's clear color (as defined in Project Settings) or using a custom color. Setting a clear color will make a solid background. Sometimes that's all that is needed, but you can also use a proper sky view for your own game world.

If the Background mode is set to Sky, you'll have two options: **PanoramaSky** or **ProceduralSky**. You can create a new type of sky by clicking the property field in Inspector and selecting the option to create a new one.

ProceduralSky

This type of sky is generated by the engine. If you don't have a sky image available but want a more realistic view than a solid background, this is a good option. It's also great for quickly prototyping stages in the open. Note that this might take a toll on performance, so it's better suited for testing. The procedural sky has a few properties that allow you to customize the default look.

▶ In the **Sky** section, you can select the colors for the sky and the horizon, as well as how much they'll blend by using a curve setting.

▶ The **Ground** section has similar options for the bottom section of the environment.

- ► The **Sun** section has properties to change the appearance and position of the sun. **Latitude** controls how high in the sky the sun appears, and **Longitude** changes its position around the horizon. The **Angle Min/Max** property changes the size of the sun and its halo, respectively, while the **Curve** property controls the blending of these elements.

PanoramaSky

A pale blue sky with a bright sun might be a great prototyping tool, but it will rarely fit the atmosphere of your game. When you need a custom skybox, you can create a PanoramaSky resource for your environment sky. This type of sky takes a single image and uses it as the sky texture. This works best with HDR panoramic images, hence the name of the resource.

NOTE

Radiance Size

A common property for both type of Sky resources is the **Radiance Size**. This property dictates how much of the sky affects the environment in terms of quality. A larger value will have greater detail but will also require more of the hardware. The default of 512 is a good choice, though it can be fine-tuned if needed.

Ambient Light

The environment can provide a default ambient light to a scene. This light is omnipresent and has no specific direction, so it does not cast a shadow. It can be used, among other things, to create dark rooms without any lighting, yet avoiding pitch-black scenes. There are three properties in this section:

- ► **Color:** the color of the ambient light. If it's black, there will be no light.
- ► **Energy:** how much the light affects the scene.
- ► **Sky Contribution:** how much the sky will contribute to the ambient light color.

Fog

A nice ambient effect is fog. This covers distant objects with a mist, improving the game's immersive feel. There are a few interesting options in this section of the Environment resource.

Besides being able to enable or disable the fog effect, you can also set its color. It's usually set to a color that blends well with the sky. There's also an option for **Sun Color**, which dictates the scattering of light. This effect might need a change of angle to be visible in the scene. The scattering can be weakened or disabled by setting the **Sun Amount** property.

FIGURE 18.1
The fog effect applied to a scene

The **Depth** property of the fog customizes how it will be affected by distance. You can set the distance where it begins and set a curve of how much it will blend with the distance. It is also possible to add fog by setting its related properties. **Height Min and Max** adjusts where the fog starts and ends relative to the vertical axis. The height curve dictates how the blending with the environment works: a value closer to 0 will make hard edges, while values higher than 1 will make the fog appear to be thinner.

NOTE

Light-Transmitting Fog

If you have lights in a scene, it might be interesting to turn on the **Transmit Light** property of the fog. This makes light permeate the fog, improving visibility. Not only is this more realistic, it can help you guide the player to where he should go without getting lost in the mist.

Glow and Auto-Exposure

When a camera goes from a dark place to a bright one, it must adjust the exposure so the picture doesn't get too white, and vice-versa: it needs to increase exposure to capture the image of a darker place. The **Auto Exposure** properties of environments in Godot does exactly that. It is not enabled by default, but it is readily available. It's possible to configure how much it affects the scene (**Scale**), the minimum and maximum brightness (**Min/Max Luma**), and the speed of transition when the ambient light changes.

The **Glow** property goes hand-in-hand with auto exposure. This property can make bright objects glow and can make great scene transitions when the ambient light changes from one place to another. Here's a breakdown of the glow properties:

- **Levels:** enables or disables individual levels of glow. Lower levels have greater effect.
- **Intensity:** controls how much of the effect is applied.
- **Strength:** sets the power of the glow effect on objects.
- **Bloom:** controls the bleeding of light around objects.
- **Blend Mode:** controls how the glow is added to a scene.
- **HDR Threshold:** determines the point at which the Glow property should start applying the effect.
- **HDR Scale:** sets how the HDR is scaled to the effect.
- **Bicubic Upscale:** enables bicubic filtering to upscale the glow, instead of bilinear filtering. This can avoid a blocky look.

Screen Space Effects

Godot has support for a couple of screen space effects: Screen Space Ambient Occlusion (SSAO), which gives the ability to compute in real time places where shadows should form because light cannot reach those areas, and Screen Space Reflections, which calculates points where light should be reflected. Both effects depend on point of view, because they're based on what is on the screen.

You can tweak the SSAO effect to look better in your scenes. The **Radius** property determines how the shadows will spread, while the **Intensity** property changes how dark they will be. The **Bias** property acts as a threshold for the ambient occlusion to start. **Color** and **Blur** are usually better suited for testing purposes only, because without blur, the shadows look pixelated.

TIP

Ambient Occlusion

Each material can have its own ambient occlusion set by a custom texture. This allows for a better and more precise occlusion shadow that is independent of view. Of course, it requires more work for the artist, but it requires less work for the player's hardware. It can also be used as a complement to the SSAO effect on the environment.

Depth of Field Blur

A common effect of still and video cameras is how they tend to blur distant and near objects. While this is caused by how cameras and lenses operate, it can be a very valuable effect to apply to a game scene. By blurring unrelated objects, you can guide the player to focus on a specific point in a large ambient scene.

Godot provides depth-of-field blurring separately for near and far objects. You can selectively use one or both (or none), depending on your needs. This effect is also set in the environment, and has the same options for both near and far objects:

- ▶ **Distance:** where the blur should start (or finish).

- ▶ **Transition:** the speed of the transition between an object moving from unfocused to focused.

- ▶ **Amount:** the intensity of blur applied to unfocused elements.

- ▶ **Quality:** the quality of the blur effect. Setting a Higher quality demands more of the hardware, but it looks better.

Adjustments

Keeping with the photographic camera analogy, sometimes you need to adjust the settings to capture a better image. Of course, "better" is subjective, but both films and games use visuals to tell a story, and you should use the image that best conveys the message you're trying to communicate.

Godot's Environment resource offers the option to add very simple adjustment settings. You can fine-tune the brightness, contrast, and saturation of the scene, and set a custom gradient for custom color correction.

NOTE

Tone Mapping

Godot works internally with a linear color space. This means it uses raw color values instead of adjusting for how the eye perceives them. This might sound bad, but it is actually the opposite: by using the linear space, the final image can be further processed to adjust the output curve, showing or hiding details.

If your scene looks too dark or too bright, try playing with the environment's tone-mapping settings. This can also be used for bright flashes in animation.

Global Illumination

Usually, lights do not get completely absorbed by objects; instead, they bounce off objects to illuminate other places. This effect requires extra processing in Godot to apply reflected light to other surfaces, but it pays off in terms of image quality. Another important point of global illumination is how materials that emit light affect their surroundings.

Godot has a peculiar way of handling global illumination with the ![GIProbe icon] GIProbe node. You place one (or more) nodes in the scene, set the region it covers, and click on the ![Bake icon] Bake button on the toolbar. That's all you need to do. To change which objects affect the scene, you can set the **Use In Baked Light** property of each Geometry Instance (which can be ![MeshInstance icon] MeshInstance, ![Particles icon] Particles, or ![Sprite3D icon] Sprite3D, for example).

Baked Light

The global illumination generated by the GIProbe is prebaked; that is, the process is done in Editor, and the data is saved to be used in real time. This ensures a higher quality and less usage of the player's hardware. It also means that if changes are made to emissive objects in the game, the global illumination won't change and cause imprecision.

While moving emissive materials may cause trouble with the GIProbe, reflective materials work great. Dynamic objects are illuminated by indirect light resulting from the bounces (see Figure 18.2).

FIGURE 18.2
A simple scene illuminated only by the light emitted from the ball in the center

Besides the extents of the GIProbe, there are a few other properties in the node:

▶ **Subdiv:** sets the number of subdivisions to probe. Increasing this number will increase the quality and also the memory usage and time it needs to bake.

▶ **Dynamic range:** sets up the light's dynamic range multiplier.

▶ **Energy:** determines how powerful the bounced light will be.

▶ **Propagation:** determines how slowly the reflected light will degrade.

▶ **Bias:** sets a threshold to determine whether the light will bounce off an object.

▶ **Normal Bias:** how normal objects affect the direction of the light.

▶ **Interior:** disregards the environment sky when computing illumination.

▶ **Compress:** determines whether to compress the GIProbe data.

▶ **Data:** sets custom preprocessed data. Can be useful when sharing data between multiple probes.

Reflection Probes

Since Godot uses the PBR workflow, materials can have multiple sources for reflections. One of these sources is the ◼ **ReflectionProbe** node. This is a special node that basically captures everything in a certain area, and the objects in that area use the probe as a reflection source.

If the scene has multiple passages and rooms, you'll need to set up a Reflection Probe for each one. This ensures that all reflections are correctly applied. Godot has a nice way to blend adjacent probes without hard edges.

The probes also have a special setting for interiors. If enabled, Godot will ignore the environment sky and consider only the light sources inside the scene. There's a **Box Projection** option that is better suited for interior places, since it maps the reflection to the sides of the probe and ensures a higher-quality reflection in closed spaces.

Extents and Origin

The main configuration of a Reflection Probe node consists of the extents and origin. The **Extents** property makes a box in which it will look for reflections, and should be set to surround a room or area of your scene. Note that the extents are measured from the node's position to its border.

The **Origin** property sets up the center of the area. Usually, the default (center of the box) is ideal, but sometimes it can be over, under, or inside an object, which will break the reflections. Set it to a place around the center of the room, where it can be seen by most objects.

Setting up Probes

Let's try to set up a couple of probes to see how it's done:

1. Create a new scene and add a 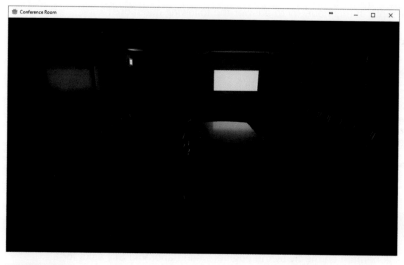 Spatial as the root. You can add some objects to the scene so it's not empty.

2. Add a GIProbe node as a child of the root.

3. You'll see a green reticulated box in the Editor. It determines the probe's actuation range.

4. Click on the Move tool.

5. Move the GIProbe around to position it away from the origin.

6. There are three circular handles, one for each axis. Move them around to make the box cover a certain area.

7. Now add a ReflectionProbe node as a child of the root, Spatial.

8. Move it around away from the origin (see Figure 18.3).

9. Using the three handles on the box edges, change the area covered by the box.

10. In the center of the Reflection Probe box, there are three handles close together. Each of them moves the origin of the probe on an axis.

11. Set the origin of the reflection to a different location.

FIGURE 18.3
A simple conference room scene shows the effect of the Global Illumination and Reflection probes.

Summary

This hour showed you the environmental effects of the Godot engine. You learned how to set up and tweak the World Environment for your scene. You saw how to use global illumination to your advantage. You also learned about Reflection Probes and how they help with reflective materials.

Q&A

Q. Do I need multiple GIProbes in a scene?

A. GIProbes doesn't have any blending features, so using multiple probes close together isn't advised. However, in a large scene, some small areas might have GIProbes where indirect light makes a difference.

Q. Do I need a reflection probe for reflections to work?

A. No. Reflective materials work by themselves. But Screen Space Reflections in the environment and reflection probes will enhance the quality of reflections.

Q. What environment will be used: the one from the camera or the World Environment node?

A. The editor will show only the one from the World Environment. The running game or camera preview will show the one from the active camera if it is set.

Workshop

To better grasp the concepts of this hour, try to answer the following questions.

Quiz

1. Where are the default environment settings?

2. What is the difference between **ProceduralSky** and **PanoramaSky**?

3. Can the environment fog be reduced in bright spots?

4. What are the two screen space effects?

5. True or False: you should set one Reflection Probe per room or passage.

Answers

1. In the file called **default_env.tres**, or where it is set in Project Settings.

2. Procedural Sky is generated on the fly by the engine, while Panorama Sky asks for a premade texture.

3. Yes. The **Transmit Enabled** property must be set for it to show.

4. Screen Space Ambient Occlusion (SSAO) and Screen Space Reflection (SSR).

5. True. Each room or passage should have its own probe for better reflection quality.

Exercises

To get yourself acquainted with environments and probes, try to execute the following exercises.

1. Create a new scene and add a ⊙ **Spatial** as the root node.

2. Add a ⊕ **WorldEnvironment** node.

3. In Inspector, click on the **Environment** property. On the menu that appears, select **New Environment**. This will create a new ⊕ **Environment** resource.

4. Click on the property again to edit the environment.

5. In the **Background** category, set the **Mode** property to **Sky**.

6. Click on the **Sky** property and create a new ☁ **ProceduralSky**.

7. In the **Tone Map** category, change the settings and see how the scene changes.

8. Enable the **Auto Exposure** option.

9. Change the **Scale** and see how the scene is affected.

10. In a similar manner, change the **Luma** settings to see their effects.

11. Add some ◰ **MeshInstances** to the scene with simple shapes and materials.

12. Try to change other environment properties and see how they affect the scene.

HOUR 19
Sound

What You'll Learn in This Hour:

▶ Using player nodes to emit sound
▶ Making use of positional audio with the Doppler effect
▶ Adding effects to your sounds
▶ Changing audio effects on certain game locations

In this hour, you will see the possibilities of using audio effects in Godot. You will learn how to add background music and sound effects, how to use the automatic positional audio features, and how to add audio effects to post-process sounds in-game. You'll also learn how to use multiple buses and how to change the effects of audio based on the location of the emitting source.

Playing Sounds

Often overlooked, sound is a very important part of a game's atmosphere, as it helps increase player immersion in the game world. There are essentially two ways of playing audio inside Godot: directly to the output (as is common for background music) and from the position of the player in the scene (usually for sound effects). This means you can have a stereo or surround setup without additional effort.

Importing audio files

Godot supports two audio formats out of the box: .wav and Ogg Vorbis. Ideally, you should use .wav files for short sound effects, since they are faster to parse and play, and Ogg Vorbis for longer tracks such as music, because this format has compression and occupies less disk space. In any case, Godot won't force you to use a specific file, since music and effects are treated the same way by the engine.

NOTE

Streams vs. Samples

If you're coming from Godot 2, you might notice the absence of distinction between streams and samples in Godot 3. In older versions, streams were used for music and samples for effects. Godot 3 removes this distinction and can play both types from the same audio player node.

There's no special treatment to import audio files, so you'll do it the same way as for other resources: simply copy them to your project folder. They'll appear in the file system dock as usual. Figure 19.1 shows the import options for both WAV and Ogg Vorbis files (see Figure 19.1).

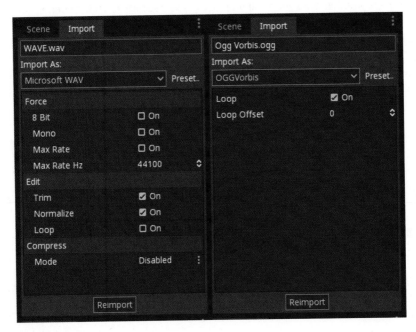

FIGURE 19.1
Import options for WAVE and Ogg Vorbis files

AudioStreamPlayer

The simplest way to play an audio file is to use the AudioStreamPlayer node. This node can be used both in 2D and 3D scenes, since it inherits directly from Node. It plays sounds straight to the output, disregarding the positional effects.

After adding this node to the scene, you'll need to set up an audio stream to play. This property (see Table 19.1) can be loaded with any type of audio file supported by Godot. Then you can enable the Playing property in Inspector to start playing the sound. It will loop, if set to do so; otherwise, it will stop once the audio is finished.

TABLE 19.1   AudioStreamPlayer Properties

Property	Description
Stream	Sets the audio stream to be played. This can be any type of audio stream resource supported by Godot.
Volume dB	Adjusts the gain of the audio in decibels. A value of 0 means no change in volume. A negative value means a reduction in sound, while a positive value makes the sound louder.
Playing	Sets whether or not the sound is playing. You can check this in the Editor to hear the audio or set it via code to start or stop playing.
Autoplay	Determines whether the sound will be played automatically when the scene starts.
Mix Target	The final target of the audio. This can be set to Stereo, Surround, or Center. Stereo plays standard binaural sound, Surround uses the player's home theater system to play positional audio, and Center aurally focuses the audio in the center.
Bus	The audio bus is the sound output. Buses will be discussed in greater detail later in this hour.

TRY IT YOURSELF ▼

Playing Audio

Let's try to make something in the Editor play a sound. Assuming you already have an audio file in your project folder, you'll just need to follow these steps:

1. Create a new scene in the Editor.

2. Add an **AudioStreamPlayer** node (don't select the 2D or 3D variant).

3. Drag the audio file from the file system dock to the **Stream** property in Inspector.

4. Click on the **Audio** tab in the bottom panel. The audio bus layout will show up.

5. Enable the **Playing** property in Inspector. The sound will start and the master bus meter will light up to show the audio levels.

6. Disable the **Playing** property and enable **Autoplay** instead.

7. Save and play the scene. There's no meter in the running game, but you should be able to hear the sound playing.

TIP
_____

AudioStreamRandomPitch

A type of stream that is not tied to any audio format is **AudioStreamRandomPitch**. This is a special type of resource that plays the audio with a different pitch each time it starts. It can make sound effects such as hits and bullets sound a bit different every time, decreasing the audio fatigue of the user.

You can create this effect in Inspector. It has two properties: the audio stream, where the actual sound comes from, and the random pitch variation as a percentage. A value of 1 for the random pitch property will make the stream always sound the same, while larger values will make it deviate from the original pitch.

Note that the pitch variation goes in both directions (the sound will sometimes have more bass, and at other times, more treble). The tempo of the sound is also affected, since changing pitch while maintaining tempo is a time consuming process and can't be done in real time.
_____

Positional Audio

Godot offers a very simple way to enable positional audio in your games. **Positional audio** means the volume of the sound changes in each speaker of a stereo or surround-sound setup so that the listener can associate the sound with a particular direction.

To enable positional audio, use the 🎵 AudioStreamPlayer2D node for 2D games and 🎵 AudioStreamPlayer3D for 3D games. They can be put anywhere inside the game world, and the player will listen to the sound coming from that place, relative to where the current camera is placed. The sound will be automatically sent to the correct speaker, based on where the player is inside the world and the direction he is looking.

TIP
_____

Audio Players as Children

Since positional audio usually comes from a specific game object, it's interesting to put the stream player node as children of that object. The sound will seem to come from it without any extra effort, since the player will follow the transform of its parent. This simplifies the creation of realistic ambience sounds without worrying about the sound source position.
_____

Positional Audio in 2D

In a 2D environment, positional audio is achieved with the 🎵 AudioStreamPlayer2D node (see Table 19.2). Since a 2D world has no depth, this only affects left and right panning.

If the node is in the center of the viewport, it will sound the same on both channels. It will play louder in the left channel and at a lower volume in the right the farther the node goes to the left, and the opposite when it is going right. When the node goes too far, it will start losing volume until it's completely mute, so you don't need to explicitly stop sounds that are too far away to be heard.

TABLE 19.2   AudioStreamPlayer2D Specific Properties

Property	Description
Max Distance	The maximum distance the node can be heard in full volume. It will be attenuated when it's farther than that value from the camera.
Attenuation	Sets the attenuation curve. As with other curves, 1 is linear, smaller values are ease-out, and greater values are ease-in.
Area Mask	Sets which area layers can affect this player. Area effects will be presented in following sections.

Positional Audio in 3D

When you have a 3D space available, the positional audio gets more interesting. With a depth dimension, you can create user surround audio (if the user has the equipment to play it). For this, you'll use the AudioStreamPlayer3D node (see Table 19.3).

Sounds that are far from the player start losing volume, independent of the direction those sounds travel. They also will use stereo or surround panning, depending on the direction relative to the camera. It is possible to define an emission angle to the sound source to direct the sound and muffle it for listeners outside the range (like a speaker does in real life) (see Figure 19.2).

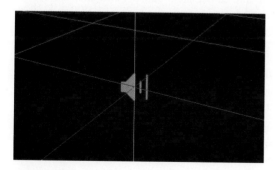

FIGURE 19.2
The spatial audio player feature helps you place where the sound will come from.

NOTE

Audio Listener

Other game engines have the concept of an Audio Listener that represents the user "ear" inside the world, but this is not quite the case for Godot. The sound listener is the current camera by default, so there's no extra step to set up a listener.

In case you need a listener in the world that is not in the same position as the camera, you can override it by adding a Listener node and enabling its **Current** property.

TABLE 19.3   AudioStreamPlayer3D Specific Properties

Property	Description
Attenuation Model	Determines how the sound should attenuate when the source is farther away. It can follow an inverse, a square inverse, or a logarithmic curve.
Unit dB	Increases the base sound volume in decibels.
Unit Size	Defines how much distance the sounds needs to attenuate. Larger values mean the node must be farther away to have a significant attenuation.
Max dB	Sets the limit of gain for the sound source. This prevents the audio from becoming too loud.
Max Distance	Sets how far the node must be from the source before it starts attenuating the sound.
Out of Range Mode	Determines what to do when the sound source is too far away to be heard. You can pause the sound when it's inactive, or keep playing it with zero volume.
Area Mask	Like its 2D counterpart, this sets which area layers can affect this player.
Emission Angle	If enabled, makes the source act like a speaker and emit the sound in a narrow direction. Listeners outside the range will hear the sound as muffled.
Degrees	The wideness of the sound source, if the emission angle is enabled.
Filter Attenuation dB	Determines how loud the sound is if the listener is outside the range of the emission angle. Lower values increase the amount of muffle in the sound.
Cutoff frequency	The frequency above which the sounds will be cut when the attenuation is being applied. This value applies both to the emission angle and the distance attenuation.
dB (Attenuation Filter)	Defines the amount of attenuation for frequencies below the cutoff point. Lower values will make the sound more muffled.
Doppler Tracking	Enables or disables the Doppler effect for this source. "Idle" and "Fixed" refer to the processing frame, the same as the `_process()` and `_fixed()` callbacks of a script.

Doppler Effect

The Doppler effect is the compression and expansion of sound waves when the sound source and listener are moving in relation to each other. This makes the frequency of the sound go higher if the source is approaching the listener, and lower if it's moving away. The practical effect is the sound distortion that you hear from the siren of a fast ambulance and from the horn of a moving train or truck.

Enabling such an effect in Godot is very simple. First, enable Doppler tracking in the current ▓ **Camera** node. Then do the same to the AudioStreamPlayer3D node that acts as your sound source. The choice for "Idle" or "Fixed" should adjust to the needs of your game, so you should try both and see what works best.

Once the Doppler effect is enabled, if the sound source or the camera is moving, you will hear the distortion in the sound.

Audio Buses

People with audio backgrounds will be familiar with the concept of buses. Essentially, a bus is a route for audio signals that can either go to another bus or directly to the output. Each bus can have its own volume and chain of effects, giving you the flexibility to process audio any way you want and reuse effects.

The **Master** bus is the main bus, and can't be renamed or deleted. Every audio signal eventually goes to the Master bus, and from there, it follows the user's audio output.

TIP

Using the Master Bus

It might be tempting to change the volume or apply effects to the Master bus (see Figure 19.3). However, you should avoid it. This bus is the final link in the chain for all game audio, so effects would be applied to everything. While this might be intended, it may also bite you if you want to add another sound without those effects.

Instead, create a new bus for global effects and route all other sounds there. This way, you can add sounds that bypass those global effects if need be. This is useful even for typical master effects, such as a limiter.

FIGURE 19.3
The Master bus as it is by default

Bus Layout

Clicking the **Audio** button in the bottom panel will bring up the Bus Layout Editor. Here, you can add and remove buses, change and edit their effects, and adjust their volumes.

It's also possible to create, save, and load layouts. Note that a layout is enabled for the project and not for individual scenes. You can change the bus layout during runtime by calling the `set_bus_layout()` function of the **AudioServer** singleton.

NOTE

Default Bus Layout

When you make changes to the bus layout, Godot automatically creates a file called `default_bus_layout.tres` and saves it on the root of your project. As the name implies, this is a default bus layout for the entire project, and it can be easily recalled by clicking the **Load Default** button on the Bus Layout Editor.

Changing Buses and Effects

In this exercise, you'll use some of the functions of the bus layout Editor.

1. Click on the **Audio** button of the bottom panel to bring up the bus layout Editor, if it's not open already.

2. Create a new bus by clicking the **Add Bus** button at the top of the panel (see Figure 19.4).

3. Rename the new bus "Effects."

4. Click on the **Add Effect** button of this bus and select **Distortion**.

5. Select the **Distortion** effect by clicking on its name. You can see and change the effect properties in Inspector.

6. Create a new bus and call it "Reverb."

7. Add a **Reverb** effect to this new bus.

8. On the bottom of the bus, there is a dropdown menu with **Master** selected. Change this dropdown to **Effect** instead. This is the target output of the new bus.

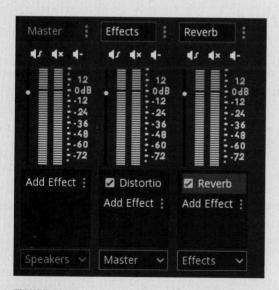

FIGURE 19.4
The bus layout after adding buses and effects

Bus Chain

As indicated in the previous exercise, you can select the target output for every bus in the layout, so you can make a sound go into a series of buses before finally reaching the output. This can be useful for adding effects to specific sounds by making them go into a targeted bus that proceeds to send the audio to another effect bus.

However, there are a few rules to this layout. First, the buses have only one output. You cannot make copies of the sound to send to another bus (this is usually called "sends" in professional audio software, but Godot does not have this function). The second rule is that you can only send the output to buses to the left of the current one. This avoids signal loops.

You can move buses by clicking and dragging them to the desired positions. The output target will be changed automatically if you set the bus into a position that puts it to the left of the previous target bus.

Solo, Mute, and Bypass

There is a set of three buttons in each bus that can solo, mute, and bypass the bus. Here's a simple breakdown:

- **Solo:** Mutes all other buses except the one playing. You can solo multiple buses, and all the ones that are soloed will be active.

- **Mute:** Inactivates the bus by setting the volume to zero. Sounds sent to muted buses won't be played.

- **Bypass:** Ignores all the effects and makes the sound pass through the bus as if all the effects were disabled. Note that you can also disable effects individually by clicking on the checkboxes beside them.

Area Effects

Besides the positional audio in terms of speaker sets, Godot has effects that can be applied to sound when the audio player is inside a certain game area. This allows effects such as increased reverb when the player character is inside a cave, or a muffled sound when the character is underwater.

2D Audio Area Effect

If you are making a 2D game, you can also avail yourself of the area effects. First you'll need an area, which can be set up with the **Area2D** node (the same node that interacts with the physics engine).

The [icon] **Area2D** node has a special property that can redirect its sounds to a specific audio bus. You can change the effects applied to the [icon] **AudioStreamPlayer2D** sound by sending it to a different bus loaded with the desired effects.

Like in the physics engine, you'll need to add a [icon] **CollisionShape2D** node (or a [icon] **CollisionPolygon2D**) as a child of the [icon] **Area2D** so it has an actual area of effect. When the audio player is inside the shape (based on its position property), its sound will be redirected to the other bus.

3D Audio Area Effect

In 3D, the area effect is a bit more powerful, since you can have a Reverb Bus. It still has the same properties as the 2D counterpart, so it can redirect the sounds played inside it to another bus. Note that you still must add a child [icon] **CollisionShape** (or [icon] **CollisionPolygon**) to determine the affected area.

If enabled, the **Reverb Bus** property creates a copy of the sounds played inside the area and directs it to the specified bus. This is quite common in professional audio mixing, because you can send multiple sounds to the same reverb bus while maintaining the characteristics (and effects) of the individual audio sources. Table 19.4 shows the specific properties of the [icon] **Area** node that are related to the Reverb Bus.

TABLE 19.4   Area Reverb Bus Properties

Property	Description
Enable	Enables the audio copy to the reverb bus.
Name	The name of the bus to which the audio copy will be sent.
Amount	The volume of the audio that will be sent to the reverb bus as a percentage of the original audio. This effectively affects the amount of reverb (or any other applied effect) that the user will hear.
Uniformity	The uniformity of the effect inside the area, such as how the position of the object will affect the panning of the reverb bus. A value of 0 means the audio signal to the bus will be completely dependent of the position of the source. A value of 1 means complete independence, so the original audio will be sent to the reverb bus.

Dynamic Audio

While Godot has a very easy setup for using positional audio and adjusting volume based on distance, sometimes you'll need a fine-grained control to change sound properties during gameplay. Like other aspects of Godot, you can control audio via animations and scripting.

Controlling Audio via Animations

Changing audio properties via animations is the simplest way to trigger audio effects and creating fade effects. Since they have great control over nodes in the scene, they're great for changing the properties of an ⏹ AudioStreamPlayer node, but animations can't change global properties like bus volumes and effects.

Animating Stream Player

Follow these steps from an empty scene to create an audio animation:

1. Add a ⏺ Node to serve as the root.

2. Create an ⏹ AudioStreamPlayer and set its stream to a song.

3. Add an ⏹ AnimationPlayer and create a new animation.

4. Set the animation to Autoplay on Load.

5. Change the length of the animation to 10 seconds.

6. Select the ⏹ AudioStreamPlayer node. In Inspector, click on the key button for the Play property to create a key frame. Godot will ask if you want to create a track, so click on Create.

7. Go to the 1-second mark in the animation.

8. Enable the Play property and create another key frame.

9. Go to the 9-second mark in the animation.

10. Disable the Play property and create another key frame for it.

11. Go to the 3-second mark in the animation.

12. Create a track for the Volume dB property by clicking on its key button.

13. Go to the 5-second mark in the animation.

14. Set the Volume dB to -40 (negative forty) and create a key frame.

15. Create another key frame at the 6-second mark.

16. Go to the 8-second mark in the animation.

17. Set the Volume dB back to zero and make a key frame.

18. Save and play the scene. The sound will start playing, fade out, fade in again, then stop playing. While these step-by-step instructions may be convoluted, the steps in the Editor are simple and allow you to create powerful effects with ease.

Controlling Audio via Scripting

Animations are very powerful, but sometimes they are not enough. With scripting, you can get around that and do more than change volume and trigger sounds.

If you use the **AudioServer** singleton, you can call functions that change the bus layout and all its properties. You can enable or disable specific effects, change their values, or even add effects to the chain. It's possible to change the volume of specific buses and replace the target output. Check Godot's documentation to see the available functions in the AudioServer class.

TIP

Tween Node

While you can't use animations directly, the **Tween** node can help you achieve similar effects when doing things via scripts. You can set up interpolation for a bus volume or an effect parameter by using functions in the AudioServer singleton.

Summary

This hour explained the audio system inside the Godot engine. You learned how to play sounds directly to the output and how to make it vary according to the object's position, both in 2D and in 3D. You saw how to create and use buses, set up a bus chain, and add sound effects. Finally, you learned how to change effects based on the audio source's position.

Q&A

Q. How can I control audio latency?

A. Via the Output Latency property in Project Settings. Note that decreasing the value might cause buffering issues, which will be audible in the form of clicks. You won't generally have to use this setting unless you're making time-sensitive games.

Q. Can Godot convert sound formats?

A. No. Godot supports only WAVE and Ogg Vorbis, and cannot convert files between formats. You can use free software such as Audacity to convert audio files to a format supported by Godot.

Workshop

Let's recall the contents of this hour by answering some questions.

Quiz

1. What are the nodes responsible for playing sounds?

2. True or False: Every audio played in Godot is affected by position.

3. How do you enable the Doppler effect?

4. True or False: It's not possible to change audio properties during the game.

Answers

1. There are three: **AudioStreamPlayer**, **AudioStreamPlayer2D**, and **AudioStreamPlayer3D**.

2. False. Sounds played with **AudioStreamPlayer** won't be affected by position (in fact, it does not even have a position).

3. Enable the Doppler Tracking property in the stream player node and on the **Camera**.

4. False. Audio properties and effects can be changed via animation or via scripting.

Exercises

In this exercise, you will create a simple audio scene with Doppler and area effects.

1. Create a new scene and add a **Spatial** node as the root. Save the scene.

2. Add a **MeshInstance** node.

3. Set the **Mesh** property to a new **SphereMesh**.

4. Add an **AudioStreamPlayer3D** as a child of the MeshInstance.

5. Set the **Stream** property to a song you have on your project. Enable the **Autoplay** property.

6. Create a **Camera** node as a child of the root. Put it in a position to see the MeshInstance.

7. Set the **Doppler Tracking** property of the camera to **Fixed**.

8. Do the same to the **AudioStreamPlayer3D** node.

9. Create an **Area** node as a child of the root.

10. Add a **CollisionShape** as a child to the area.

11. Set the **Shape** property to a new **BoxShape**. Set its values to (5, 5, 5).

12. Select the **MeshInstance** node and set its **Translation** property to (0, 0, -50).

13. Open the Audio Bus Layout panel.

14. Create two new buses: **FX** and **Reverb**.

15. In the FX bus, add a **LowPass** effect. Set its cutoff frequency to 500 Hz and resonance to 1.

16. In the Reverb bus, add a **Reverb** effect. You can leave it with its default parameters.

17. Select the ⬛ **Area** node.

18. Enable the **Audio Bus Override** property and set the bus to "FX."

19. Enable the **Reverb Bus** property. Set the name to "Reverb" and the amount to 1.

20. Add a script to the root node.

21. Set the script contents to the following code:

```
extends Spatial
export var speed = 10.0
func_process(delta):
    $MeshInstance.translation += speed * delta * Vector3(0, 0, 1)
```

22. Save and play the scene. Use headphones or a surround setup to hear the sounds better. Notice how the audio changes based on the position. The Doppler effect can be noticed by a change in pitch when the node passes through the camera. Also note the reverb and low-pass effect when the ball passes within the area.

HOUR 20
Particle System

What You'll Learn in This Hour:

► What particles are and why you should use them
► How to add 2D particles to the scene
► How to modify 2D particles to suit your wishes
► How to add 3D particles to the scene
► How to modify 3D particles to suit your wishes

Say you're building a platform game where the player runs over grassy tiles. To make it look amazing, blades of grass and dust clouds fly into the air with every footstep. You could achieve this effect by creating many Sprites with every footstep, make them fly away randomly, and delete them several seconds later. But that would be a pain to make, and a huge performance hog. Instead, one can use particles!

In this hour, you'll learn what particles are and when to use them. You'll also learn how to add 2D and 3D particles to your scene and how to edit their (many) properties to make them behave.

2D Particles

A particle is the smallest unit of something. For example, a single raindrop is a particle. When lots of particles of the same type work together (to create rain in this case), we call it a particle system. Using a particle system is extremely useful for two major reasons:

► You can instantiate/delete many particles without a significant effect on the performance of the game.

► You can control all these particles and make them work together without writing a line of code.

Common uses for particles are rain, snow, fire, sparks, stars, smoke, and other visual effects.

The Particles2D Node

To add particles to your game, choose the 🔲 **Particles2D** node.

A single 🔲 **Particles2D** node can only control a single type of particle. It can't do raindrops and smoke at the same time, for example.

To set the image for the particle, go to the node's properties and load the image in the **Textures > Texture** field (Figure 20.1).

FIGURE 20.1
The default Godot icon set as the particle texture.

The Process Material

Once the texture is loaded, it will display in the editor, but nothing will happen. To process the texture as a particle, we need to create a **Process Material**. Go to the properties, find the **Process Material > Material** field, and create a new 🔲 **ParticlesMaterial** (Figure 20.2).

FIGURE 20.2
A standard ParticlesMaterial loaded as the Process Material.

Why use a whole new material for this? Because process materials process the particles on the GPU — the graphics processing unit of every computer. This is seperate from the CPU, which is the main computational unit used for game logic and everthing else.

Now you should see the particles moving and animating in the editor! This default 🔲 **ParticlesMaterial** does only one thing: add gravity to each particle. It can, however, do much more.

To edit the material, click on it in the Inspector. You'll be greeted by a huge list of properties (Figure 20.3).

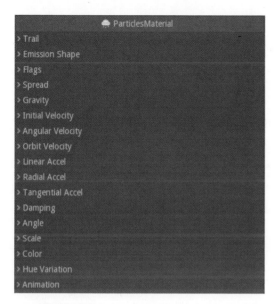

FIGURE 20.3
All the properties of a ParticlesMaterial.

Don't be intimidated; it's all pretty self-explanatory. Let's walk through the most important properties:

▶ **Emission Shape**: Determines where particles start their lives. By default, it's set to **Point**, which means they all start at the same point. Another common option is the **Sphere**, which means every particle starts somewhere within a circle.

▶ **Direction**: Determines the direction particles will move.

▶ **Spread**: The range of directions in which particles are created. If you set it to **180** (degrees), particles appear in every direction (it emits from −180 degrees to 180 degrees, which is 360 degrees total). If you set it to **90**, particles only appear on one side.

▶ **Gravity**: The gravity exerted upon the particles, which goes downward by default (as you'd expect). By setting it to **Vector3(0,0,0)**, you remove all gravity.

▶ **Initial Velocity**: The velocity at which each particle starts moving. The direction of this velocity is determined by the direction and the spread.

▶ **Angular Velocity**: The velocity at which each particle starts rotating.

▶ **Linear Accel**: How quickly a particle's moving velocity accelerates.

▶ **Radial Accel**: How quickly a particle's rotating velocity accelerates.

- ▶ **Damping**: How quickly a particle's velocity decelerates. For example, in an explosion, each particle starts with a huge velocity but slows down the further it gets from the blast. It acts like friction.

- ▶ **Angle**: The angle at which each particle starts. (Note that this does not mean the direction the particle moves. It literally means the rotation of the particle Sprite.)

- ▶ **Scale**: The scale at which each particle starts.

- ▶ **Color**: The hue modification for each particle. Using the Color Ramp property, you can make the color change over time. (For example, a flame might start bright white and end in a faint red.)

- ▶ **Hue Variation**: Using this, you can give each particle a slightly different color to get more variation.

Random Properties

As you probably noticed, almost every property also has a Random field. This property is a slider that goes from 0 to 1. When it's 0, there is no randomness. When it's 1, there is complete randomness. For example, say we set the Velocity property to 50, then set Velocity Random to 1. Every new particle will has a random velocity between 0 and 50 (Figure 20.4).

FIGURE 20.4
An example of the Random property in the editor.

Curves

Additionally, many properties have a Curve field. This allows you to change the property over time, similar to the Color Ramp. For example, you might want particles to start at a certain size but end as a different size.

To create a curve, click on the property field and select **New CurveTexture**. Once created, click on it to edit the texture. This should open a new **Curve** window at the bottom of the editor (Figure 20.5). Here, you can edit the curve by dragging around points and modifying the bend. You should see results immediately in the editor.

FIGURE 20.5
The Curve editor window. This particular curve starts
the particles on full scale (1.0) but ends the particles
so small, you can't see them anymore (0.0).

Creating a Flame/Torch

In this Try It Yourself, we'll create a simple particle system that simulates a flame or a torch.

1. Create a **Particles2D** node.

2. Create or find an image of a white square or a white circle. Set this image as the **Texture**.

3. Create a **Process Material**. Disable the gravity, set the **direction** to −45, and increase the initial velocity. This ensures that the particles fly upwards.

4. Create a **Color Ramp**. Click on the property to create a new **GradientTexture**. Click the **GradientTexture** to edit it. In the edit window, create a new **Gradient**.

5. Edit the gradient. Create new points and make a gradient that moves from white to orange to red. It should look like Figure 20.6.

FIGURE 20.6
A gradient. You can create new points by clicking
anywhere, delete points by right-clicking on them, and
edit the color of the point by clicking on the big solid
square on the right.

6. Create a **Scale** curve so that particles get smaller and smaller as they get higher and higher.

7. Play around with other properties to get the most realistic fire you can possibly make.

Particles2D Settings

Whereas the Process Material determines what process the particle goes through, the properties of the 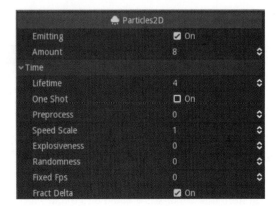 Particles2D node determine how a particle starts and ends (Figure 20.7).

FIGURE 20.7
The properties of the Particles2D node.

Let's take a look at what everything means:

▶ **Emitting**: When this is turned "on," the node will continually emit particles. When turned "off," it does nothing.

▶ **Amount**: The number of particles created. When a particle dies (at the end of its lifetime), a new one is automatically created (at the start of its lifetime) to keep the number steady. The time between particles being created, therefore, depends on the **Lifetime** property.

▶ **Lifetime**: How long a particle lives in seconds. In Figure 20.7, particles will live four seconds. This means that every 4/8 = 0.5 seconds, a new particle is created.

▶ **One Shot**: When turned "off," the default behavior of particles is used, which means they are constantly generated. When turned "on," the node will shoot all of its particles at once and then stop.

▶ **Preprocess**: Determines how many seconds of particle simulation is preprocessed. Preprocessing means before the particles are shown, the node already calculates a few seconds of simulation and saves it. This is useful if, for example, you start a scene with many particle nodes immediately emitting. If you don't preprocess, the screen will likely lag for a few seconds when the scene is loaded.

▶ **Speed Scale**: Used to speed up or slow down the particles. A number higher than 1 will speed everything up. A number lower than 1 will slow everything down. (This also influences the settings in the Process Material, not just how fast particles are created.)

▶ **Explosiveness**: By default, there's a constant interval between new particles that are created. By setting a high explosiveness, you change this. Many particles are created shortly after each other at the start of their lifetimes instead of distributing their creation evenly along their lifetimes. It's an explosion of particles.

▶ **Randomness**: Adds overall randomness to all (physics-related properties of) particles.

Creating an Explosion

In this Try It Yourself, we'll create a particle system to simulate a bomb exploding.

1. Create a ▦ **Particles2D** node.

2. Again, use an image of a white square or a white circle. Set this image as the **Texture**.

3. Create a **Process Material**. Disable the gravity and set the **Spread** to 180. Set a very high initial velocity and use some damping.

4. Create some randomness in the initial scale of particles. You can create a **Scale** curve, but this time, make the particles bigger as they get further away.

5. Create a **Color Ramp** again. This time, let it fade from white to white, but make the alpha of the end color 0. This makes the particles fade away the further they get from the blast.

6. In the node settings, create a huge amount (say, 50 or 100) of particles. Set the **Explosiveness** to 1 and turn **One Shot** "on."

7. Now, every time you toggle **Emitting** "on," it will explode.

Animated Particles

You can animate particles the normal way (with keyframes), but it probably won't look good. All particles follow the exact same animation, regardless of when they started.

In 2D, we can animate particles with a spritesheet (Figure 20.8). Instead of providing an image as texture, you can provide an image containing multiple frames of an animation. Using the **H Frames** and **V Frames** properties, you can cut it into frames.

FIGURE 20.8
A spritesheet as texture, cut into the right dimensions.

Now, go to the **Process Material** and then to the **Animation** property dropdown menu (Figure 20.9). If you set the **Speed** property to anything higher than 0, it starts animating the particles by going through the frames from left to right and top to bottom. At the bottom, there's also a toggle to make the animation **Loop**.

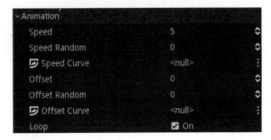

FIGURE 20.9
The animation properties of the Process Material.

Local Coordinates versus Global Coordinates

In a sense, the ![] **Particles2D** node is the parent of all its particle children. That's why, by default, it actually behaves like a parent node. If you move the ![] **Particles2D** node, all of its particles move with it, even the ones that are already halfway through their lifetime. This property is called **Local Coords** (Figure 20.10), and is found under **Drawing**.

FIGURE 20.10
The Local Coords property.

By default, it is turned "on." This means every particle's position is remembered local to its parent and follows wherever the parent goes.

If you turn it "off," this does not happen. Every particle remembers its own position in the scene. When the ![] **Particles2D** node moves, all existing particles do not respond. Only new particles start from the new position.

When should you turn off Local Coords? For example, you have a race car in your game and there's smoke leaving the exhaust pipe. It looks odd if the smoke moves with the car—it should go in the other direction. The smoke is independent of the car, so that's when you'll want to use global coordinates instead.

Scripting Particles

Just like every other node, the ⬚ **Particles2D** node can be scripted. Every property is accessible and editable with GDScript. However, because particles aren't nodes themselves, you can't script each individual particle. (You should be glad you can't, as it's what makes them so extremely fast.)

As a quick example (Listing 20.1), the following function is called on a particle node to make it explode.

LISTING 20.1   Scripting Particles

```
func explode():
    set_explosiveness(1.0)
    set_oneshot(true)
    set_emitting(true)
```

3D Particles

As you probably know by now, 2D and 3D are each other's mirrors in Godot. Whatever node exists in 2D also exists in 3D. So, naturally, the ⬚ **Particles2D** node has a 3D alternative called the ⬚ **Particles** node.

The Particles Node

The ⬚ **Particles** node emits 3D particles. Instead of a texture, it requires a mesh. If you look in the properties, however, you'll find not a mesh property, but a property called **Draw Passes** (Figure 20.11).

FIGURE 20.11
The Draw Passes property with one pass set to a cube.

The reason for this is that the ⬚ **Particles** node can emit multiple meshes at the same time. By increasing the **Passes** property, more passes are added below the first one. Each of those can be set to a (different) mesh, and all of the passes are combined with the particle that's emitted.

Order is important here. The meshes are drawn from the first pass to the last. So, if we add a mesh to pass 2 that is much bigger than the cube, it completely hides the cube.

The Good News

Everything else in 3D works the same as in 2D! You need to set at least one **Draw Pass** and a **Process Material**, then you're good to go. You can edit the same set of properties with the same effect.

Using 2D in 3D

In Hour 13 (3D Graphics), it's mentioned that 2D nodes work in 3D as well, but they're fixed to the camera. The same is true for the 📷 **Particles2D** node—it can create flat 2D particles in a 3D game.

One may be tempted to think this is easier and leads to better performance than 3D particles. For example, if your player is shooting bullets, you can replace them with flat images instead of actual bullet meshes. While it sounds good, it's not what the node was made for, and the calculations you'd have to do (to reposition the particles properly) are not worth the effort.

Instead, it's often best to use a flat Plane or Quad mesh that hold the 2D texture that you want in 3D space.

TIP

The Bullet Example

We used bullets as an example because many beginning game developers use it when they first embark on a particle adventure. In real games, however, it's never used this way.

Why not? First and foremost, particles are for visual effect only and are supposed to be unpredictable. An explosion (generally speaking) looks the same on every computer, but the details will be random, and thus different. In the case of a bullet, you need to control exactly where it goes.

Second of all, your game will most likely shoot hundreds of bullets per second, and it has to check whether any of them collided with anything. On top of that, they move too fast to see. No computer can handle this, not until we get quantum computers.

Instead, games often shoot a straight line from the player's gun and see what object it hits first. Then they draw a bullet hole on that object and drop a shell casing for effect. No bullet is actually shot. (It feels like a magician's trick, doesn't it?)

About Performance

The previous tip neatly leads to our next subject: performance. Particles were invented to increase performance of scenes with many, many objects or visual effects of the same type. So, for most use cases, particles won't be a performance problem.

It must be said, though, that a 3D mesh requires more computational power than a 2D texture. You're likely to hit the limit much earlier with the 📷 **Particles** node than with the 📷 **Particles2D** node. The easiest solution is to keep your meshes as simple and straightforward as possible.

Alternatively, you can abandon the Particles node altogether and see if the MultiMeshInstance node is faster.

Smart Use of Particles

Particles are mostly used for visual effect. They can create smoke, fire, rain, dazzling sparkles, and much more to make your game look amazing and real. This also means, however, that they are useless when off-screen.

If you have many particles in your game and you notice they are hurting the game's performance, you might save a lot by disabling all particles that are off-screen.

Summary

In this hour, you learned how to add the 2D and 3D particle nodes to your game. You learned the steps that enable them to work and display something. (In 2D, this means adding a texture and process material. In 3D, this means adding a draw pass and process material.) You learned how to edit the process material and set properties to get the particle effect you want. You learned how to make properties change over time with ramps and curves. You also learned how to edit the node's properties to gain even more control over your particles. Finally, you learned about performance and practical use of particles.

Q&A

Q. In the "bullet example" tip, you mentioned it's possible to check if particles collide. How do I do that?

A. Unfortunately, in Godot 3.0 there is no such option, but there is in Godot 3.1. Additionally, there are other particle nodes not mentioned, such as the particle attractor, which attracts all particles within its vicinity (like a magnet or the gravity of a planet).

Q. Is there a limit to the number of particles a node can emit? Or the amount of particle nodes in a scene?

A. If you test this, you'll see the limit is around 100,000 (for the number of particles). As usual, there's no limit to the amount of particle nodes; you just need one for every single particle effect. However, if you ever hit a limit, you can be sure that you've gone too far and must kick down your particle use a notch.

Q. What happens to the particles when I rotate or scale the parent node?

A. Everything rotates and scales with it, even the gravity. That's why if you want to make your particles jump upwards at the start, for example, it's not useful to rotate the node 180 degrees. It makes the gravity go upwards as well.

Workshop

Now that you have finished the hour, take a few moments to review and see if you can answer the following questions.

Quiz

1. True or False: one **Particles(2D)** node can emit multiple types of particles.

2. True or False: each individual particle can be scripted.

3. The ___ determines when a particle starts and ends; the ___ determines how the particle develops over time.

4. True or False: it's impossible to animate particles.

5. To get an explosion, one must edit the ___, turn on ___, and turn off/on ___.

6. True or False: the **Particles** node can also use 2D textures.

7. True or False: you cannot have a **Particles** node with zero draw passes.

8. Say you're making a game with a flying character, using a jetpack. Smoke and fire are released underneath him all the time, using particles. Would you turn the **Local Coords** property on or off?

9. Continuing from the last question, how would you turn the smoke from dark gray (at the start) to transparent (at the end)?

Answers

1. False. They can only emit one type.

2. False. They work together as a system and are mainly used for visual effects with no influence on the actual gameplay.

3. Particles(2D) node, Process Material

4. False; you can animate them with keyframes (though it's recommended to use curves for that) or by adding a spritesheet as texture.

5. Explosiveness, One Shot, Emitting

6. False. It can only use meshes.

7. True. You always need at least one (with a mesh in it).

8. Off. The character moves around, and the particles should not move with him once released.

9. Create a Color Ramp. Set a gradient, which starts with dark gray (with alpha channel set to 255), and ends with the same dark gray (but with alpha channel set to 0).

Exercises

Exercise 1: Make rain pour from the current mouse position.

1. Create a **Particles2D** node. Set the texture to something that looks like rain. (A thin, long rectangle that's blue-ish and slightly transparent usually works.)

2. Tweak all the properties until you're satisfied.

3. Create a script on the node. Give it an update function and update the position to the mouse position.

Exercise 2: Make fireworks explode when you click at the mouse position.

1. Create another **Particles2D** node. Tweak the properties so that it's explosive and creates many particles that fly off in random directions and have different colors. (You can also play around with scale.)

2. Create a script on the node. Give it an input function and perform `set_emitting(true)` if the mouse is clicked. (Make sure the particle node has the right position.)

3. Alternatively, you can write a script to move the particle node upward (decreasing its y-position). Once it has reached a certain height near the top of the screen, that's when the fireworks explode.

Exercise 3: Perform the previous exercises, but for the **Particles** node instead.

HOUR 21
Viewports and Canvas

What You'll Learn in This Hour:

▶ Viewport and its use cases
▶ Managing your rendering through Canvas Layers
▶ Mixing 2D and 3D scenes
▶ Adding a split-screen feature to a game

In this hour, we start playing with viewports. So far, we've talked a lot about how to assemble different nodes types into a Scene Tree that represent our world. However, given that we are not building a weather forecast simulation, well want to render things by displaying images on the user's screen. This is what the viewport is about: opening a window into our world to the user.

While this seems a very generic role, this also means that viewports allow us to implement a wide range of features:

▶ Create advanced GUI

▶ Mix multiple scenes into one

▶ Take screenshots of your game

▶ Mix 2D and 3D

▶ Add advanced effects like rearview mirror

▶ Allow split-screen

In short, if you're planning to create more than simple demos, you will most likely need viewports sooner or later, so let's choose sooner and start learning about them.

Viewports

If you've already read Hour 13 by now, you should have a rough idea what a viewport is and what Godot does with it.

The viewport is seen as a bridge between our world scene and the low-level parts of Godot like the visual server responsible for rendering a scene as a frame.

Most of the time, the viewport is a shy beast: so far, we've hardly encountered it, and all our projects rendered fine. This is because the very root node of our scene (the one we get by calling **get_node('/root')** in GDScript) is itself a ▢ **Viewport** automatically created by Godot when the game starts (Figure 21.1).

FIGURE 21.1
Once our game starts, the root node is always a viewport that's automatically added.

Given that the viewport is going to render each frame of our world, we have to tell it where to place itself and what to face before doing the rendering. This is done by adding a 📷 **Camera** (or 📷 **Camera2D** if you're doing 2D) child node. Note that a viewport can have multiple cameras, but only one at a time is configured as current.

Obviously, if a viewport doesn't have a camera set, it will stick with the default configuration (remember the blue rectangle that is present by default in the 2D editor). This is fine for simple 2D games like the one we did in Hour 5, but quickly falls short when we need more advanced features like scrolling. If you do a 3D game, however, a 📷 **Camera** is mandatory, or your screen will be black.

So far, if talking about the camera made sense, viewport seems more like a technical detail of how Godot handles rendering. This is because our use cases were fairly simple, so let's imagine something a bit more complicated.

For example, we are building a 3D action game, and at some point, the player enters a room with a television screen on. A decade ago, we had no choice but to display fixed images on the TV screen due to power limitations. However, things have changed (and Godot has arrived), so a much more modern approach is to create a scene somewhere, render it, and display the result on the TV screen (hence, etymologically speaking, it's really a television).

Translated into Godot, this means we will create a new ■ **Viewport** node, assign it a child scene so it's played on the TV, and a 📷 **Camera** node that acts as a real television camera. Finally, back in our main scene, we will connect the television screen ◪ **MeshInstance** material's texture to the ■ **Viewport**'s texture (see Listing 21.1).

LISTING 21.1   Connecting to a Viewport's Texture

```
func host_game(port):
    var viewport = get_node('Viewport')
    # For a 2D Sprite
    var sprite = get_node('Sprite')
    sprite.texture = viewport.get_texture()
    # For a 3D MeshInstance
    var mesh = get_node('Mesh')
    mesh.material_override.albedo_texture = viewport.get_texture()
```

Of course, in our main scene we also have a 📷 **Camera** representing the player view and configuring the root ■ **Viewport** (the one created automatically by Godot) that produces the frame displayed on the user's screen.

One more thing that's worth mentioning is that the ■ **Viewport** node has an Own World property that can be set to either use or not use the main scene.

To illustrate this, let's continue with our example: instead of a television displaying a show, there's a security monitor connected to a camera (a real one this time) somewhere in the level. To do that, the security camera becomes another view on the world (just like the player has its own).

The same way the player has a ■ **Viewport** (which happened to be the default root one, but it doesn't matter) and a 📷 **Camera** to render the world, we will create a ■ **Viewport** with only a 📷 **Camera** child node for the security camera.

On the contrary, to render a show completely unrelated to our main scene, enabling the Own World property prevents us from mixing the scenes together and rendering bad code, especially considering global configuration to a scene like ⊕ WorldEnvironment's skybox (Figure 21.2).

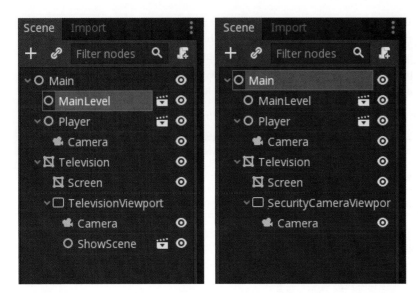

FIGURE 21.2
Different Scene Trees for the TV show (left) and the security camera. Note that.
TelevisionViewport's Own World property is enabled, unlike the SecurityCameraViewport.

Another great feature of viewport is that it allows us to mix 2D and 3D together! This is really useful every time you want to add a 2D minimap in a 3D game, for example.

You should get the idea now: first we create a ▦ **Viewport** node child of our main scene containing all the nodes for our subscene.

Then we create a surface (a 😊 **Sprite** for 2D, a ◰ **MeshInstance** in 3D) in our main scene and connect its texture (or its material's texture for a ◰ **MeshInstance**) to the ▦ **Viewport**'s texture.

Note that 2D and 3D are rendering separately, so you don't have to use the ▦ **Viewport**'s Own World property to avoid mixing your 2D and 3D scenes (well, unless your 3D scene inside your 2D main scene uses a viewport on 2D scenes . . . you're not doing that, right?).

One last cool thing about viewports: they are not limited to graphics. You can enable 2D or 3D positional audio (using the 🎥 **Camera** to configure the position of your listener) and have your viewport play sound accordingly. You can also choose whether or not the inputs sent by the player are passed to a ▦ **Viewport**, or you can send arbitrary inputs to it.

NOTE

Watch Out With Input Singleton

When processing inputs, most of the time, we use the Input singleton (for example, doing `Input.is_key_pressed(KEY_UP)`. However, as a singleton, this is something that is global to the entire game and thus ignores the viewport's "Disable Input" property!

The bottom line is, to use viewport's "Disable Input," you should only process your input with a `gui_input(event)` method (Figure 21.3).

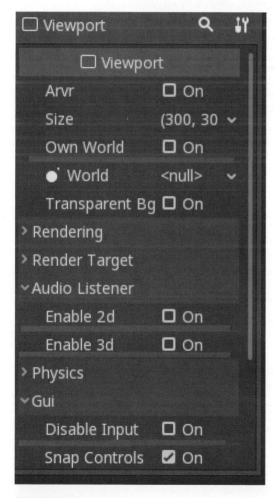

FIGURE 21.3
Viewport properties to configure in order to share
(or not) with the parent Viewport.

▼ TRY IT YOURSELF

Take Screenshots from Within a Game

1. Take any of the games we already created and start modifying the input handling to trigger a **_screenshot()** function when the enter key is pressed.

2. In the **_screenshot()**, we get back the main viewport node, select its texture, and extract its data as a new **Image**.

3. The texture outputs an upside-down image, so we have to flip its on its y axis.

4. Finally, we can simply save the **Image** as a file. See Listing 21.2.

   LISTING 21.2   Screenshot Function

   ```
   func _screenshot():
       var img = get_viewport().get_texture().get_data()
       img.flip_y()
       img.save_png('screenshot.png')
   ```

It's that easy!

NOTE

Vflip

Due to the way Godot does its rendering, by default, the Viewport's texture outputs an upside-down image. To solve this, you can enable the Vflip property in the Viewport or simply call the **flip_y()** method on the resulting image.

Canvas Layers

Now that we are head-deep into rendering, it's good to mention another cool tool provided by Godot to make our life easier: the **CanvasLayer**.

When making a 2D game, the order of drawing elements is really important, given that it determines whether your character stands under or over a tree, for instance.

A simple solution for this trouble is to use the Z property to sort our nodes' drawing order. This works great at first, but when our scene starts growing in complexity, it becomes increasingly harder to make sure no subscenes have a node with the wrong Z value.

On top of that, this trick doesn't work at all when dealing with a 3D game where we want to have a GUI.

This is where the CanvasLayer steps in. As its name suggests, it wraps all of its child nodes into a single rendering layer. Then Godot does the rendering of our scene layer by layer, starting with the CanvasLayer with the lower value of its Layer property.

NOTE

Default CanvasLayer

Every node that is not child of a CanvasLayer is considered by Godot to be part of the default layer, which has a value of 0. So, when adding a CanvasLayer, remember to set its Layer property to a negative value if it's in the background or a positive one for a foreground layer.

A very common use case of CanvasLayer is with 2D platforms to create the separation between fixed background, parallax scrolling background, middle-ground (where the player interacts with the world), and foreground for the GUI. In fact, Godot even provides a special layer node called ParallaxBackground to simplify the implementation of parallax scrolling.

TRY IT YOURSELF ▼

Play with Parallax Scrolling

1. Create a simple 2D scene with a fixed background and a player-controlled ship. To make things easier, you can use the assets from Hour 5's game.

2. Add a child Camera2D node to the ship and disable its Drag Margin H&V properties to make it follow the ship's movements exactly.

3. Now add ParallaxBackground to the scene. Make sure it displays between the background and the player (a good idea would be to use some CanvasLayer for the background and player, and remember that ParallaxBackground is already a CanvasLayer).

4. Configure the ParallaxBackground's base scale property (0 means no parallax scrolling on this axis). See Figure 21.4.

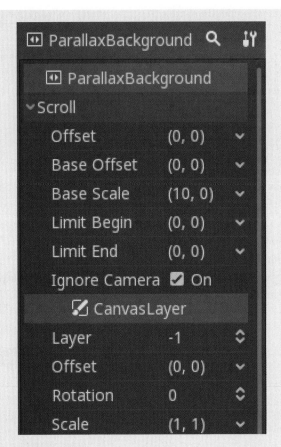

FIGURE 21.4
Configuring ParallaxBackground.

5. Add one or more ▣ **ParallaxLayer** child nodes to the ▣ **ParallaxBackground**, each one containing multiple Sprites of asteroids. You can customize the Scale property to specify how fast each one will move on each axis. See Figure 21.5.

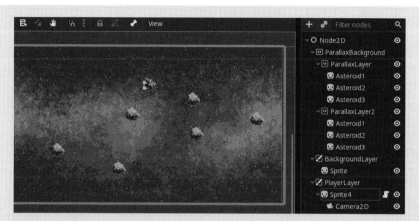

FIGURE 21.5
The Scale property specifies how fast each one will move on each axis.

6. Now play the scene and observe how the different **ParallaxLayer** nodes move compared to the player. See Figure 21.6.

NOTE

Keep the Number of Layers Low

Keep in mind that adding ![icon] **CanvasLayer** has a cost given there's less freedom for the Godot renderer to process our nodes in batches. A good rule of thumb would be to only use a couple of ![icon] **CanvasLayer** in your main scene (typically world rendering, in-game GUI, and a paused menu for a 3D game) and keep the Z axis ordering in the subscenes.

Split-Screen

One really cool feature in ![icon] **Viewport** is the split-screen: we can divide our screen into two (or more) parts, each one usually controlled by a different player.

From what we've learned so far, we can implement this by dividing our screen into multiple ![icon] **Sprite** nodes, each connected to a ![icon] **Viewport** with a camera node.

If we think about it, this is not a really elegant solution: it would be much better to have a ![icon] **Control** node instead of this 2D ![icon] **Sprite** to have useful features like anchor or margin. Besides, we have to do the texture connection with a bit of code, which adds to the complexity.

The solution to these concerns, of course, lies in a new type of node provided by Godot: the ![icon] **ViewportContainer** node. Think of it as a ![icon] **Control** node that connects directly with its first child ![icon] **Viewport** node.

▼ TRY IT YOURSELF

Add Split-Screen to a Scene

1. Create a simple 3D scene. Typically, it's a mesh (don't forget to add a material to it) and a light. See Figure 21.6.

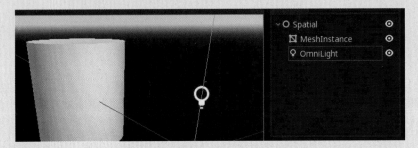

FIGURE 21.6
Mesh and light.

2. Create another scene with a regular **Node** as its root and our simple 3D scene as children.

3. Now add multiple ViewportContainers, configure their size to divide the screen between them, and enable their Stretch properties.

4. For each ViewportContainer, add a Viewport and Camera. Move the cameras to show different angles of the scene. See Figure 21.7.

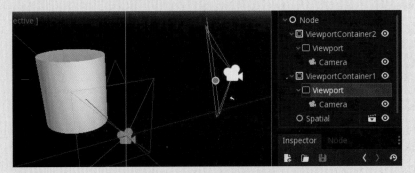

FIGURE 21.7
Cameras show various angles.

5. Finally, play your scene. As expected, we have multiple views of the scene. See Figure 21.8.

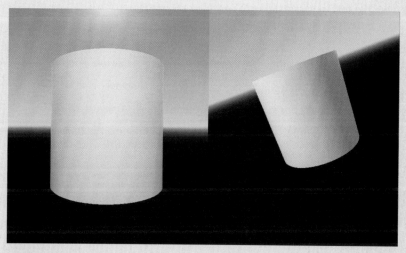

FIGURE 21.8
Multiple views of the scene.

Summary

In this hour, we saw how useful **Viewport** is when dealing with advanced subjects like nested scenes, multiple views on the same scene, or mixing 2D and 3D scenes together. On top of that, we saw how useful **CanvasLayer** is for ordering the drawing of a complex scene and how to combine **ParallaxBackground** and **ParallaxLayer** nodes to create parallax scrolling efficiently. Finally, we learned how to add the very common split-screen feature to a game.

Q&A

Q. My 3D scene is not rendered by my viewport!

A. Make sure you didn't forget to add some illumination to your scene. Also, check how you do your connection between the **Viewport** texture and the surface using it. Finally, make sure you configured the Size property of the **Viewport**.

Q. My viewport produces an upside-down image.

A. You forgot to check the Vflip property of your **Viewport**. Also, if it is connected to a **MeshInstance**, it's possible its Transformation property is the cause.

Q. My Parallax background is not moving.

A. Parallax moves relative to the camera, so make sure it is moving (and not just your character). Check if the **ParallaxBackground**'s Base Scale or **ParallaxLayer**'s Scale properties are not set to 0 on one of their axes.

Workshop

See if you can answer the following questions to test your knowledge.

Quiz

1. What are the differences between the ■ Viewport and the ▣ Camera nodes?

2. How do you configure the ■ Viewport to render the frames displayed on the user's screen?

3. In which layer are the nodes rendered that don't belong to a ▧ CanvasLayer?

4. Why is it useless to give a wrap to a ⬚ ParallaxBackground node a ▧ CanvasLayer parent node?

Answers

1. The ▣ Camera node configures the ■ Viewport; the ■ Viewport does the actual rendering of the scene.

2. It's always the root ■ Viewport (aka /**root** node), automatically created by Godot.

3. They will render in the default 0 layer. Keep in mind that layers are rendered from lower to greater value.

4. ⬚ ParallaxBackground is already a ▧ CanvasLayer by itself.

Exercises

1. Try to add a split-screen feature to the game we created in Hour 17 to provide a side and top view.

2. Merge multiple games into a single one by using the ■ ViewportContainer and configuring each ■ Viewport to manage its own world.

3. Now go inception-style by controlling a game from within another game:

   ▶ Create a 3D scene with an arcade game machine (basically a big rectangle ◩ MeshInstance with another plane and ◩ MeshInstance representing the screen) and a player (another rectangle ◩ MeshInstance) with a camera.

   ▶ Attach a ■ Viewport playing the game from Hour 5 to the arcade machine screen.

   ▶ If the game-within-the-game originally uses the **Input** singleton, convert the input processing to use a _**gui_input**() method (typically by creating you own custom **Input** class this is updated each frame by _**gui_input**()).

   ▶ Now inject input to the game-within-the-game ■ Viewport from script. The simplest way to do this is to provide some ⬛ Button nodes. Another more advanced way is allowing the player ◩ MeshInstance to move (or control its view and send a ⬇ RayCast there) and detecting its collision with other ◩ MeshInstance representing the arcade machine's buttons.

Networking

- Basic concepts about networking for games and how to use UDP and TCP protocols to compete
- Godot high-level networking
- RPC system
- Master and slave synchronization

With this 22nd hour, it's time to deal with networking. Synchronizing players across the world to make them feel they play the same game at the same time has always appeared as a daunting task. Having a multiplayer mode feature has to be considered early on in the game development process to avoid long and painful rewriting of core components. Fortunately, Godot once again saves the day thanks to a shiny high-level networking interface!

TCP, UDP, and Why It Matters

First things first: when talking about networking protocol, what immediately comes to mind is the TCP/IP stack that powers basically all of the internet. The reason behind this is clear: TCP works well with the complexity of the internet (remember, it is not called "the web" for nothing!) and makes you feel like everything is simple in the first place:

- It is connection-based, so your server won't mix the requests sent by multiple clients.
- It guarantees reliability, so you're sure to get notified if requests cannot reach their destination.
- It guarantees in-order receiving.
- A request can be almost as big as you want, because TCP takes care of splitting them into packets of the correct size.

All of these points are pretty awesome, but they come at a cost: latency. When a packet is lost, TCP asks the sender again, and when packet n arrives, TPC cannot process it if packet n-1 is still in the wild. This is not a big concern for most applications on the internet (you just wait a bit longer to get your webpage loaded), but not for a real-time application such as a game!

Enter UDP, a much rawer protocol that sends a packet to a remote computer: packet lost, ordering, sender identity, and multiple receptions of the same packets are none of its concerns. You can use UDP for fine-tuning over handling networking. This allows you to go much faster at the price of complexity.

This is where Godot's high-level networking system comes in: it handles UDP complexity for us and integrates it inside its Scene system, making a multiplayer game seem like a single-player game where you set each node to either synchronize with a remote player or send synchronization information about its current state to other players.

NOTE

Use Raw UDP/TCP

In addition to its high-level networking system, Godot also offers classical UDP and TCP client/server capability with **StreamPeerTCP**, **TCP_Server**, and **PacketPeerUDP** classes. This is useful if you want to write your custom game server or connect to a third-party API.

Managing Connections

Enough with theory! To connect multiple Godot instances, we need to configure one of them as a server and connect the others as clients to it (Listing 22.1).

LISTING 22.1   Creating Connection

```
# For the server
func host_game(port):
    var host = NetworkedMultiplayerENet.new()
    host.create_server(port)
    get_tree().set_network_peer(host)

# For the clients
func join_game(ip, port):
    var host = NetworkedMultiplayerENet.new()
    host.create_client(ip, port)
    get_tree().set_network_peer(host)
```

We create a **NetworkedMultiplayerENet** instance, configure it as a server or client, and define it as the one to use for our **Scene Tree**. Note that the Godot network API is defined in the abstract **NetworkedMultiplayerPeer** class, from which **NetworkedMultiplayerENet** is an implementation using the ENet library.

Once our network peer is defined on each Godot instance, we are notified of network activity by signals:

▶ **network_peer_connected:** A new Godot instance joins the server. This signal is triggered on each peer (not only on the server) and the newly connected ones get this signal numerous times (one per peer is already connected before it arrives).

▶ **network_peer_disconnected:** Triggered on each peer when someone left (except on the leaving peer).

▶ **connected_to_server:** Triggered on the newly connected peer once connection has been achieved.

▶ **connection_failed:** Triggered when the connection has failed with the server.

▶ **server_disconnected:** Connection with the server has been lost, so other peers get a network_peer_disconnected signal.

NOTE

Beware of Firewalls

Be careful when choosing a port for your game! While it is easy to remember, low number ports (like TCP 80 used by HTTP) are most of the time only accessible to users with advanced privileges (e.g., administrator). So, you should choose a port higher than 1023 and make sure it is not already in use by some other application.

Finally, when you want to close the connection, simply remove the network peer from the **Scene Tree** (Listing 22.2).

LISTING 22.2   Closing Connection

```
func finish_game(port):
    get_tree().set_network_peer(null)
```

Note that this works the same for both the client and server sides.

Remote Procedure Call

Let's make our multiple Godot instances talk! For this, we can use what is called RPC (Remote Procedure Call), which consists of triggering from a peer the call of a procedure on one or multiple other peers. Be careful that you are talking of "procedure" and not "function," because the second procedure doesn't return any value to the caller (so it's a fire-and-forget call). Godot provides the following RPC methods:

▶ **Node.rpc:** Regular RPC call; use it to call one of the node's procedure.

▶ **Node.rset:** Same as RPC, but used to remotely set a node's property.

> ▶ **Node.rpc_id/rset_id:** Instead of sending the procedure to all of the peers, we can use those methods to only send the procedure on a given peer by providing its network ID.

> ▶ **Node.rpc_unreliable/rset_unreliable/rpc_unreliable_id/rset_unreliable_id:** Finally, these are the unreliable versions of the precedent methods. This means it's possible your procedure won't be received at all (remember how UDP works?).

Remote and Sync Keywords

That said, RPC can be a dangerous tool if not well controlled: what would happen if you allowed a complete stranger from across the globe to call any function of your Godot instance? (Remember Hour 12, when you had access to the entire user's filesystem from Godot?) To prevent anything like that, a function (or a property) must be explicitly flagged as allowed to be called by RPC with a keyword (Listing 22.3):

> ▶ **sync:** the procedure is called by all peers (including the caller).

> ▶ **remote:** the procedure is only called on the remote peer and not on the caller.

LISTING 22.3   Using Remote and Sync Keywords

```
var speed = Vector2(0, -200)
sync var alive = true

remote func update_pos_for_remotes(new_pos):
    position = new_pos

func _process(delta):
    if is_network_master():
        position += speed * delta
        if position.y < 0:
            position.y = 0
            rset("alive", false)
        rpc_unreliable("update_pos_for_remotes", position)
```

Note: Beware of network congestion.

Keep in mind that using RPC, even unreliable, on each frame is costly and won't scale well beyond the local network or a few player games, so use the fixed timer for such a task.

Listing 22.3 illustrates how to use these keywords: we have a node falling down, and when it hits the ground, it gets killed. Once per frame, **process** gets called to update the state of the node on the peer responsible for it (that's what **is_network_master()** tells you, but more on this later).

Now this peer needs to tell the other ones about the new position of this node. Thus, it uses the RPC call on **update_pos_for_remotes**, which updates all of the peers except itself. Note that we use **rpc_unreliable** here given that the call is done for every frame, so missing one is not as much of a concern.

Finally, when the node hits the ground, we need to set the property **alive** to **false**. This time, even the peer responsible for the node must have this property updated, so we flag it as **sync** and let the **rset** call update every peer, including ourselves at the same time.

Slaves and Masters

Even if **remote** and **sync** are pretty cool, they fall short on something: exploit protection. Given that any peer can do a RPC on **remote** or **sync** procedure that will impact all the other peers, it's pretty easy for a client to impersonate the server and trick the game.

In our previous example, we could have a malicious client using the **rset** (alive, false) to kill a node even if it is not responsible for it.

To solve this, Godot has a concept of master/slave that is set on a per-node basis for each peer. Remember the **is_network_master()** from the last paragraph? It returns **true** if the peer on which the code is executed is in charge (i.e., the master) of the current node.

By default, the server is set as master of all the nodes in the **Scene Tree**. Later on, when clients start connecting, they can agree that a node is managed by a specific peer. This means you should make sure a node has only a single peer declared as master; otherwise, strange things will happen.

Also note that the default **set_network_master()** configures a node slave/master property (Listing 22.4) as well as all of its children in the **Scene Tree**, but you can disable this behavior by setting **false** as a second parameter.

LISTING 22.4   Declaring a Peer Master of a Node

```
var player_scene = preload("res://scenes/player.tscn")

func peer_joined(peer_id)
    var player = player_scene.instance()
    get_tree().get_root().add_child(player)
    player.set_network_master(peer_id)
```

Now you can **use is_network_master()** (Listing 22.5) to separate the task that should only run on the master, typically processing a player's user input.

LISTING 22.5   Filtering Input Processing Depending on Node's Master Property

```
func _update(delta)
    if is_network_master():
        if Input.is_action_pressed("ui_up"):
            # Do something
```

Mixing **sync/remote** and **is_network_master()** can be cumbersome, so the **master** and **slave** keywords have been created to simplify things. As you can guess from their names, a procedure flagged with **master** is only executed on the peer declared as master for the node. On the other hand, **slave** is executed on the other peers (Figure 22.1).

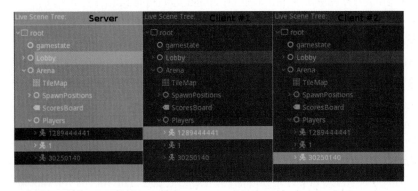

FIGURE 22.1
Typical live Scene Tree view of each peer with master (in green) and slave (in red) nodes.

This allows really powerful synchronization patterns in which a master gets notification from slaves (with the latter using RPC on a **master** procedure) and sends a synchronization command to them (RPC on a slave procedure) while being sure no malicious slave can impersonate himself (a slave using RPC on **slave** procedure gets only called on itself!).

In noncompetitive or co-op games, exploits are a small concern. Depending on your use case, it can be necessary to avoid using **remote** and **sync** keywords, given how they can be used by any slave and offer no protection against malicious use.

LISTING 22.6   Replacing Sync by Slave

```
slave func update_score(new_score)
    score = new_score

func _on_player_killed():
    if is_network_master():   # Score should be handled only by the master
        rpc("update_score", score + 100)
        update_score(score + 100)
```

A common pattern to replace **sync** is to declare your procedure as a **slave** (Listing 22.6), then call it both as RPC (to synchronize all of the slave peers) and directly as a regular function (to execute the function locally). This way, you'll get the procedure called everywhere when triggered from the master without the risk of exploits when used by a malicious slave.

TRY IT YOURSELF ▼

Test the Synchronization

A great way to understand networking is to try it on a really simple project:

1. Create a very basic GUI with a couple of buttons and a label. See Figure 22.2.

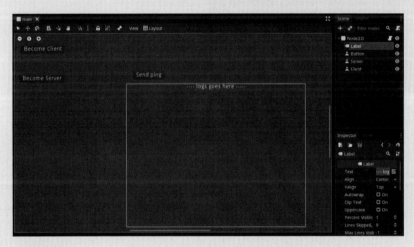

FIGURE 22.2
A basic GUI.

2. Connect the functions provided in Listing 22.1 to the client/server buttons.

3. Create a **_update_text** function, adding a line of log to the Label and multiple functions calling this **_update_text**, while flagging with different network attributes. See Figure 22.3.

```
 3  onready var label = get_node('Label')
 4
 5  func _update_text(txt):
 6  ›ı    label.text = label.text + '\n' + txt
 7
 8  sync func _sync_update_text(txt):
 9  ›ı    _update_text('sync ' + txt)
10
11  master func _master_update_text(txt):
12  ›ı    _update_text('master ' + txt)
13
14  slave func _slave_update_text(txt):
15  ›ı    _update_text('slave ' + txt)
16      .
17  remote func _remote_update_text(txt):
18  ›ı    _update_text('remove ' + txt)
19
20
21  func _on_Button_pressed():
22  ›ı    rpc('_sync_update_text', 'ping !')
23  ›ı    rpc('_master_update_text', 'ping !')
24  ›ı    rpc('_slave_update_text', 'ping !')
25  ›ı    rpc('_remote_update_text', 'ping !')
```

FIGURE 22.3
Finding a static mesh asset in the content browser.

4. Connect the ping button to a function making **rpc**, **rpc_id** or direct call of our network function.

5. Finally, launch your project and test with multiple configurations. It's really informative to mess around to see what happens (like having multiple servers or setting multiple peers as master).

Visual Script

As you just saw, networking is a lot about scripting: you must dynamically configure who is slave and master (given peers are not known beforehand), then use RPC to call script functions as a procedure. So far, we've only showed examples with GDScript because it is the most common way to script with Godot, but this doesn't mean you cannot use VisualScript for networking (Figure 22.4).

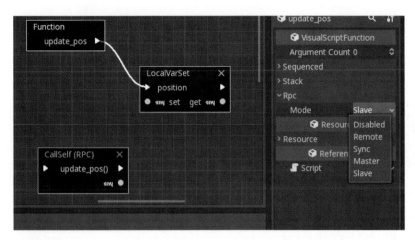

FIGURE 22.4
Using networking with VisualScript.

As you can see in Figue 22.4, VisualScript provides an RPC dropdown menu to configure the network attribute on a function. To call the procedure, you can use the **CallSelf** box configured on the RPC method (this is exactly the same as calling **Node.rpc** with GDScript).

Summary

In this hour, you learned about networking and how Godot simplifies this area through its high-level networking system. You saw how to configure and connect client and server. Then you learned how to use RPC to synchronize across network peers. Finally, you learned how to use the keywords **sync**, **remote**, **master**, and **slave** to decorate your procedures and use more powerful synchronization patterns by using the per-peer and per-node master/slave properties. Networking is a complex beast with many concerns (typically designing your procedures to avoid exploits from malicious clients, or keeping the amount of data low to synchronize and avoid latency), but you already have a good overview of what Godot has to offer.

Q&A

Q. Is there a way to determine ahead of time the network ID of the peers?

A. Server ID is always 1, so it can be safely hardcoded in your game; however, clients get unique, randomly generated IDs at connection time.

Q. How can you determine if the current node is master or slave?

A. You can use the **Node.is_network_master()** method, which returns a Boolean.

Q. Can I set up a dedicated server for my game with Godot?

A. By default, Godot ships as a full-grown game engine with 2D/3D renderer and audio engine. This is perfectly normal when used by a player, but gets really annoying when you want to make it run on a headless server without GPU and a fraction of the CPU and RAM of a modern gaming PC.
However, a server version of Godot is available on the official website (it currently supports Linux 64bits, which is a great choice as a server).

Workshop

See if you can answer the following questions to fix your knowledge.

Quiz

1. What happens if you do a RPC on a sync procedure from a slave node?

2. What is the difference between master/slave and client/server?

3. Can I have two masters on the same node in my game?

4. What happens if I don't explicitly define who's the master for a node?

5. Given a **sync func foo()** function, what is the difference between **foo()**, **rpc('foo')**, and **rpc_id(1, 'foo')**?

Answers

1. The procedure gets called on all the peers (including ourselves).

2. Server/client is only a matter of a network connection. Master/slave defines which peer manages a given node and sends synchronization to the others.

3. Strictly speaking, you can, but both peers will refuse to execute slave RPC and won't send master RPC through the network, so your game will desynchronize pretty fast. So don't do that.

4. By default, the server is the master of all nodes.

5. **foo()** calls the function locally only, **rpc('foo')** calls the function locally and on each peer (given function is marked **sync**), and **rpc_id(1, 'foo')** calls the function only on the remote peer with ID 1 (i.e., the server).

Exercises

The best way to work with networking is to take an existing single-player game and convert it to a multiplayer game:

1. Modify the space shooter from Hour 5 to add a lobby so that the game only starts when a client connects to a server. Once started, client and server each have their own game independent from each other.

2. Now start synchronizing by providing a spectator mode so that only the server process with which the player inputs and synchronizes game state is a connected client. This is done by flagging its functions as sync and using RPC instead of direct calls.

3. Finally, provide a co-op mode: when a peer connects, add a new ship to the scene (a new peer should be master of this ship node). Don't forget to check **is_network_master**() before processing player input to have a peer controlling only its own ship.

HOUR 23
Game 3: Networked Bomberman Clone

What You'll Learn in This Hour:

▶ Handle networking in a real game
▶ Use the **TileMap** and **TileSet** tools to create a map
▶ Combine the **Sprite** and **AnimationPlayer** for your animations
▶ Use **AutoLoad** to make a script global

In this hour, we will create our final game. It is a clone of the Nintendo Entertainment System-era legendary game *Bomberman*, but with a killer feature the original didn't have in its time: networked multiplayer. The game consists of multiple players evolving in a top-down labyrinth with the ability to plant bombs to break walls and kill other players, increasing their scores. This game is pretty classic, and making a single-player version of it shouldn't be too much trouble after what we've learned from games 1 and 2, so it will allow us to focus more on the networking aspects.

Concept and Design

Each player is controlled by its own instance of the game. Ideally, each instance is on its own computer with a real human player. But if you lack spare computers and/or friends with whom share your joy of Godot, it's perfectly fine to start the game multiple times on your own computer and switch from one window to another to control each player in turn.

As said earlier, players evolve in a tiled-based labyrinth, so they can move vertically and horizontally with the arrow keys and plant bombs with the space bar. Once planted, a bomb will wait two seconds before blowing up. Given it's a tiled-based game, the bomb detonates following vertical and horizontal tiles (it doesn't propagate in diagonal tiles).

The detonation propagates until it has reached two tiles or hits a solid wall. On the other hand, softer walls are destroyed by the explosion, and players are killed.

When killed, a player returns to its beginning position, and its killer gets 100 more points (unless the player committed suicide, thus getting –50 points)

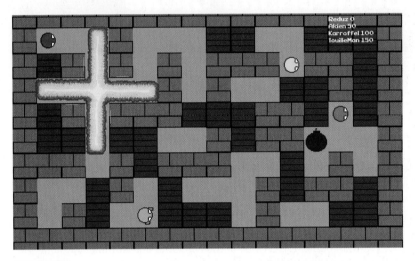

FIGURE 23.1
Screenshot of the final game.

Given that it's a multiplayer game, we need to build a main menu to choose whether we want to start the game as a server or to join an existing game as a client. Finally, we need a lobby in which players wait once they join until the server decides it's time to start the game.

Bootstrap the Project

You know the drill: create a new project and add the classic folders (scene, scripts, etc.) to have a nicely organized project.

FIGURE 23.2
Our project directory.

Before we start jumping on the code, you should copy the fonts and Sprite resources from the Hour 23 folder. Of course, when reading this tutorial, don't hesitate to have a look at the scripts or open this project with the Godot editor if you get stuck.

Setting Up the Scenes

As usual with Godot, we first divide our game into small scenes, allowing us to break down complexity and improve modularity:

TABLE 23.1 Scenes Needed for the Game

Scene	Description
Menu and Lobby	Given how simple the menu and lobby scenes are, we can combine them into a single scene and choose which one to display (or none once the game is started).
	This scene consists of a ⊙ **Control** node (this is the base node for UI) with two ⊙ **Control** children (one for the menu, one for the lobby), each one composed of a mix of ▢ **Label**, ⬛ **Button**, and ⬛ **Input**.
Arena	This is our main scene where the instantiated player scenes evolve and the bomb and explosion scenes are created. We also have to handle the labyrinth here, which is the perfect use case for a ▦ **TileMap** node and the starting position for players with **Position2D** nodes. Finally, this scene is responsible for displaying the score for each player through a simple ▢ **Label**.
Player	The player scene consists of a 🐾 **KinematicBody2D** with a ⬛ **CollisionShape2D**, which allows us to easily move it and handle its collisions. We also need a ☺ **Sprite** and an ▦ **AnimationPlayer** to display the player on the screen and animate it when it is moving. Finally, a ⏲ **Timer** node is used to avoid the player spamming bombs.
Bomb	Given that the bomb won't move once planted, we can represent it with a ⬛ **StaticBody2D** with a ⬛ **CollisionShape2D**. Just like for the player, we use ☺ **Sprite** and ▦ **AnimationPlayer** nodes to help players spot when a bomb is about to blow up. Speaking of this, a ⏲ **Timer** allows us to configure when the explosion occurs.
Explosion	Because an explosion propagates by following the tiles, we can rely on the arena's tilemap to handle collisions. This means our explosion scene has to display a per-tile explosion animation using a ☺ **Sprite** and an ▦ **AnimationPlayer**.

As we saw in Hour 21, one of the big advantages of the Godot high-level network system is that it allows us to first focus on developing a single-player game, then add multiplayer capability to it by declaring how nodes should synchronize together. To follow this idea, we'll start by making a single-player *Bomberman* game, then we'll switch our focus to making it multiplayer.

Making the Scenes

Let's look at how to make the scenes.

Creating Player, Bomb, and Explosion Scenes

Start with the most important scene: the player. Often, it is one of the most complex scenes of the game. However, our game is still small, so there is no reason to panic. Hour 9 told us that for a 2D platform game, ⬡ **KinematicBody2D** is the best root node for player-controlled scenes, given that it isn't affected by physics while it still allows us to detect a collision and move it accordingly if needed.

As you already know, a ⬡ **KinematicBody2D** needs a collision shape to work, so we'll add a ◼ **CollisionShape2D** and configure its **Shape** property. Given that our player will move on tiles, we may be tempted to use a rectangular shape the size of a tile. However, this causes continuous collisions that often end up with our node becoming stuck. So, it's a much better solution to use a circle collision shape that's slightly smaller than the size of a tile.

Speaking of which, we should choose the tile size of 32 pixels, so we will scale all of our Sprites and collision shapes to this size.

We will also add as a child to the root node: a ⧗ **Timer** node to control the rate of fire of the player. We'll set its **Wait Time** to one second, and, given that this timer is triggered by code when a bomb is planted, select the **One Shot** property and make sure **Autostart** is disabled.

NOTE

Collision Shape and Scaling

A reminder from Hour 9: be careful when scaling collision shapes. Make sure they are uniform and have nonnegative values. Otherwise, strange things will happen with your physics.

It's time to make the player visible. We could use the simple ◕ **AnimatedSprite** for this task, but to add a bit of variety, we'll choose the more powerful ◕ **Sprite** and ▦ **AnimationPlayer** combo this time. We aren't in Kansas anymore.

First, add the ◕ **Sprite** node as a child of the root, then configure it using the **Texture** property. Click on load and select "sprites/player1.png." At this point, you should realize that the image we loaded is not a single Sprite but a spritesheet (an image containing one next to other, multiple Sprites), so configure the ◕ **Sprite** accordingly with the **Animation:Vframes** and **Animation:Hframes** properties (in our case, the spritesheet contains one row and three columns, so **Vframes = 1** and **Hframes = 3**).

Now we can use the **Frame** property to pass through the animations and choose the default one. As you can see, our spritesheet is composed of three Sprites: an idle pose and two steps that compose a primitive walking animation (Figure 23.3).

FIGURE 23.3
Sprite configuration on the player node.

Using the **Frame** property by hand (or even scripting its update with GDNative) is a no-go when you can use a shiny tool like the ▦ **AnimationPlayer**. Add this node (make sure it is a direct child of the root) and start configuring its animations.

Click on the ▦ **AnimationPlayer**, and the animation menu will open on the lower part of the editor. Click on ⬚ to create a new animation and call it **idle**. Now use the Scene Tree viewer to select the **Sprite** node. In the Inspector, find the **Animation:Frame** property and make sure its value is **0**. Now click on ⬚, a popup that asks you if you want to add a new track to your animation. Click "create."

FIGURE 23.4
Idle animation for the player.

You have created your first animation composed of . . . one frame. This seems silly putting it this way, but this means you can now easily improve the one-frame idle animation. Once the walking animation is triggered, you'll need to trigger this simple idle animation, or the player will walk forever.

Speaking of the **walking** animation, it is the same thing as idle animation, except you click two times on the button next to the **Animation:Frame** property (once per frame). This time, be careful to configure the **Length** and **Step** property of your animation; otherwise, you will end up with something clunky (typically frame 1 at 0 seconds, frame 2 at 0.1 seconds, then frame 1 again 0.9 seconds later when the animation loop's given default Length is 1 second). Also, don't forget to set the track to **Discrete**; otherwise, the default continuous mode blends your two frames together and you'll end up with a single frame playing continuously (Figure 23.5).

FIGURE 23.5
Walking animation for the player.

Finally, you should have a third and last animation to do the **respawn** on. Do the same steps, but this time, don't change the Sprite, but make it blink (it will help the player spot where his character has respawned). To do so, use the next to the **Visibility:Visible** property. Note that this is where using an AnimatedSprite for our animation would fall short (Figure 23.6).

FIGURE 23.6
Respawn animation for the player.

Creating the Bomb Scene

The bomb scene is pretty similar to the player scene:

1. Create a ▣ **StaticBody2D** node as root and rename it "Bomb."

2. Add a child ▣ **CollisionShape2D** and activate its **Disabled** property. The idea is that a player plants a bomb on the tile on which it currently stands, so you'll want to wait a bit before enabling the bomb physics to let the player leave the tile and avoid glitches.

3. Add a ⏳ **Timer**, rename it "EnableCollisionTimer," and configure it with **Wait Time = 0.5, One Shot = True**, and **Auto Start = True**.

4. Create a 🙂 **Sprite** and set the **Texture** to the "sprites/bomb.png." Like for the player, it is a 3 × 1 spritesheet that makes the bomb get redder the closest it is to exploding.

5. Finally, create and use ▦ **AnimationPlayer**, configure a **default** animation lasting 2 seconds, and change the bomb color at 0, 1, and 1.5 seconds. Activate the **Playback:Active** checkbox to start the animation when the node gets created.

Note that we don't need to create a ⏳ **Timer** to control when the bomb will blow: we will obtain similar results by connecting to the **animation_finished** event provided by our ▦ **AnimationPlayer**.

Creating the Explosion Scene

The explosion scene is even simpler:

1. Create a 🙂 **Sprite** node as root, call it "Explosion," and assign to it the "sprites/explosion.png" image. This time, the spritesheet is a 3 x 7 representing a seven-frame center and side and end explosion animations.

2. Add an ▦ **AnimationPlayer** and create three animations: "explosion_center," "explosion_side," and "explosion_side_border," each 0.35 seconds long with steps of 0.05 seconds.

Creating the Arena Scene

We start with a ◉ **Node2D** as root of the scene (don't forget to rename it "Arena" for the sake of clarity). Strictly speaking, this node is not really useful, but it allows you to better divide the subnodes.

To construct the labyrinth, you can create a scene for each type of block, then instantiate and place them by hand on the Arena scene. However, this is a really cumbersome task, and we have a much better tool to achieve this: the ▦ **TileMap** node. As it name indicates, this type of node allows you to easily select and place tiles on your scene.

But before you can use a ▦ **TileMap**, you'll need to build a ▦ **Tileset** that defines different tiles to be placed. For our game, we need three types of tiles:

▶ **BackgroundBrick:** represents the ground where the players will walk

▶ **SolidBrick:** represents the wall of the arena; the player cannot cross them, and explosions are stopped

▶ **BreakableBrick:** blocks players like SolidBrick; player is destroyed once hit by an explosion

Create a new scene, call it "scenes/tileset-source.tscn," and add a root ⬤ **Node2D**. Now, we are going to add 🙂 **Sprite** children nodes, with each of them representing a tile. Make sure to give a meaningful name for each of these nodes, as the tiles will keep them once imported into the ▦ **TileMap**.

For each 🙂 **Sprite**, load "sprites/bricks.png" in the **Texture** property (once again, it's a 3 × 1 spritesheet, so correct **Vframes** and **Hframes** accordingly) and configure the **Frame** property so that each tile is different.

On top of that, add a ▦ **StaticBody2D** with a ▦ **CollisionShape2D** (with a ▦ **RectangularShape2D** of 32 × 32) child to the SolidBrick and BreakableBrick (Figure 23.7).

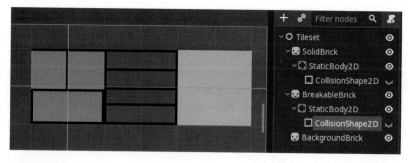

FIGURE 23.7
TileSet source scene.

Now open the menu **Scene –> Convert To . . . –> TileSet** and save the tileset as "scenes/tileset.res."

Back to the arena scene. Add a ▦ **TileMap** child node, configure the ▦ **Tileset** property to load the shiny new tileset, and start painting the map with tiles (Figure 23.8).

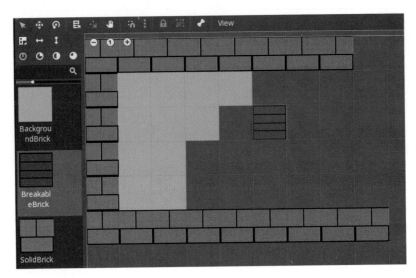

FIGURE 23.8
Drawing the tilemap.

Once you're happy with the results of your map, move on by adding spawn positions for the player. Add a ⊙ **Node2D** and name it "SpawnPositions." Inside it, add four ✛ **Position2D** where you want your players to start. (Of course, they should be placed on a BackgroundBrick, since you don't want a player to get stuck in a wall.)

Now, create another ⊙ **Node2D** and name it "Players," which is the node where you'll register all player scenes to easily iterate through them (more on this in the scripting part).

Finally, create a simple ▣ **Label** node named "ScoresBoard" that displays the score of each player.

FIGURE 23.9
Scene Tree of the player, bomb, explosion, and arena.

NOTE

Make the Draw Order Right

Even in 2D, the Z axis is useful to determine what is displayed on top of what. Here, we want the z value for the arena scene to stay at the default value of 0, then set it higher for bomb, player, and explosion, in this order.

Scripts and Input

To control the player, first attach a script to the player scene root node, save it as "scripts/player. gd," and start tweaking it (see Listing 23.1).

LISTING 23.1   Player Movements with Kinematic Body — player.gd

```
const WALK_SPEED = 200
var dead = false
var direction = Vector2()
var current_animation = "idle"

func _physics_process(delta):
    if dead:
        return

    if (Input.is_action_pressed("ui_up")):
        direction.y = - WALK_SPEED
    elif (Input.is_action_pressed("ui_down")):
        direction.y =   WALK_SPEED
    else:
        direction.y = 0

    if (Input.is_action_pressed("ui_left")):
        direction.x = - WALK_SPEED
    elif (Input.is_action_pressed("ui_right")):
        direction.x =   WALK_SPEED
    else:
        direction.x = 0

    move_and_slide(direction)

    rotation = atan2(direction.y, direction.x)
    var new_animation = "idle"
    if direction:
        new_animation = "walking"
    if new_animation != current_animation:
        animation.play(new_animation)
        current_animation = new_animation
```

It shouldn't be a surprise now: create a **_physics_process()** function to control the movement of the player. Use the **move_and_slide()** function provided by the ![] **KinematicBody2D**, which automatically takes care of moving the player and handling collisions for you. Update the animation if needed (because re-setting the animation at each frame would make it only play the first frame of it).

Continue by creating a **_process** function to allow the player to plant bombs (Listing 23.2).

LISTING 23.2   Player Planting Boms

```
var can_drop_bomb = true
var tilemap = get_node("/root/Arena/TileMap")

func _process(delta):
    if dead:
        return
    if Input.is_action_just_pressed("ui_select") and can_drop_bomb:
        dropbomb(tilemap.centered_world_pos(position))
        can_drop_bomb = false
        drop_bomb_cooldown.start()

sync func dropbomb(pos):
    var bomb = bomb_scene.instance()
    bomb.position = pos
    bomb.owner = self
    get_node("/root/Arena").add_child(bomb)

func _on_DropBombCooldown_timeout():
    can_drop_bomb = true
```

Like its name suggests, connect **_on_DropBombCooldown_timeout()** to the player DropBombCooldown timer.

Bomb and Explosion

Start by creating "scripts/bomb.gd" and connect it to the bomb scene (see Listing 23.3). This script does three things: first, it enables the ![] **CollisionShape2D** once the ![] **Timer** has finished, then it waits for ![] **AnimationPlayer** to end spawn explosion scene instances according to the type of tiles present on the ![] **TileMap**, and last, but not least, it finishes by destroying itself (because it blew up, remember?).

LISTING 23.3   Bomb Explosion Expanding Algorithm

```
extends StaticBody2D

const EXPLOSION_RADIUS = 2

onready var explosion_scene = preload("res://scenes/explosion.tscn")
onready var tilemap = get_node("/root/Arena/TileMap")
onready var tile_solid_id = tilemap.tile_set.find_tile_by_name("SolidBrick")

func propagate_explosion(centerpos, propagation):
    for i in range(1, EXPLOSION_RADIUS + 1):
        var tilepos = center_tile_pos + propagation * i
        if tilemap.get_cellv(tilepos) != tile_solid_id:
            # Boom !
            var explosion = explosion_scene.instance()
            explosion.position = tilemap.centered_world_pos_from_tilepos(tilepos)
            get_parent().add_child(explosion)
        else:
            # Explosion was stopped by a solid block
            break

func _on_AnimationPlayer_animation_finished( name ):
    ...
    # Propagate the explosion by starting where the bomb was and go
    # away from it in straight vertical and horizontal lines
    propagate_explosion(position, Vector2(0, 1))
    propagate_explosion(position, Vector2(0, -1))
    propagate_explosion(position, Vector2(1, 0))
    propagate_explosion(position, Vector2(-1, 0))
    ...
```

The important point here is how you use TileMap's **map_to_world()**, **get_cellv()** and **find_tile_by_name()** to retrieve the tiles to instantiate an explosion scene.

Speaking of explosions, it's time to create and attach its script "scripts/explosion.gd." The idea is roughly the same as in bomb.gd: use TileMap to retrieve the tile in which the explosion takes place, making sure this tile is a BackgroundTile. Then retrieve the players' nodes (now we are happy to have this "Arena/Players" node) and check for each to see if it is standing on the exploding tile (Listing 23.4).

LISTING 23.4   Explosions

```
extends Node2D

onready var tilemap = get_node("/root/Arena/TileMap")
onready var animation = get_node("AnimationPlayer")
```

```
func _ready():
    # Retrieve the tile hit by the explosion and flatten it to the ground
    var tile_pos = tilemap.world_to_map(position)
    var tile_background_id = tilemap.tile_set.find_tile_by_name("BackgroundBrick")
    tilemap.set_cellv(tile_pos, tile_background_id)
    # Now that we know which tile is blowing up, retrieve the players
    # and destroy them if they are on it
    for player in  get_tree().get_nodes_in_group('players'):
        var playerpos = tilemap.world_to_map(player.position)
        if playerpos == tile_pos:
            player.damage()
```

Just like for the bomb, we should also add a function connected to the ▓ AnimationPlayer's end of animation to free the Explosion node once it is no longer needed.

▼ TRY IT YOURSELF

Single-player *Bomberman*

With a bit of polish, your *Bomberman* game will be playable:

1. Add a player scene to the Arena/Players node.

2. Configure the arena scene as the main scene of your Godot project.

3. Hit run and start playing your *Bomberman*.

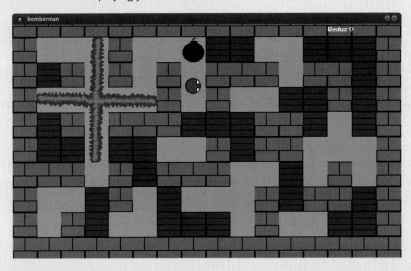

FIGURE 23.10
Our game running in single-player mode.

4. You can now add a second player to your scene and correct the player.gd script to handle different keys depending on which Player node is currently processed. Now you can have a real duel.

Enter Multiplayer

As you saw earlier, you cannot start the game right on the arena scene if your game is multiplayer: you have to let the player first choose if he wishes to host a game or join one. So, you should create the lobby scene, which cumulates the main menu with the lobby menu where users are listed. This is mainly the GUI widget placing and signaling connection, and doesn't have much to do with multiplayer, so we leave it to you (just copy/paste "scenes/lobby.tscn" and "scripts/lobby.gd" from the Hour 23 folder).

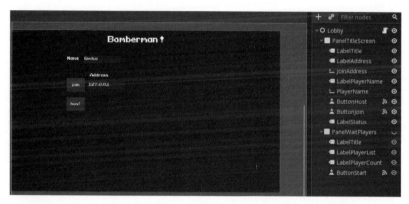

FIGURE 23.11
AutoLoad configuration for gamestate.gd.

On top of that, we should keep information about the players (e.g., nicknames) before the Arena scene is created (so we cannot store that under "Arena/Players/").

One solution is to set the lobby as the main scene, then store players' information in a script connected to the root node of this scene. This is doable; however, it's more elegant to store that information in an **AutoLoad** and have them available in all scenes, even if you decide to remove the lobby scene (for example, if you start the game as a dedicated server).

Create a new "scripts/gamestate.gd," then select **Project > Project Settings > AutoLoad**, load the newly created script, and make sure **Singleton** is set to **Enable** (Figure 23.12).

FIGURE 23.12
AutoLoad configuration for gamestate.gd.

Now, open the gamestate.gd script and copy the **host_game()** and **join_game()** functions from Listing 23.1. Those functions are called when the user clicks on the **host** or **join** buttons, along with hiding the main menu to show the list of players waiting for the game to start.

As you saw in Hour 22, a player joining or leaving the game triggers a signal that connects to a function to keep the list of players up to date (Listing 23.5).

LISTING 23.5   Gamestate Network Signals Handling

```
var players = {}
func _ready():
    get_tree().connect("network_peer_connected", self, "_player_connected")
    get_tree().connect("network_peer_disconnected", self,"_player_disconnected")
    get_tree().connect("connected_to_server", self, "_connected_ok")
    get_tree().connect("connection_failed", self, "_connected_fail")
    get_tree().connect("server_disconnected", self, "_server_disconnected")

func _player_disconnected(id):
    # Each peer get this notification when a peer diseapers,
    # so we remove the corresponding player data.
    var player_node = get_node("/root/Arena/Players/%s" % id)
    if player_node:
        # If we have started the game yet, the player node won't be present
        player_node.queue_free()
    players.erase(id)

func _connected_ok():
    # This method is only called from the newly connected
    # client. Hence we register ourself to the server.
    var player_id = get_tree().get_network_unique_id()
    # Note given this call
    rpc("register_player_to_server", player_id, player_nickname)
    # Now just wait for the server to start the game
    emit_signal("waiting_for_players")

func _connected_fail():
    _stop_game("Cannot connect to server")

func _server_disconnected():
    _stop_game("Server connection lost")
```

Here, the **_stop_game()** function disables the network and switches back to the main menu, but that is up to you.

More interesting is the RPC call on **register_player_to_server()** function. The idea is to have the joining client call the server to communicate his nickname. In return, the server tells him if he can join the game (if the game is not yet started and if there are less than four players). It turn, the server calls the clients with RPC to notify them of the newly joined one and vice versa (Listing 23.6).

LISTING 23.6   Gamestate Register New Player

```
master func register_player_to_server(id, name):
    # As server, we notify here if the new client is allowed to join the game
    if game_started:
        rpc_id(id, "_kicked_by_server", "Game already started")
    elif len(players) == MAX_PLAYERS:
        rpc_id(id, "_kicked_by_server", "Server is full")
    # Send to the newcomer the already present players
    for p_id in players:
        rpc_id(id, "register_player", p_id, players[p_id])
    # Now register the newcomer everywhere, note the newcomer's peer will
    # also be called
    rpc("register_player", id, name)
    # register_player is slave, so rpc won't call it on our peer
    # (of course we could have set it sync to avoid this)
    register_player(id, name)

slave func register_player(id, name):
    players[id] = name
```

Eventually, the user on the server will lose patience and hit the start game button. This sends an RPC to everybody (including himself) on the **start_game()** procedure (Listing 23.7).

LISTING 23.7   Gamestate Start Game

```
sync func start_game():
    # Load the main game scene
    var arena = load("res://scenes/arena.tscn").instance()
    get_tree().get_root().add_child(arena)
    var spawn_positions = arena.get_node("SpawnPositions").get_children()
    # Populate each player
    var i = 0
    for p_id in players:
        var player_node = player_scene.instance()
        player_node.set_name(str(p_id))  # Useful to retrieve the player node with
a node path
        player_node.position = spawn_positions[i].position
        ...
        player_node.set_network_master(p_id)
        arena.get_node("Players").add_child(player_node)
        i += 1
    ...
    emit_signal("game_started")
```

Here, we create the arena scene and add to it a player scene instance per peer connected. Be careful to configure each player scene instance with a different master corresponding to its peer; otherwise, only the server will be able to play.

Synchronization in Player, Bomb, and Explosion

If we now try to run the game in multiplayer, we can start a server, connect the client, and even create the Arena scene on each connected peer with all our on players on it.

But the hard truth hits us as soon as we start sending inputs to our game: there is no synchronization between peers on the player, bomb, and explosion scenes. Now is the time to fix this.

Concerning the player scenes, we already configured them to be owned by their respective peers. This means we can easily use a **is_network_master()** call to run the code responsible for processing inputs on the master peer only (Listing 23.8).

LISTING 23.8   Player Controlled Only by its Master Peer

```
func _physics_process(delta):
    if not is_network_master():
        return
    if not dead:
        if (Input.is_action_pressed("ui_up")):
            ...
        rpc('_dropbomb', tilemap.centered_world_pos(position))
    ...
func _process(delta):
    if not is_network_master() or dead:
        return
    if Input.is_action_just_pressed("ui_select") and can_drop_bomb:
        ...
        move_and_slide(direction)
        _update_rot_and_animation(direction)
    # Send to other peers our player info
    # Note we use unreliable mode given we synchronize during every frame
    # so losing a packet is not an issue
    rpc_unreliable("_update_pos", position, direction)

sync func _dropbomb(pos):
    var bomb = bomb_scene.instance()
    bomb.position = pos
    bomb.owner = self
    get_node("/root/Arena").add_child(bomb)

slave func _update_pos(new_pos, new_direction):
    position = new_pos
    direction = new_direction
    _update_rot_and_animation(direction)
```

Now the trick is to separate the code responsible for handling inputs from the one that actually updates the node's state (this is, what we do for **dropbomb()**). Note that sometimes it's easier to create a function specially dedicated to the slave synchronization: here, we work directly on the master position and direction properties, then use **_update_pos()** on the slaves. This has two advantages: first, it avoids creating temporary values to store the new direction and position before calling the RPC, then it allows us to use **rpc_unreliable** to call the slaves (the call is done on each frame, so we don't care if we lose synchronization from time to time), given that the master always keeps the real value of those properties.

What about the bomb and explosion scenes, you may ask? Well, good news first: our bomb scene is totally deterministic across the peers, so we don't have to do anything for it. Regarding the explosion scene, given that it is created by the bomb, you can be sure it will spawn in the right place and blow at the right time. The trick is that, given how the players are synchronized with an unreliable RPC, you shouldn't check for collision with them on each peer (otherwise, one peer may be lagging and a player may be considered killed when others aren't killed).

The solution is simply to delegate the explosion scene's player collision check to the server, which will RPC the **player.damage()** for synchronization (Listing 23.7).

LISTING 23.7 Explosion Player Collision Controlled by Master

```
func _ready():
    ...
    if not is_network_master():
        return
    # Now that we know which tile is blowing up, retrieve the players
    # and destroy them if they are on it
    for player in get_tree().get_nodes_in_group('players'):
        var playerpos = tilemap.world_to_map(player.position)
        if playerpos == tile_pos:
            player.rpc("damage", owner.id)
```

Finally, you can add a **sync** keyword to our **Player.damage** function, and the game should be complete. Congratulations!

NOTE

Who's Master, Who's Slave?

Remember, if not configured explicitly, master/slave properties inherit their parent, and the default root scene master is the server. So in our game, even if we create bombs with the Players node with various masters, we always add them to the arena scene, which is controlled by the server. In the end, it's the server that is master of all the bomb (and explosion) scenes.

▼ TRY IT YOURSELF

Become a Cheater

It's easy to exploit when networking, and we will illustrate this by abusing the **sync Player.damage()** procedure:

1. Copy your game project in another folder.

2. Open the "scripts/player.gd" file and modify the **_process()** function to do an abusing RPC call of the **player.damage()** procedure (see Listing 23.9).

3. Start the original game as server (you can spawn some clients as well) and start the modified one as client.

4. Now, try planting a bomb with the malicious server. The other players get killed instantly (and each peer, including the server).

   What happened? As we discussed in Hour 22, **sync** and **remote** can be called by any peer (slave or master, it doesn't matter), so you should be careful on what you allow them to trigger.

LISTING 23.9   Player Adds Kill

```
func _process(delta):
    if not is_network_master():  # don't do the exploit on our own player node !
        if Input.is_action_just_pressed("ui_select"):
            rpc("damage", id)
    ...
```

Summary

In this hour, we completed another game from scratch! This time, we used the powerful ▦ AnimationPlayer that can use anything in your scene to create animation, and we also mixed the ▦ TileMap with 🧍 KinematicBody2D players to re-create the NES-era style of gameplay. On top of that, we added to the game network capabilities and multiplayer, and saw how to modify its scenes to do synchronization in a deterministic way while trying to keep away from cheaters.

Q&A

Q. **My client cannot join the server.**

A. Make sure you have configured the same port on both client and server. If the two are not on the same computer, you should verify the IP address as well and make sure there isn't a firewall messing with them. (Did we tell you networking is a complicated thing?)

Q. Can I configure client networking before a server one?

A. You can configure networking in any order. If client is ready before server, it will poll for it until it is ready. However, keep in mind that a timeout will occur if the server takes too long to respond.

Workshop

See if you can answer the following questions to test your knowledge.

Quiz

1. What can I animate with a AnimationPlayer?

2. What do I need to use TileMap?

Answers

1. Every property in any node; it's that powerful.

2. You need a Tileset that is generated from a scene composed of a Sprite. You can also add collision nodes and shapes to handle physics. However, keep in mind that you cannot assign scripts to these nodes.

Exercises

There are some parts of the game we left on the side to simplify things. Now would be a good time to implement them:

1. Add variety among the players by giving each a different color.

2. Handle respawn feature: once hit, a player should move to its initial position, then a blinking animation triggers, during which it cannot move.

3. Create the scoring system: hitting a player gets 100 points, killing yourself makes you lose 50 points. And remember, each feature should be synchronized across the network and cheater-free.

HOUR 24
Exporting the Project

What You'll Learn in This Hour:

▶ Things to consider when exporting for each platform
▶ Creating Export Presets
▶ Modifying Export Parameters

In this hour, we'll learn about the process of deploying the project to the end users. First, we'll take a look at how to export differently for each platform. Then we're onto creating the Export Presets and using them to manage export options. Finally, we'll look at these options and how they affect the exported binaries.

Platform-specific Considerations

Each platform is unique. Features that are available in one platform might not exist in another. For example, exporting for some mobile platforms might have access to unified leaderboards, but rendering quality might not be as good as a desktop's due to limited power. This can be defined in the Project Settings.

Project Settings Override

To override a setting for specific platform, click on that item, choose "Override For" (Figure 24.1), then select the platform. A new setting item is created, and you can use it to define a value for that platform (Figure 24.2).

FIGURE 24.1
"Override For" option

FIGURE 24.2
Disabling HDR for mobile platforms only

Export Presets

Export Preset is a way to manage export parameters for a platform. Most of the time, you want to separate parameters between Debug (Testing) and Release build, since Debug build contains data useful for debugging, but this data takes up a lot of space and is not really useful for end users. Using Export Presets, you can easily switch between building Debug and Release binary, and you don't have to set export options all over again each time you export for other platforms.

Export Templates

Export Templates are Godot engine without the Editor exported for each platform. You can launch the Export Template Manager from the Editor menu > Manage Export Templates. On this dialog (Figure 24.3), you can download the templates and install, reinstall, and uninstall templates.

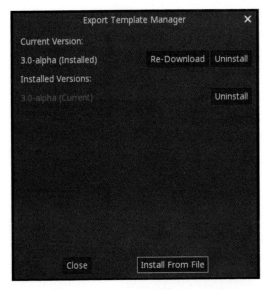

FIGURE 24.3
Export Template Manager

Imported templates are saved in the Engine's data *directory/templates/<template_name>*.

Export Template Version

It is very important that both Export Templates' version and the Editor's version are the same. The exported game might not behave as expected when they don't match.

Export Dialog

With the correct version of export templates installed, you can now create Export Presets and export the game using Export Dialog (Figure 24.4). It can be accessed from Project > Export.

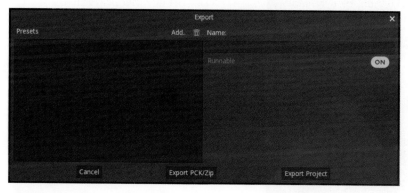

FIGURE 24.4
Blank Export Dialog

To create Export Preset, click the "Add" button (Figure 24.5) and choose the platform.

FIGURE 24.5
Adding an Export Preset

If you add a preset without the corresponding Export Template (Figure 24.6), a warning is displayed at the bottom upon selecting the preset, and you're not able to export the project (Figure 24.7).

FIGURE 24.6
Export Dialog with presets

FIGURE 24.7
Warning on missing Export Template

Export Options

Export Options are located at the right side of the Export Dialog. You customize the parameters from here. You can also specify which files to be included or excluded.

Options

In this tab (Figure 24.8), there are various platform-specific options, including texture formats, binary types, application names, and versions. Export templates are also overridden from here. You may want to do this when you make changes to the Engine internals and compile your own export template specific to the project.

FIGURE 24.8
Options tab

Resources

Here, you can choose which files to include and exclude in the final package. Use a comma to separate entries (Figure 24.9).

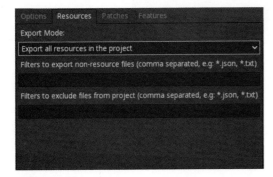

FIGURE 24.9
Resources tab

Patches

This tab creates a patch (Figure 24.10) from a package file of an earlier version.

FIGURE 24.10
Patches tab

Features

This tab summarizes parameters from the Options tab. The features listed (Figure 24.11) determine which value to use in the Project Settings. If a platform-specific value exists for the listed platform or feature, it is used instead of the global value. You can also add custom features here.

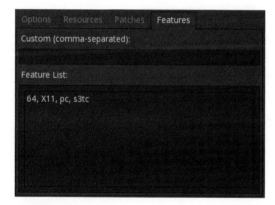

FIGURE 24.11
Features tab

Export

There are two export buttons in the lower part of Export Dialog, one for exporting PCK/Zip only, another for both executable file and PCK. Both files must be in the same folder; otherwise, the game cannot start. Clicking on the button shows Save File Dialog. Choose the destination and give it a name. Finally, click OK, and your game is now playable on that platform.

Summary

In this hour, you learned about exporting the project. You now know how to set default values for each platform. You learned about Export Preset and Export Templates and where to manage them in the Editor and in the file system. You also learned about Export Dialog and adding presets. You learned some basic Export Options and what each tab does. Finally, you learned how to export the executable file.

Q&A

Q. **What is the main difference between the Debug and Release templates?**

A. The Debug template contains information useful in debugging with tools such as "gdb." This information includes functions' names and their position in the source code, source file names, and paths in C++. Overall, it approximately takes an additional 100 megabytes of the final executable file.

Q. **What is the relation between Templates and the Editor?**

A. Templates and Editor compile from the same version of C++ source code. However, Templates are compiled without tools (tools = no), while Editor is compiled with tools enabled (tools = yes). In the other words, Templates are Godot engine without the Editor.

Workshop

Let's recall the contents of this hour by answering these questions.

Quiz

1. Where can you find the imported Export Templates in the file system?

2. True or False: can you use any version of Export Template?

Answers

1. Godot appdata directory/templates/<template_name>.

2. False. The Template's version must match the Editor's.

Exercises

Try to execute these exercises to get acquainted with this topic.

1. Export any projects you've made so far to the same platform as the Editor.

2. Export the project to HTML5 platform and run it using your favorite web browser.

HOUR 25
Native Code

What You'll Learn in This Hour:

- ▶ Using GDNative to replace slow GDScript code
- ▶ Using third-party code via GDNative
- ▶ How the Godot source code is structured
- ▶ What common datatypes are used in the engine's source
- ▶ Creating custom modules

Godot's open source nature lends itself to customization and letting users add their own code. There are a few documented ways of using native code in composition with Godot, making it possible to shape Godot the way you want it to be.

In this hour, you'll learn how to set up a basic shared library that can be used from within Godot using GDNative. This shared library contains code that performs calculations that are more complicated in GDScript than they are in direct machine code. In another example, you'll see how to link this library to another dynamic library, making GDNative a gateway for third-party code.

After that, you'll see how Godot source code is structured and where to find parts of the code. This is also an introduction to modules, which are extensions to the engine that get statically compiled into the binary.

NOTE

Development Environment

Most of Godot's core development happens in Linux, Windows and macOS, as the build environment is more mature in Linux systems. This chapter shows how to build GDNative libraries and Godot itself in Linux systems. The process is similar for other platforms, but Linux is the easiest to get into. To learn about the differences of these platforms, please visit the official documentation, as it has more information on that.

GDNative

GDNative is the C API that interfaces with Godot. This C API is used from external dynamic libraries. Because it is written in C, it uses a variety of languages, like C++, D, Rust, Nim, Go, or even Python. There is also the GDNative class in Godot's API, which lets any scripting language load and call dynamic libraries. This is the simplest way to make use of dynamic libraries, but things like NativeScript (explained in the second section) let you integrate the code from these libraries even more into Godot.

Replacing Slow GDScript Code

GDScript is an interpreted scripting language that gives it a lot of flexibility, but the downside is that the raw computing performance is worse than running straight native code.

Consider the GDScript code in Listing 25.1 that writes values into a multi-dimensional array.

LISTING 25.1   Values in a Multi-Dimensional Array

```
extends Node

var field_height = 21
var field_width  = 21

var circle_center = Vector2(11, 11)
var circle_radius = 5

func _ready():
    printraw("---------------\n")

    var data = []
    data.resize(field_height)
    for i in range(field_height):
        data[i] = []
        data[i].resize(field_width)
        for j in range(field_width):
            data[i][j] = field_value(i, j)
            printraw(data[i][j])
        printraw("\n") # newline
    printraw("---------------")

func field_value(y, x):
    var pos = Vector2(x, y)
    var distance = circle_center - pos

    if abs(distance.length()) <= (circle_radius / 2):
        # inner layer
        return '#'
```

```
    if abs(distance.length()) <= circle_radius:
        # outer layer
        return '/'

    # not inside the circle
    return ' '
```

Also consider the output in Listing 25.2. This code creates a "circle" with two layers. The outer layer has all #s in it and the inner layer has all /s.

LISTING 25.2   Circle Output

```
          /
       ///////
      /////////
      ////#////
      ///###///
     ///#####///
      ///###///
      ////#////
      /////////
       ///////
          /
```

The _ready method creates a 2D array by resizing an array and adding a new array (which gets resized as well). Each element in that array gets a value assigned that is determined by the field_value method.

The field_value method takes both indices of the current element position inside the array as arguments. It calculates the distance to the center of the circle to determine the kind of symbol to input.

Iteration can be slow in GDScript sometimes, making it unsuitable for huge procedural generation algorithms. If we wanted to write the same code in C using GDNative, we would come up with something like what is shown in Listing 25.3.

LISTING 25.3   Using C in GDNative

```
#include <gdnative.h>

#include <math.h>

#define FIELD_WIDTH 21
#define FIELD_HEIGHT 21

#define CIRCLE_CENTER_X 11
#define CIRCLE_CENTER_Y 11
#define CIRCLE_RADIUS 5
```

```
void GDN_EXPORT godot_gdnative_init(godot_gdnative_init_options *o)
{
    // Nothing for now.
}

int field_value(int y, int x)
{
    godot_vector2 pos;
    godot_vector2_new(&pos, x, y);

    godot_vector2 circle_center;
    godot_vector2_new(&circle_center, CIRCLE_CENTER_X, CIRCLE_CENTER_Y);

    godot_vector2 difference = godot_vector2_operator_substract(&pos,
&circle_center);

    float distance = fabs(godot_vector2_length(&difference));

    if (distance <= CIRCLE_RADIUS / 2)
        return '#';

    if (distance <= CIRCLE_RADIUS)
        return '/';

    return ' ';
}
godot_variant GDN_EXPORT create_circle(void *data, godot_array *args)
{
    godot_array field;
    godot_array_new(&field);

    godot_array_resize(&field, FIELD_HEIGHT);

    for (int i = 0; i < FIELD_HEIGHT; i++) {
        godot_array row;
        godot_array_new(&row);

        godot_array_resize(&row, FIELD_WIDTH);

        for (int j = 0; j < FIELD_WIDTH; j++) {
            godot_variant value;
            godot_variant_new_int(&value, field_value(i, j));

            godot_array_set(&row, j, &value);

            godot_variant_destroy(&value);
        }
```

```
        godot_variant row_variant;
        godot_variant_new_array(&row_variant, &row);

        godot_array_destroy(&row);

        godot_array_set(&field, i, &row_variant);

        godot_variant_destroy(&row_variant);
    }
    godot_variant ret;
    godot_variant_new_array(&ret, &field);

    godot_array_destroy(&field);
    return ret;
}
```

TIP

Variant Data-type

Variant is the data-type that can hold all other data-types inside it. It's like a `var` in GDScript. It carries type information so the code knows how to process the data inside it properly.

TIP

GDNative Initialization Functions

Every shared library that is used in Godot needs to have a `godot_gdnative_init` function. That function is called once the library loads. A `godot_gdnative_terminate` function is called when it gets unloaded. This is useful when third-party code needs to be de-initialized.

As you can see, C code can be very verbose because all the constructors and destructors are called manually. Also, there is no automatic conversion to Variant, which adds even more noise to the code. It is wise to only resort to a GDNative solution if GDScript or other scripting solutions are really under-performing.

In order to use this new algorithm that's expressed in the C code, we need to create a GDNativeLibrary. A GDNativeLibrary is a resource that abstracts the file paths to the native libraries on all Godot-supported platforms (see Figure 25.1).

FIGURE 25.1
The GDNativeLibrary.

Now that the GDNativeLibrary exists as a GDScript (or any other scripting language, for that matter), we can load and use the library (see Listing 25.4).

LISTING 25.4   Using the GDNativeLibrary

```
extends Node

func _ready():

    printraw("------------\n")

    var lib = GDNative.new()
    lib.library = load("res://draw_circle_library.tres")

    lib.initialize()

    var array = lib.call_native("standard_varcall", "create_circle", [])

    for row in array:
        for ch in row:
            printraw(char(ch))
        printraw("\n")

    lib.terminate()


    printraw("------------\n")
```

Using Third-party Libraries

One common use for GDNative is to make third-party libraries usable in Godot without having to create modules (more on modules later). This is as simple as compiling the library like previously shown, but linking to other libraries.

Here is a small example (Listing 25.5) that makes use of the "stb image write" single-header-file library to draw a circle into an image and then write it to a disk.

LISTING 25.5   Drawing a Circle with STB Image Writer

```
#include <godot/gdnative.h>

#include <math.h>
#include <stdlib.h>
#include <string.h>

#define STB_IMAGE_WRITE_IMPLEMENTATION
#include "stb_image_write.h"

#define FIELD_WIDTH 200
#define FIELD_HEIGHT 200
```

```
#define CIRCLE_CENTER_X 100
#define CIRCLE_CENTER_Y 100
#define CIRCLE_RADIUS 50

void GDN_EXPORT godot_gdnative_init(godot_gdnative_init_options *o)
{
    // Nothing for now.
}

void field_value(int y, int x, uint8_t *r, uint8_t *g, uint8_t *b)
{
    godot_vector2 pos;
    godot_vector2_new(&pos, x, y);

    godot_vector2 circle_center;
    godot_vector2_new(&circle_center, CIRCLE_CENTER_X, CIRCLE_CENTER_Y);

    godot_vector2 difference = godot_vector2_operator_substract(&pos,
&circle_center);

    float distance = fabs(godot_vector2_length(&difference));
    if (distance <= CIRCLE_RADIUS / 2) {
        *r = 255;
        *g = 0;
        *b = 255;
        return;
    }

    if (distance <= CIRCLE_RADIUS) {
        *r = 255;
        *g = 0;
        *b = 0;
        return;
    }
    *r = 255;
    *g = 255;
    *b = 255;
}

godot_variant GDN_EXPORT create_circle(void *data, godot_array *args)
{
    godot_variant ret;
    godot_variant_new_nil(&ret);

    uint8_t *image_data = malloc(3 * FIELD_HEIGHT * FIELD_WIDTH);

    for (int i = 0; i < FIELD_HEIGHT; i++) {
        for (int j = 0; j < FIELD_WIDTH; j++) {
```

```
                uint8_t r;
                uint8_t g;
                uint8_t b;
                field_value(i, j, &r, &g, &b);

                uint8_t *start_pixel = image_data + (FIELD_WIDTH * 3 * i + j * 3);
                start_pixel[0] = r;
                start_pixel[1] = g;
                start_pixel[2] = b;
            }
        }
    stbi_write_png("circle.png", FIELD_WIDTH,
FIELD_HEIGHT, 3, image_data, 0);

    free(image_data);

    return ret;
}
```

Because this is a header-only library, there are no extra steps involved to get it to compile. As an example of using a shared library, we link to libcurl and get the version string (see Listing 25.6).

TIP

Using Third-party Libraries

In this next example, we use libcurl to get some data from a library. Make sure you have the library installed and that the linker can find it; otherwise, it won't work.

LISTING 25.6   Using libcurl to Retrieve Data

```
#include <godot/gdnative.h>

#include <string.h>

#include <curl/curl.h>

void GDN_EXPORT godot_gdnative_init(godot_gdnative_init_options *o)
{
    // Nothing for now.
}

godot_variant GDN_EXPORT godot_libcurl_version(void *data, godot_array *args)
{
    godot_variant ret;

    char *version_string = curl_version();
```

```
godot_string gdstring;
godot_string_new_data(&gdstring, version_string, strlen(version_string));

godot_variant_new_string(&ret, &gdstring);

godot_string_destroy(&gdstring);

return ret;
}
```

Now we can get the libcurl version (see Figure 25.2) from GDScript and other languages
(Listing 25.7).

LISTING 25.7   libcurl with GDScript

```
extends Node

func _ready():

    var lib = GDNative.new()
    lib.library = load("res://curl.tres")

    lib.initialize()

    var version = lib.call_native("standard_varcall", "godot_libcurl_version", [])

    $Label.text = version

    lib.terminate()
```

It works similarly for static libraries. Add the .a/.lib file to the compile command, and it works out
of the box.

libcurl/7.55.1 OpenSSL/1.1.0f zlib/1.2.11 libpsl/0.18.0 (+libicu/59.1) libssh2/1.8.0 nghttp2/1.23.1

FIGURE 25.2
Libcurl and OpenSSL.

Creating a NativeScript Using C

NativeScript is a script that uses an underlying shared library for its code instead of source code. Writing NativeScripts in C can be quite verbose and error-prone, so there are some bindings to other languages to make it easier. Other languages include D, Nim, Go, Rust, and C++.

When using a GDScript or VisualScript, Godot inspects the contents of those files directly. It can see available methods, the properties, and exported signals. With shared libraries, it's not that simple, because Godot can't parse the binary code on all platforms and decide which symbols are important or not. Also, Godot has signals that have no direct counterpart in native code. So, a registering mechanism is used in NativeScripts: the library tells Godot what it has to offer. This is done in the `godot_nativescript_init` function.

In this example (Listing 25.8), we define a class "Adder," which adds up numbers. It's not very useful, but the setup needed to create a simple example and a more complex one is exactly the same.

LISTING 25.8 Adder Adds Up Numbers

```
#include <godot/gdnative.h>
#include <godot_nativescript.h>

void GDN_EXPORT godot_gdnative_init(godot_gdnative_init_options *o)
{
    // Nothing for now.
}

void *adder_new(godot_object *o, void *method_data)
{
    int *call_count = godot_alloc(sizeof(int));
    *call_count = 0;
    return call_count;
}

void adder_destroy(godot_object *o, void *method_data, void *userdata)
{
    int *call_count = userdata;
    godot_free(call_count);
}

godot_variant adder_add(godot_object *o, void *method_data, void *userdata,
int num_args, godot_variant **args)
{
    int *call_count = userdata;
    (*call_count)++;

    int a = godot_variant_as_int(args[0]);
    int b = godot_variant_as_int(args[1]);

    int result = a + b;
```

```
    godot_variant res;
    godot_variant_new_int(&res, result);

    return res;
}

godot_variant adder_get_call_count(godot_object *o, void *method_data, void
*userdata, int n, godot_variant **a)
{
    int *call_count = userdata;

    godot_variant res;
    godot_variant_new_int(&res, *call_count);

    return res;
}

void GDN_EXPORT godot_nativescript_init(void *handle)
{
    godot_instance_create_func create_func = {};
    create_func.create_func = &adder_new;

    godot_instance_destroy_func destroy_func = {};
    destroy_func.destroy_func = &adder_destroy;

    godot_nativescript_register_class(handle, "Adder", "Node", create_func,
destroy_func);

    {
        godot_method_attributes method_attr;
        method_attr.rpc_type = GODOT_METHOD_RPC_MODE_DISABLED;

        godot_instance_method method = {};
        method.method = &adder_add;

        godot_nativescript_register_method(handle, "Adder", "add", method_attr,
method);
    }
    {
        godot_method_attributes method_attr;
        method_attr.rpc_type = GODOT_METHOD_RPC_MODE_DISABLED;

        godot_instance_method method = {};
        method.method = &adder_get_call_count;

        godot_nativescript_register_method(handle, "Adder", "get_call_count",
method_attr, method);
    }
}
```

As you can see, the class gets registered in the `godot_nativescript_init` function, along with its method. The `godot_method`, `godot_create_func`, and `godot_destroy_func` structures each have `method_data` and `free_func` fields. Some bindings might reuse the same functions for different methods, but they need to pass some custom data to know what to actually perform. This data is passed to these functions in the `method_data` field. If the data is heap allocated, `free_func` is called on the data before the library gets unloaded.

In the simple C example, we don't need these features, so we leave both fields 0, which is done by using the `{}` initialization.

The `create_func` gets called when the script instance gets created. The function is supposed to return a pointer to the object data that the script needs, so it's like a pointer in C++. This pointer is passed to all functions that are registered on that class for all of the objects as the `user_data` parameter. A structure with fields is allocated, the pointer returns, and all of the methods access the member variables through that pointer. In the case of the `Adder`, it is a pointer to an integer in which we store the number of times the `add` method gets called. The `get_call_count` method returns the number so it can be inspected from another script.

Now that the library is in place, you can create a new NativeScript file. It's like a GDScript file, but it doesn't contain source code. Instead, there's a link to a GDNativeLibrary and the name of the class used. One library can contain multiple classes, so it's necessary to specify which one should be used.

Because the Adder class extends node, we can use it as an AutoLoad. Select the `.gdns` file and name it "Adder," then you can use it from any GDScript (see Listing 25.9).

LISTING 25.9   Adder in AutoLoad

```
extends Node

func _ready():
    var res = Adder.add(13, 37)
    print(res)

    res = Adder.add(4, 2)
    print(res)

    print(Adder.get_call_count())
```

This creates the following output:

```
# output
50
6
2
```

Modules

Modules are parts of Godot source code that represent an extension of the engine functionality. Many features of Godot are implemented in modules; for example, GDScript or the TileMap Node. Modules are statically compiled into the Godot binary and have access to all other classes and functions defined inside Godot.

Because modules are usually independent from each other and only depend on core functionality—but not the other way around—it's possible to disable modules at compile time.

For example, if a game doesn't use the TileMap Node, it's possible to disable the tilemap module to reduce the size of the game's binary.

Godot Source Structure

In order to write modules, you first have to have a basic understanding of the way Godot's source code is structured. If you obtain the source code, you will see these top-level directories:

▶ **core:** This folder contains all of the core data types, including Vectors, Variant, Arrays, HashMap, Set, and many more. Godot's object system is defined here as well. So, in short, it contains all of the basic building blocks.

▶ **doc:** Contains the documentation data that's accessible in the script editor.

▶ **drivers:** Contains the code that implements interfaces of the engine using a specific third-party library or technology; for example, the OpenGL renderer and the PNG image loader. When a driver is platform-specific (for example, the rendering code for a console), it'll be found in its corresponding "platform" directory.

▶ **editor:** Because the editor is just a "game" in Godot, it needs to be written somewhere. This is where. The whole editor is defined in the EditorNode class. The export templates get compiled without editor sources, so this whole directory gets ignored when building these export templates.

▶ **main:** Contains the code for the main loop. It defines how one iteration of the game loop executes.

▶ **misc:** Contains mostly scripts for special situations. It also includes git commit hooks you can use when working on a pull request for the engine.

▶ **modules:** This is where custom modules are placed. Modules extend the engine; they aren't fundamental, but they still offer functionality. For example, GDScript is a module just like TileMap or ENet (networking). This is where we need to place our custom modules for the engine to find them.

▶ **platform:** Godot runs on many platforms. It abstracts APIs to make working with these platforms easier. This is where the actual implementation of these interfaces is defined for each platform.

▶ **scene:** The source code for all the different node types are defined here, including 3D, 2D, and control. Everything is in here.

▶ **servers:** The servers are the low-level systems that are in charge of the main features of the engine: rendering, physics, audio, etc. Servers have an asynchronous API and are a fairly higher-level abstraction than usual to achieve better portability. The scene system abstracts this architecture away from the user.

▶ **third-party:** Godot makes use of multiple third-party libraries. These are included in this directory, along with licensing information.

Compiling Godot

Godot uses the **scons** build system. To build Godot, you need to execute the following command in the Godot source directory:

▶ `scons p = x11 -j n`

▶ **scons:** Is the name of the build program. It executes the code in the `Sconstruct` file.

▶ **P:** Is shorthand for `platform`.

▶ **x11:** Is the platform for which we're building. In this case, it's Linux/X11. You can also write `platform=x11`. Other platforms to build are: `windows`, `osx`, `iphone`, and `javascript`. For platforms that are not your host platform, you need some form of cross compiler on your system.

▶ **–j n:** Where `n` is the number of **jobs.**

The latter argument specifies the number of "jobs" used to build Godot. One job is one compiler process used to build your program. So, if you specify `-j 4`, four compiler processes will run in parallel. This can cause problems on Windows due to file locking. If your compilation throws errors because files cannot be opened, try to leave this option out or set use 1 as `n`.

On some systems that have a more recent version of OpenSLL installed, it may be necessary to pass the argument `builtin_openssl=yes` to the scons command.

TIP

Compiling on Different Platforms

Godot builds on many different platforms, and on some (looking at you, Windows), you need to perform some extra steps to compile Godot. The official documentation has more information about the compilation process for different platforms.

Custom Modules

Because the design of Godot is to "keep it simple," in general, there may be missing functionality for some games. For example, a module to connect two devices via Bluetooth may be needed for a game that makes use of it to implement some form of local multiplayer across devices. This functionality is unneeded in the majority of games, so it's not a good idea to include this functionality as a core part of the engine.

This is where custom modules are popular. They let users extend the engine with functionality that's needed for their games.

Modules are rather easy to create and distribute, but they require a recompilation of the engine. Here is the directory structure of the module:

```
adder
register_types.h
register_types.cpp
adder.h
adder.cpp
SCsub
config.py
```

When scons starts to build Godot, it searches in the `modules/` directory. Every subdirectory represents a module (Listing 25.10).

LISTING 25.10   Searching for Modules

```
# SCsub

Import('env')

env.add_source_files(env.modules_sources, "*.cpp")
```

The SCsub file is a scons subbuildscript, which tells scons how to build the module. The config.py is a file that only needs two methods: `can_build`, which returns True or False depending on if the module is built on that current platform or not, and `configure`, which is used to change scons settings if needed (Listing 25.11).

LISTING 25.11   The conifg.py File

```
# config.py

def can_build(platform):
    return True

def configure(env):
    pass
```

Scons adds a file called `register_types.cpp` to the build queue for every subdirectory.

This file needs to include a function called `register_MODULENAME_types`, where MODULENAME is the name of the subdirectory (Listing 25.12). This function is used to register types defined in the module. It's a lot like the registering process in GDNative. Godot needs to know what classes and types are available.

LISTING 25.12   Including register_MODULENAME_types

```
// register_types.h
void register_adder_types();
void unregister_adder_types();

And:
// register_types.cpp
#include "register_types.h"

#include "core/class_db.h"

#include "adder.h"

void register_adder_types() {

    ClassDB::register_class<Adder>();
}

void unregister_adder_types() {
}
```

Like in the GDNative example, we create a class called "Adder" that adds numbers and has a way to tell us how often the method gets called (Listing 25.13).

LISTING 25.13   Adding Adder

```
// adder.h
#ifndef ADDER_H
#define ADDER_H

#include "core/reference.h"

class Adder : public Reference {
    GDCLASS(Adder, Reference)

    int call_count = 0;
```

```
public:
    static void _bind_methods();

    int add(int a, int b);
    int get_call_count();
};


#endif
```

To create a class we can use from the scripting system, we need to be able to register that class to ClassDB. The macro `GDCLASS(name, base)` needs to be used as the first thing in the class declaration. This macro code implements some methods needed for the introspection system of ClassDB to work properly (Listing 25.14).

LISTING 25.14   Registering the Class to ClassDB

```
// adder.cpp
#include "adder.h"

void Adder::_bind_methods() {
    ClassDB::bind_method(D_METHOD("add", "a", "b"),
                &Adder::add);
    ClassDB::bind_method(D_METHOD("get_call_count"),
                &Adder::get_call_count);
}
int Adder::add(int a, int b) {
    call_count++;
    return a + b;
}

int Adder::get_call_count() {
    return call_count;
}
```

NOTE

Introspection

Introspection is the ability to see and query properties of certain types of classes. Classes in Godot have the `get_method_list` and `get_property_list` methods for that purpose. A lot more of those methods are available in the ClassDB singleton.

The `bind_methods` is the method that needs to register all of the other properties that the class exposes. This is done using the `ClassDB::bind_method` method. The `D_METHOD` macro is for including debug information about the method in debug builds. In export templates, these do not generate debug information.

After that, we recompile the engine with `scons p = x11 -j n`, where n is the number of jobs.

Everything should compile without errors.

Now, you can use the Adder class in a GDScript to test if everything works (Listing 25.15).

LISTING 25.15   Adder Testing

```
extends Node

func _ready():
    var adder = Adder.new()

    var res = adder.add(13, 37)
    print(res)

    res = adder.add(4, 2)
    print(res)

    print(adder.get_call_count())
```

As you can see, the NativeScript and module version are very similar in usage. Other high-level language bindings for NativeScript can make the implementation of it look much more like the module implementation, but every binding handles things differently, so the examples here were in C, because NativeScript and GDNative are pure C APIs.

Summary

This was a short introduction to using native code with Godot, be it via GDNative or modules. What was shown here is only a small part of what is possible to achieve. The truth is that a chapter in a book isn't enough to talk about everything that the engine source code has to offer and how to interact with it to get the most out of Godot. There are many ways to get in contact with developers to get more information about how to make better use of the engine's APIs. Hopefully, this chapter gave you a first impression of what the workflow looks like!

Q&A

Q. **What is the difference between a NativeScript and a module?**

A. A NativeScript is like a GDScript—but it uses native code. A module gets compiled into the engine and can add more functionality to the core of the engine than a GDNative library can.

Q. **Can every language that can produce C-callable code be used to create GDNative libraries?**

A. Yes, yet some languages are easier to use with GDNative than others. This is the case because of many different things like Garbage Collection or binary compatibility.

Q. **How can a GDScript/VisualScript/[Insert other scripting language here] method be called from a NativeScript?**

A. It can be done by using the `Variant.call()` method or the `Object.call()` method. The `Object.call()` method is be called by using so-called "method binds," which we didn't have time to explore here.

Workshop

Answer the following questions to make sure you understood the content of this hour.

Quiz

1. Where do modules need to be put in the Godot source code to be compiled?

2. What files need to be present for Godot to find and compile modules?

3. Why do libraries need to be linked in a GDNativeLibrary resource?

4. For what are the `godot_gdnative_init` and `godot_gdnative_terminate` functions used?

5. For what is the `godot_nativescript_init` function used?

Answers

1. Modules need to be put inside the `modules/` directory.

2. Every module needs to include a `config.py` and `SCsub` file. These are used to check if the module can be compiled and to let the build system know which files should get compiled and how.

3. Godot runs on multiple platforms, which use different formats for native libraries. The GDNativeLibrary includes paths for every library for every platform. This way, native code can run on all platforms that support GDNative.

4. Those functions are supposed to be used for setup and de-initialization of possible third-party libraries.

5. It's used to register script classes to Godot, much like how the `_bind_methods` method is used in modules.

Exercises

Try to make a button that spawns Sprites that fall down and increase a counter when they leave the screen:

1. Read the source file `main/main.cpp`; it contains the code that starts off any Godot application.

2. Explore the GDScript module in `module/gdscript`. If you're familiar with compiler development, you can try to add your own language construct (like a do-while loop, for example).

3. Look at the `core/object.h, core/object.cpp,` and `core/reference.h` files. They contain the definition of the Object system with its signal and group subsystems, as well as the implementation of Reference-Counting—the main memory management system used in Godot.

Index

W

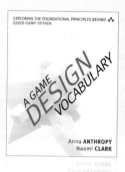

 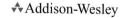

SAMS

REGISTER

THIS PRODUCT

informit.com/register

Register the Addison-Wesley, Exam Cram, Prentice Hall, Que, and Sams products you own to unlock great benefits.

To begin the registration process, simply go to **informit.com/register** to sign in or create an account. You will then be prompted to enter the 10- or 13-digit ISBN that appears on the back cover of your product.

Registering your products can unlock the following benefits:

- Access to supplemental content, including bonus chapters, source code, or project files.
- A coupon to be used on your next purchase.

Registration benefits vary by product. Benefits will be listed on your Account page under Registered Products.

About InformIT — THE TRUSTED TECHNOLOGY LEARNING SOURCE

INFORMIT IS HOME TO THE LEADING TECHNOLOGY PUBLISHING IMPRINTS Addison-Wesley Professional, Cisco Press, Exam Cram, IBM Press, Prentice Hall Professional, Que, and Sams. Here you will gain access to quality and trusted content and resources from the authors, creators, innovators, and leaders of technology. Whether you're looking for a book on a new technology, a helpful article, timely newsletters, or access to the Safari Books Online digital library, InformIT has a solution for you.

THE TRUSTED TECHNOLOGY LEARNING SOURCE

Addison-Wesley | Cisco Press | Exam Cram
IBM Press | Que | Prentice Hall | Sams

SAFARI BOOKS ONLINE